VOGUE® KNITTING
VERY EASY KNITS

VOGUE® KNITTING

VERY EASY KNITS

THE BEST OF VERY EASY VERY VOGUE

Edited by Trisha Malcolm

THE BUTTERICK® PUBLISHING COMPANY
NEW YORK

B

THE BUTTERICK® PUBLISHING COMPANY
161 Avenue of the Americas
New York, New York 10013

Editor-in-Chief
Trisha Malcolm

Editor
Annemarie McNamara

Art Director
Christine Lipert

Technical Illustration Editor and Page Layout
Elizabeth Berry

Managing Editor
Daryl Brower

Yarn Editor
Veronica Manno

Copy Editor
Jacquelyn Smyth

Editorial Coordinator
Kathleen Kelly

Editorial Assistants
Amy Patrick
Charlotte Parry
Jean Guirguis

Photo Archivist
Sherry Onna Handlin

Production Managers
Lillian Esposito
Winnie Hinish
Caroline Politi

Cover Designer
Joe Vior

Executive Vice President and Publisher, Butterick® Company, Inc
Art Joinnides

President and CEO, Butterick® Company, Inc
Jay H. Stein

Library of Congress Cataloging-in-Publication Data

Vogue knitting: very easy knits/ edited by Trisha Malcolm.
p. cm.
ISBN 1-57389-012-X Trade
ISBN 1-57389-029-4 Paper
1. Knitting Patterns. I. Malcolm, Trisha, 1960-
II. Butterick Publishing Company. III. Title: Very easy knits.
TT820.V626 1999   99-15021
746.43'20432–dc21   CIP

Manufactured in China

3 5 7 9 10 8 6 4

Introduction

Since its relaunch in 1982, *Vogue Knitting* magazine has endeavored to bring readers classic, yet up-to-the-minute fashions, with clear, easy-to-follow instructions that would allow anyone the pleasure and enjoyment of creating beautiful handknit garments. Included in each issue are Very Easy Very Vogue patterns, designs whose basic stitches and simple finishing make them ideal for knitters with busy schedules or for novice knitters eager to put their new skills into practice. With the ever-increasing pace of life today, and the resurgence of interest in all things knit, these patterns have reached their height of popularity. This collection of the best of Very Easy Very Vogue to appear over the last seventeen years of *Vogue Knitting* magazine is especially designed with you, our readers in mind, so you'll always have a good selection of quick-to-knit garments on hand.

A book filled with simple-to-accomplish, but unmistakably stylish projects was such a wonderful concept, our editors were instantly inspired. With something so right to motivate us, the hours spent poring over past issues searching for the very best designs was more pleasure than work. But, of course, that isn't to say it was easy. There were so many really wonderful sweaters to choose from, the difficulty wasn't finding which to include, but which not to.

Once the patterns were selected, the next step was exploring our vast fashion archives for film. For some styles, the original photograph from the magazine was chosen. For others, we decided to take advantage of one of the many different views available. Where applicable, we included additional photographs in order to highlight the special features of a particular design.

While many of the original yarns were still available, others were no longer being manufactured and a substitute had to be found. Our yarn editor spent hours knitting swatches in search of the perfect match. Still, the challenge did not end there. Once the ideal yarn was found, there was the matter of finding a comparable color. Once in a while an identical color was available. If that wasn't the case, a similar shade or palette had to be suggested. We've listed the original yarn wherever substitutions have been made, just in case someone has leftovers tucked away.

We know you'll enjoy the variety of patterns offered. We made a point to include styles to suit every season, taste, and occasion. So if you think you haven't the time or just plain talent to knit something fabulous, then it's time to think again!

With this one-of-a-kind collection, timeless, easy-to-knit fashions are within the reach of every knitter...

Table of Contents

Before You Begin

This book was designed as an anthology of patterns. For more precise technical explanation, refer to Vogue Knitting—The Ultimate Knitting Book *(New York: Pantheon Books). See page 159 to order.*

YARN SELECTION

Some of the yarns, or colors, used in the original patterns are no longer available. We have provided substitute yarns readily available in the U.S. and Canada at the time of printing. The Resources on page 158 lists addresses of yarn distributors—contact them for the name of a retailer in your area or for mail-order information.

If you wish to substitute a yarn, check the gauge carefully to ensure the finished garment will knit to the correct measurements. To facilitate yarn substitution, *Vogue Knitting* grades yarn by the standard stitch gauge obtained in stockinette stitch. There is a grading number in the Materials section of each pattern. Look for a substitute yarn that falls into the same category—the suggested gauge on the ball band should be comparable to that on the Yarn Symbols Chart (right).

After successfully gauge-swatching in a substitute yarn, you'll need to determine yarn requirements. First, find the total length of the original yarn in the pattern (multiply number of balls by yards/meters per ball). Divide this figure by the new yards/meters per ball (listed on the ball band). Round up to the next whole number. The answer is the number of balls required.

GAUGE

Always knit a gauge swatch before beginning to ensure a successful project. Normally, gauge is measured over a four-inch (10cm) square. Using the needles and yarn suggested, cast on enough stitches to knit a square at least this size. Gauge is usually given in stockinette stitch, but if the pattern calls for a specific stitch, work this stitch for the swatch. Measure stitches carefully with a ruler or gauge tool. If the swatch is smaller than the stated gauge (more stitches per inch/cm), try larger needles. If it is larger (fewer stitches per inch/cm), use smaller needles. Experiment with needle size until the gauge exactly matches the one given before proceeding.

If a pattern calls for knitting in the round, this may tighten the gauge, so if the gauge was measured on a flat swatch, take another reading after beginning the project.

YARN SYMBOLS

The following symbols 1-6 represent a range of stitch gauges. Note that these symbols correspond to the standard gauge in stockinette stitch.

① **FINE WEIGHT**
(29-32 stitches per 4"/10cm)
Includes baby and fingering yarns, and some of the heavier crochet cottons.

② **LIGHTWEIGHT**
(25-28 stitches per 4"/10cm)
Includes sport yarn, sock yarn, UK 4-ply and lightweight DK yarns.

③ **MEDIUM WEIGHT**
(21-24 stitches per 4"/10cm)
Includes DK and worsted, the most commonly used knitting yarns.

④ **MEDIUM-HEAVY WEIGHT**
(17-20 stitches per 4"/10cm)
Also called heavy worsted or Aran.

⑤ **BULKY WEIGHT**
(13-16 stitches per 4"/10cm)
Also called chunky. Includes heavier Icelandic yarns.

⑥ **EXTRA-BULKY WEIGHT**
(9-12 stitches per 4"/10cm)
The heaviest yarns available.

READING PATTERNS

Read all instructions thoroughly before starting to knit a gauge swatch and again before beginning a project. Familiarize yourself with abbreviations (see Knitting Terms and Abbreviations, opposite). Refer to the *Vogue Knitting* book for clear explanations of any stitches or techniques you may not be familiar with.

Generally, patterns are written in several sizes. The smallest appears first, and figures for larger sizes are given in parentheses. Where only one figure appears, it applies to all sizes. Highlight numbers pertaining to your size before beginning.

Knitted measurements are the dimensions of the garment after all the pieces have been sewn together. Usually, three measurements are given: finished chest; finished length; and, sleeve width at upper arm. The finished chest measurement is the width around the entire sweater at the underarm. For cardigans, the width is determined with the front bands buttoned. Finished length is measured from the highest point of the shoulder to the bottom of the ribbing. Sleeve width is measured at the upper arm, after all increases have been worked and before any cap shaping takes place.

Schematics are a valuable tool for determining size selection and proper fit. Schematics are scale drawings showing the dimensions of the finished knitted pieces.

Work figures given inside brackets the number of times stated afterward. Directions immediately following an asterisk are to be repeated the given number of times. If the instructions call for working even, work in the same pattern stitch without increasing or decreasing.

KNITTING TERMS AND ABBREVIATIONS

approx approximately

beg begin(ning)

bind off Used to finish an edge and keep stitches from unraveling. Lift the first stitch over the second, the second over the third, etc. (UK: cast off)

cast on A foundation row of stitches placed on the needle in order to begin knitting.

CC contrast color

ch chain(s)

cm centimeter(s)

cont continue(ing)

dc double crochet (UK: tr-treble)

dec decrease(ing)—Reduce the stitches in a row (knit 2 together).

dpn double pointed needle(s)

foll follow(s)(ing)

g gram(s)

garter stitch Knit every row. Circular knitting: knit one round, then purl one round.

hdc half-double crochet (UK: htr-half treble)

inc increase(ing)—Add stitches in a row (knit into the front and back of a stitch).

k knit

k2tog knit 2 stitches together

lp(s) loops(s)

LH left hand

m meter(s)

M1 make one stitch—With the needle tip, lift the strand between the last stitch worked and next stitch on the left-hand needle and knit into the back of it. One stitch has been added.

MC main color

mm millimeter(s)

oz ounce(s)

p purl

p2tog purl 2 stitches together

pat pattern

pick up and knit (purl) Knit (or purl) into the loops along an edge.

pm place markers—Place or attach a loop of contrast yarn or purchased stitch marker as indicated.

rem remain(s)(ing)

rep repeat

rev St st reverse Stockinette stitch—Purl right-side rows, knit wrong-side rows. Circular knitting: purl all rounds. (UK: reverse stocking stitch)

rnd(s) round(s)

RH right hand

RS right side(s)

sc single crochet (UK: dc - double crochet)

sk skip

SKP Slip 1, knit 1, pass slip stitch over knit 1.

sl slip—An unworked stitch made by passing a stitch from the left-hand to the right-hand needle as if to purl.

sl st slip stitch (UK: single crochet)

SSK slip, slip, knit—Slip next 2 stitches knitwise, one at a time, to right-hand needle. Insert tip of left-hand needle into fronts of these stitches from left to right. Knit them together. One stitch has been decreased.

st(s) stitch(es)

St st Stockinette stitch—Knit right-side rows, purl wrong-side rows. Circular knitting: knit all rounds. (UK: stocking stitch)

tbl through back of loop

tog together

WS wrong side(s)

wyif with yarn in front

wyib with yarn in back

work even Continue in pattern without increasing or decreasing. (UK: work straight)

yd yard(s)

yo yarn over—Make a new stitch by wrapping the yarn over the right-hand needle. (UK: yfwd, yon, yrn)

* repeat directions following * as many times as indicated.

[ ] Repeat directions inside brackets as many times as indicated.

FOLLOWING CHARTS

Charts are a convenient way to follow colorwork, lace, cable and other stitch patterns. *Vogue Knitting* stitch charts utilize the universal language of "symbolcraft." Each symbolcraft symbol represents the stitch as it appears on the right side of the work. For example, the symbol for the knit stitch is a vertical line and the symbol for a purl stitch is a horizontal one. On right-side rows, work the stitches as they appear on the chart—knitting the vertical lines and purling the horizontal ones. When reading wrong-side rows, work the opposite of what is shown; that is, purl the vertical lines and knit the horizontal ones.

Each square on a chart represents one stitch and each horizontal row of squares equals a row or round. When knitting back and forth on straight needles, right-side rows (RS) are read right to left, wrong-side rows (WS) are read from left to right; bottom to top. When knitting in rounds on circular needles, read charts from right to left on every round, repeating any stitch and row repeats as directed in the pattern. Posting a self-adhesive note under the working row is an easy way to keep track on a chart.

Sometimes, only a single repeat of the pattern is charted. Heavy lines drawn through the entire chart indicate a repeat. The lines are the equivalent of an asterisk (*) or brackets [] used in written instructions.

KNITTING NEEDLES		
US	**METRIC**	**UK**
0	2mm	14
1	2.25mm	13
	2.5mm	
2	2.75mm	12
	3mm	11
3	3.25mm	10
4	3.5mm	
5	3.75mm	9
	4mm	8
6		
7	4.5mm	7
8	5mm	6
9	5.5mm	5
10	6mm	4
10½	6.5mm	3
	7mm	2
	7.5mm	1
11	8mm	0
13	9mm	00
15	10mm	000

Simple,
yet stylish
sweaters—
perfect
for the
new knitter

Seed-stitch pockets and edging add interest to this long-sleeved Chanel-style short jacket with round neck and buttoned cuffs. Designed by Gabriele Brouillad. Shown in size Small. The Cropped Cardigan Jacket first appeared in the Fall '96 issue of *Vogue Knitting*.

Cropped Cardigan Jacket

SIZES
To fit X-Small (Small, Medium, Large). Directions are for smallest size with larger sizes in parentheses. If there is only one figure it applies to all sizes.

KNITTED MEASUREMENTS
- Bust at underarm 37 (40, 43, 45)"/94 (101.5, 109, 114.5)cm.
- Length 17 (17, 19, 20$\frac{1}{2}$)"/43 (43, 48.5, 52)cm.
- Sleeve width at upper arm 14 (14, 14$\frac{1}{2}$, 15)"/35.5 (35.5, 37, 38)cm.

MATERIALS
- 12 (12, 13, 15) 1$\frac{3}{4}$oz/50g balls (each approx 68yd/63m) of Tahki *Cottage Chunky Knit* (wool⑤) in #594 parrot
- One pair size 9 (5.5mm) needles OR SIZE TO OBTAIN GAUGE
- Four $\frac{3}{4}$"/20mm buttons

Note
The original color used for this sweater is no longer available. A comparable color substitute has been made, which is available at the time of printing.

GAUGE
15 sts and 24 rows to 4"/10cm over St st and seed st using size 9 (5.5mm) needles.
FOR PERFECT FIT, TAKE TIME TO CHECK GAUGE.

STITCH GLOSSARY
Seed Stitch
Row 1 *K1, p1*; rep between *'s to end.
Row 2 P the k sts and k the p sts. Rep row 2 for seed st pat.

BACK
Cast on 70 (75, 80, 84) sts. Work in seed st for 3 rows.
Row 4 (WS) Purl.
Row 5 (RS) Knit. Rep rows 4 and 5 (St st) until piece measures 8 (8, 9, 10)"/ 20.5 (20.5, 23, 25.5)cm, end with WS row.

Armhole shaping
Bind off 3 (4, 5, 5) sts at beg of next 2 rows, 2 sts at beg of next 2 rows. Dec 1 st each side every other row 2 times—56 (59, 62, 66) sts. Work even until armhole measures 7$\frac{1}{2}$ (8, 9, 9$\frac{1}{2}$)"/24.5 (19.5, 20.5, 23, 24.5)cm or desired length, end with WS row.

Shoulder and neck shaping
Bind off 5 (6, 5, 6) sts at beg of next 2 rows, 4 (4, 5, 5) sts at beg of next 4 rows, AT SAME TIME, bind off center 26 (27, 28, 30) sts for neck and working both sides at once, dec 1 st each neck edge 2 times.

LEFT FRONT
Cast on 35 (38, 40, 42) sts. Work in seed st for 3 rows.
Row 4 (WS) Working first 3 sts in seed st, purl to end.

Row 5 (RS) Keeping seed st border (front edge) as established, work 32 (35, 37, 39) sts in St st. Cont in pats until front measures same as back to armhole, end with a WS row.

Armhole shaping
Shape armhole at side edge (beg of RS rows) as for back—28 (30, 31, 33) sts. Work even until armhole measures 5 (5, 6, 6$\frac{1}{2}$)"/12.5 (12.5, 15, 16.5)cm, end with RS row.

Neck shaping
Shape at beg of WS rows—neck edge (work even on RS rows), bind off 8 (9, 9, 9) sts once, 4 (4, 4, 5) sts once, dec 1 st 3 times—13 (14, 15, 16) sts rem. Work even until armhole measures same as for back.

Shoulder shaping
Shape shoulder at side edge as for back.

RIGHT FRONT
Work as for left front reversing shaping and seed st pat:
Row 4 (WS) Purl to last 3 sts, work seed st as established.

LEFT SLEEVE
To establish cuff slit Cast on 16 sts with one ball, cast on 24 sts with 2nd ball. Working both sides of slit at same time, work 3 rows in seed st.
Row 4 (WS) Purl.

Row 5 (RS) Knit. Cont in St st, inc 1 st at sleeve side edges (beg of row for narrow piece, end of row for wide piece) on 9th row once, then 6th row once, work even until piece measures 3½"/9cm from beg, end with WS row.

To join pieces (RS) Work across all sts using first ball of yarn, break off 2nd ball of yarn. Cont in St st, inc 1 st each side every 6 rows 4 (4, 5, 6) times—52 (52, 54, 56) sts. Work even until sleeve measures 17½ (17½, 18, 18¼)"/44.5 (45.5, 46, 47)cm or desired length to underarm, end with a WS row.

Cap shaping
Bind off 3 (5, 4, 5) sts at beg of next 2 rows. Dec 1 st each side every other row 15 (15, 17, 18) times. Bind off 3 (2, 1, 1) sts at beg of next 2 rows, 2 (1, 1, 1) sts at beg of next 2 rows. Bind off rem 6 (6, 8, 6) sts.

RIGHT SLEEVE
Work as for left sleeve reversing slit: Cast on 24 sts with one ball, cast on 16 with 2nd ball.

POCKETS (make 4)
Cast on 17 (17, 18, 19) sts, work in seed st for 4"/10cm. Bind off.

FINISHING
Sleeve plackets
(Note: Work overlap on wider section; pick up sts with RS facing.) Beg at bottom edge pick up and k 14 sts. Work 3 rows seed st. Bind off. Block pieces. Sew shoulder seams.

Neckband
With RS facing, beg at right front edge, pick up and k66 (66, 72, 72) sts evenly around neck edge. Work in seed st for 4 rows. Bind off. Sew on pockets 2"/5cm from cast on edge, 2"/5cm from edge and 2"/5cm apart vertically. Set in sleeves. Sew sleeve and side seams. Sew 2 buttons on each sleeve placket, sewing through both layers to hold placket in place. •

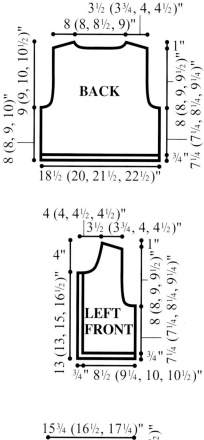

Mohair Twin Set

Knit in fuzzy, soft mohair, this easy cardigan and matching shell have touchable charm. The long-sleeve cardigan is standard fitting, with angled armholes and rolled edges. The close-fitting sleeveless shell has a round neck and rolled edges. A Vogue Original. Cardigan and shell shown in size Small. The Mohair Twin Set first appeared in the Fall '95 issue of *Vogue Knitting*.

Mohair Twin Set

CARDIGAN

SIZES
To fit X-Small (Small, Medium, Large, X-Large). Directions are for smallest size with larger sizes in parentheses. If there is only one figure it applies to all sizes.

KNITTED MEASUREMENTS
● Bust 38 (40, 42, 44, 46)"/96.5 (101.5, 106.5, 111.5, 116.5)cm.
● Length 19 (19, 19½, 20, 20½)"/48 (48, 49.5, 51, 52)cm.
● Upper arm 17 (18, 18, 19, 20)"/43 (46, 46, 48, 51)cm.

MATERIALS
Original Yarn
● 8 (8, 9, 9, 10) 1¾oz/50g skeins (each approx 104yd/95m) of Phildar *Mohair 50* (mohair/polyamide/polyester⑤) in #04 blush
Substitute Yarn
● 6, (7, 7, 7, 8) 1¾oz/50g balls (each approx 140yd/130m) of Phildar *Kid Mohair No. 4* (mohair/acrylic/nylon④) in #001 ambre
● One pair size 9 (5.5mm) needles OR SIZE TO OBTAIN GAUGE
● Size 9 (5.5mm) circular needle, 16"/40cm long

Note
The original yarn used for this sweater is no longer available. A comparable substitute has been made, which is available at the time of printing. Check gauge of substitute yarns very carefully before beginning.

GAUGE
16 sts and 22 rows to 4"/10cm over St st using size 9 (5.5mm) needles. FOR PERFECT FIT, TAKE TIME TO CHECK GAUGE.

BACK
With size 9 (5.5mm) needles, cast on 76 (80, 84, 88, 92) sts. Work in St st (k on RS, p on WS) until piece measures 10½ (10, 10½, 10½, 10½)"/26.5 (25.5, 26.5, 26.5, 26.5)cm from beg (with edge rolled), end with a WS row.

Armhole shaping
Dec 1 st each side *every* row 6 times, then every other row twice—60 (64, 68, 72, 76) sts. Work even until armhole measures 7½ (8, 8, 8½, 9)"/19 (20.5, 20.5, 21.5, 23)cm, end with a WS row.

Neck shaping
Next row (RS) Work 18 (20, 22, 24, 26) sts, join 2nd ball of yarn and bind off center 24 sts, work to end. Working both sides at once, bind off from each neck edge 3 sts twice. Bind off rem 12 (14, 16, 18, 20) sts each side for shoulders.

LEFT FRONT
With size 9 (5.5mm) needles, cast on 35 (37, 39, 41, 43) sts. Work in St st until piece measures same length as back to armhole. Work armhole shaping at side edge (beg of RS rows) as for back—27

(29, 31, 33, 35) sts. Work even until armhole measures 5½ (6, 6, 6½, 7)"/14 (15, 15, 16.5, 18)cm, end with a RS row.

Neck shaping
Next row (WS) Bind off 4 sts (neck edge), work to end. Cont to bind off from neck edge 3 sts once, 2 sts 3 times, 1 st twice. When same length as back, bind off rem 12 (14, 16, 18, 20) sts for shoulder.

RIGHT FRONT
Work as for left front, reversing shaping.

SLEEVES
With size 9 (5.5mm) needles, cast on 32 (32, 34, 36, 38) sts. Work in St st, inc 1 st each side every 4th row 0 (5, 2, 5, 8) times, every 6th row 18 (15, 17, 15, 13) times—68 (72, 72, 76, 80) sts. Work even until piece measures 20"/51cm from beg (with edge rolled), end with a WS row.

Cap shaping
Work as for back armhole shaping. Bind off rem 52 (56, 56, 60, 64) sts.

FINISHING
Block pieces lightly. Sew shoulder seams.

Neckband
With RS facing and size 9 (5.5mm) needles, beg at right front neck edge, pick up and k19 sts along right front neck edge, 36 sts along back neck, 19 sts along left front neck edge—74 sts. Work in St st for 1"/2.5cm. Bind off.

Left front band
With RS facing and size 9 (5.5mm) needles, beg at neck edge, pick up and k64 (64, 66, 68, 70) sts evenly along left front

edge, ending 1"/2.5cm from cast-on edge. Work in St st for 1"/2.5cm. Bind off.

Right front band

Work as for left front band. Set in sleeves. Sew side and sleeve seams.

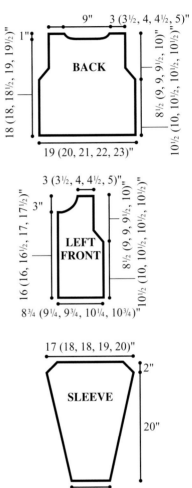

SHELL

SIZES

To fit X-Small (Small, Medium, Large, X-Large). Directions are for smallest size with larger sizes in parentheses. If there is only one figure it applies to all sizes.

KNITTED MEASUREMENTS

● Bust 34 (36, 38, 40, 42)"/86 (91, 96, 102, 106)cm.
● Length 18 (18, 18½, 19, 19½)"/46 (46, 47, 48, 49.5)cm.

MATERIALS

Original Yarn

● 4 (4, 5, 5, 6) 1¾oz/50g skeins (each approx 104yd/95m) of Lane Borgosesia/Phildar *Mohair 50* (mohair/polyamide/polyester⑤) in #04 blush

Substitute Yarn

● 3 (3, 4, 4, 5) 1¾oz/50g balls (each approx 140yd/130m) of Phildar *Kid Mohair No. 4* (mohair/acrylic/nylon④) in #001 ambre
● One pair size 9 (5.5mm) needles OR SIZE TO OBTAIN GAUGE
● Size 9 (5.5mm) circular needle, 16"/40cm long
● Stitch marker

Note

The original yarn used for this sweater is no longer available. A comparable substitute has been made, which is available at the time of printing. Check gauge of substitute yarns very carefully before beginning.

GAUGE

16 sts and 22 rows to 4"/10cm over St st using size 9 (5.5mm) needles. FOR PERFECT FIT, TAKE TIME TO CHECK GAUGE.

BACK

With size 9 (5.5mm) needles, cast on 68 (72, 76, 80, 84) sts. Work in St st until piece measures 10 (10, 10½, 11, 11½)"/25.5 (25.5, 26.5, 28, 29)cm from beg (with edge rolled), end with a WS row.

Armhole shaping

Bind off 3 sts at beg of next 2 rows, 2 sts at beg of next 2 rows, dec 1 st each side every other row twice—54 (58, 62, 66, 70) sts. Work even until armhole measures 7"/18cm, end with a WS row.

Neck shaping

Next row (RS) Work 15 (17, 19, 21, 23) sts, join 2nd ball of yarn and bind off center 24 sts, work to end. Working both sides at once, bind off from each neck edge 3 sts twice. Bind off rem 9 (11, 13, 15, 17) sts each side for shoulders.

FRONT

Work as for back until armhole measures 5"/13cm, end with a WS row.

Neck shaping

Next row (RS) Work 20 (22, 24, 26, 28) sts, join 2nd ball of yarn and bind off center 14 sts, work to end. Working both sides at once, bind off from each neck edge 3 sts once, 2 sts twice, 1 st 4 times. When same length as back, bind off rem 9 (11, 13, 15, 17) sts each side for shoulders.

FINISHING

Block pieces lightly. Sew shoulder seams.

Neckband

With RS facing and circular needle, pick up and k92 sts evenly around neck edge. Join, place marker, and work in rnds of St st (k every rnd) for 1"/2.5cm. Bind off.

Armhole bands

With RS facing and circular needle, pick up and k73 sts evenly around each armhole edge. Join, place marker, and work in rnds of St st for 1"/2.5cm. Bind off. Sew side seams. ●

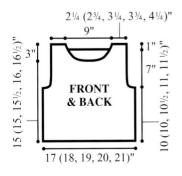

Casual elegance combined with comfort and practicality is the signature style of fashion designer Adrienne Vittadini. Figure-flattering side shaping, three-quarter raglan sleeves and a face-framing, ribbed mock turtleneck all add up to a go-with-everything wardrobe essential. Shown in size Medium. The Shaped Pullover first appeared in the Winter '98/99 issue of *Vogue Knitting*.

Shaped Pullover

SIZES
To fit Small (Medium, Large, X-Large). Directions are for smallest size with larger sizes in parentheses. If there is only one figure it applies to all sizes.

KNITTED MEASUREMENTS
● Bust 37½ (39, 41, 44)"/95 (99, 104, 111.5)cm.
● Waist 33 (34½, 36, 39)"/84 (87.5, 91.5, 99)cm.
● Length 22½ (23, 24¼, 25½)"/57 (58.5, 61.5, 65)cm.
● Upper arm 13¼ (14, 15½, 17¼)"/33.5 (35.5, 39.5, 43.5)cm.

MATERIALS
● 17 (20, 21, 22) 1¾oz/50g balls (each approx 38yd/34m) of Adrienne Vittadini/JCA *Dani* (wool ⑥) in #801 ecru
● One pair each sizes 11 and 13 (8 and 9mm) needles OR SIZE TO OBTAIN GAUGE
● Size 11 (8mm) circular needle, 16"/40cm long
● Stitch holders

GAUGE
10 sts and 14 rows to 4"/10cm over St st using size 13 (9mm) needles.
FOR PERFECT FIT, TAKE TIME TO CHECK GAUGE.

BACK
With smaller needles, cast on 49 (49, 55, 55) sts.
Next row (WS) P2, *k3, p3; rep from *, end k3, p2.
Next row (RS) K the knit and p the purl sts. Cont in k3, p3 rib as established until piece measures 2"/5cm from beg,

dec 2 (0, 4, 0) sts evenly across last WS row—47 (49, 51, 55) sts. Change to larger needles and St st.
Next row (RS) K3, k2tog, k to last 5 sts, ssk, k3. Rep this row every 6th row twice more—41 (43, 45, 49) sts. Work even until piece measures 7"/17.5cm from beg.
Next row (RS) K3, M1, k to last 3 sts, M1, k3. Rep this row every 8th row twice more—47 (49, 51, 55) sts. Work even until piece measures 13"/33cm from beg.

Raglan armhole shaping
Dec row (RS) K3, k2tog, k to last 5 sts, ssk, k3. Rep this row every [2nd, 4th] row 2 (2, 3, 4) times, then every 2nd row 9 (10, 9, 8) times, AT SAME TIME, when 23 (23, 23, 25) sts rem, work neck shaping.

Neck shaping
Cont to work armhole shaping, join 2nd ball of yarn and bind off center 13 (13, 13, 15) sts, work to end. Working both sides at once, bind off 1 st from each neck edge once. When armhole shaping is complete, bind off rem 2 sts each side.

FRONT
Work as for back until 29 (29, 29, 31) sts rem.

Neck shaping
Next row (RS) Cont to work armhole shaping, place center 7 (7, 7, 9) sts on a holder, join 2nd ball of yarn, work to end. Cont to work raglan armhole shaping, working both sides at once and binding off 2 sts from each neck edge once, then dec 1 st every other row twice. When all decs are completed, bind off rem 2 sts each side.

SLEEVES
With smaller needles, cast on 25 (25, 31, 31) sts. Work in rib as for back for 2"/5cm. Change to larger needles and St st.
Next row (RS) K1, M1, k to last st, M1, k1. Rep this row every 12th (10th, 12th, 8th) row 3 (4, 3, 5) times more—33 (35, 39, 43) sts. Work even until piece measures 15 (15, 15½, 16)"/38 (38, 39.5, 40.5)cm from beg.

Raglan cap shaping
Dec row (RS) K3, k2tog, work to last 5 sts, ssk, k3. Rep this row every [2nd, 4th] row 3 times, then every 2nd row 5 (6, 8, 10) times—9 sts. Work 1 row even.
Next row (RS) K2, k2tog, k1, ssk, k2. Place rem 7 sts on a holder.

FINISHING
Block pieces to measurements. Sew raglan caps into raglan armholes. Sew side and sleeve seams. With RS facing and circular needle, pick up and k54 (54, 54, 60) sts evenly around neck edge, including sts from holders. Join and work in rnds of k3, p3 rib for 4"/10cm. Bind off in rib. ●

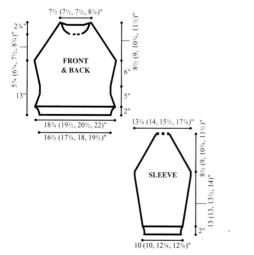

Perfect for beginners, this Vogue classic works as a cardigan or jacket—a great way to stretch your wardrobe. Oversized, the sweater features drop shoulders and garter-stitch edges for subtle texture. Shown in size 36. The Cropped Cardigan first appeared in the Winter '92/93 issue of *Vogue Knitting*.

Cropped Cardigan

SIZES
To fit 32 (34, 36, 38, 40)"/81 (86, 91, 96, 101)cm bust. Directions are for smallest size with larger sizes in parentheses. If there is only one figure it applies to all sizes.

KNITTED MEASUREMENTS
● Bust (buttoned) 38 (39½, 42, 44, 46¼)"/96.5 (100.5, 106.5, 111.5, 117.5)cm.
● Length 20 (20, 20, 21, 21)"/51 (51, 51, 53.5, 53.5)cm.
● Sleeve width at upper arm 18 (19¼, 20, 20¾, 22)"/45.5 (49, 51, 52.5, 56)cm.

MATERIALS
● 14 (14, 15, 15, 16) 1½oz/40g balls (each approx 90yd/82m) of Classic Elite *La Gran* (mohair/wool/nylon⑤) in #6551 soleil
● One pair each sizes 10½ and 11 (6.5 and 8mm) needles OR SIZE TO OBTAIN GAUGE
● Five ⅞"/2.5cm buttons
Note
The original color used for this sweater is no longer available. A comparable color substitute has been made, which is available at the time of printing.

GAUGE
11 sts and 17 rows to 4"/10cm over St st using size 11 (8mm) needles and 2 strands of yarn held together.
FOR PERFECT FIT, TAKE TIME TO CHECK GAUGE.

Note
Use 2 strands of yarn held together throughout.

BACK
With smaller needles and 2 strands held tog, cast on 52 (55, 58, 61, 64) sts. Work in garter st (k every row) for 8 rows (4 ridges on RS). Change to larger needles and St st (k on RS, p on WS). Work even until piece measures 19 (19, 19, 20, 20)"/48.5 (48.5, 48.5, 51, 51)cm from beg, end with a WS row.

Neck shaping
Next row (RS) K17 (18, 20, 21, 23), join 2nd ball of yarn and bind off 18 (19, 18, 19, 18) sts, work to end. Working both sides at once, bind off from each neck edge 3 sts once. When piece measures 20 (20, 20, 21, 21)"/51 (51, 51, 53.5, 53.5)cm from beg, bind off rem 14 (15, 17, 18, 20) sts each side for shoulders.

LEFT FRONT
With smaller needles and 2 strands held tog, cast on 23 (24, 26, 27, 29) sts. Work in garter st as for back. Change to larger needles. Work even in St st until piece measures 16½ (16½, 16½ 17½, 17½)"/42 (42, 42, 44.5, 44.5)cm from beg, end with a RS row.

Neck shaping
Next row (WS) Bind off 3 sts (neck edge), work to end. Cont to bind off from neck edge 2 sts twice, dec 1 st every other row twice. When same length as back to shoulder, bind off rem 14 (15, 17, 18, 20) sts.

RIGHT FRONT
Work as for left front, working neck shaping at beg of RS rows.

SLEEVES
With smaller needles and 2 strands held tog, cast on 27 (27, 27, 29, 29) sts. Work in garter st for 8 rows. Change to larger needles. Work in St st, inc 1 st each side every 4th row 0 (3, 6, 6, 11) times, every 6th row 11 (10, 8, 8, 5) times—49 (53, 55, 57, 61) sts. Work even until piece measures 19 (19, 20, 20, 20)"/48.5 (48.5, 51, 51, 51)cm from beg. Bind off.

FINISHING
Block pieces. Sew shoulder seams.

Left front band
With RS facing, smaller needles and 2 strands held tog, pick up and k52 (52, 52, 55, 55) sts along straight edge of left front. Work in garter st for 7 rows (4 ridges on RS). Bind off. Place markers on band for 4 buttons, with the first 1½"/4cm from lower edge, the last 3"/7.5cm from beg of neck dec and 2 others evenly between.

Right front band
Work as for left front band, working buttonholes on 3rd row (2 ridges on RS) opposite markers as foll: k2tog, yo.

Neckband
With RS facing, smaller needles and 2 strands held tog, pick up and k72 sts around neck edge, including tops of front bands. Work in garter st for 3 rows (2 ridges on RS).

Next row (RS) K2, k2tog, yo (buttonhole), *k2tog, k4; rep from * to end—61 sts. Cont to work in garter st for 3 more rows (4 ridges on RS). Bind off. Place markers 9 (9½, 10, 10½, 11)"/23 (24, 25.5, 26.5, 28)cm down from shoulders on front and back for armholes. Sew top of sleeves between markers. Sew side and sleeve seams. Sew on buttons. •

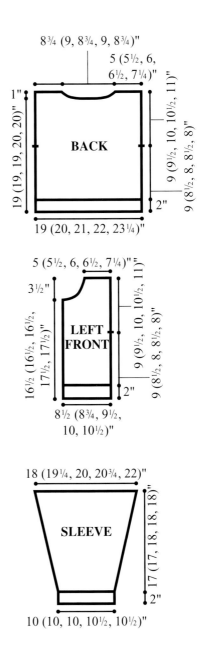

8¾ (9, 8¾, 9, 8¾)"

5 (5½, 6, 6½, 7¼)"

1"

BACK

19 (19, 19, 20, 20)"

9 (9½, 10, 10½, 11)"

9 (8½, 8, 8½, 8)"

2"

19 (20, 21, 22, 23¼)"

5 (5½, 6, 6½, 7¼)"

3½"

LEFT FRONT

16½ (16½, 16½, 17½, 17½)"

9 (9½, 10, 10½, 11)"

9 (8½, 8, 8½, 8)"

2"

8½ (8¾, 9½, 10, 10½)"

18 (19¼, 20, 20¾, 22)"

SLEEVE

17 (17, 18, 18, 18)"

2"

10 (10, 10, 10½, 10½)"

Designer Isaac Mizrahi chose a luxurious cream-colored brushed alpaca blend for this wonderfully relaxed shawl-collared pullover. Shown in size Medium. The Shawl-Collared Pullover first appeared in the Fall '98 issue of *Vogue Knitting*.

Shawl-Collared Pullover

SIZES
To fit Small (Medium, Large, X-Large). Directions are for smallest size with larger sizes in parentheses. If there is only one figure it applies to all sizes.

KNITTED MEASUREMENTS
● Bust 40 (43, 46, 49)"/101.5 (109, 117, 124.5)cm.
● Length 21½ (21½, 22, 23)"/55 (55, 56.5, 58.5)cm.
● Upper arm 13½ (13½, 14½, 16)"/34.5 (34.5, 37, 40.5)cm.

MATERIALS
● 9 1¾oz/50g balls for all sizes (each approx 152yd/140m) of Filatura Di Crosa/Stacy Charles *Ultralight* (alpaca/wool/nylon⑤) in #13 ecru
● One pair size 19 (16mm) needles OR SIZE TO OBTAIN GAUGE
● Size 17 (12.75mm) circular needle

GAUGE
6 sts and 10 rows to 4"/10cm over St st using size 19 (16mm) needles and 3 strands of yarn held tog.
FOR PERFECT FIT, TAKE TIME TO CHECK GAUGE.

Notes
1 A selvage st is worked at beg and end of every row and not included in measurements.
2 Use 3 strands of yarn held tog throughout.

BACK
With straight needles and 3 strands of yarn held tog, cast on 32 (34, 37, 39) sts.

Work in St st for 12½ (12½, 12½, 13)"/32 (32, 32, 33)cm, end with a WS row.

Armhole shaping
Bind off 1 st at beg of next 2 rows.
Dec row (RS) K2, k2tog, work to last 4 sts, SKP, k2. [P 1 row. Rep dec row] 1 (1, 2, 2) times—26 (28, 29, 31) sts. Cont in St st until armhole measures 7½ (7½, 8, 8½)"/19 (19, 20.5, 21.5)cm.

Shoulder shaping
Bind off 3 (4, 4, 4) sts at beg of next 2 rows, 4 (4, 4, 5) sts at beg of next 2 rows. Bind off rem 12 (12, 13, 13) sts for back neck.

FRONT
Work as for back until armhole measures 5 (5, 5½, 6)"/12.5 (12.5, 14, 15)cm, end with a WS row.

Neck shaping
Next row (RS) Work 9 (10, 10, 11) sts, join a 2nd ball of yarn and bind off center 8 (8, 9, 9) sts, work to end. Working both sides at once, dec 1 st at each neck edge every row twice, AT SAME TIME, when same length as back to shoulder, shape shoulder as for back.

SLEEVES
With straight needles and 3 strands of yarn held tog, cast on 18 sts. Work in St st, inc 1 st each side every 14th (14th, 10th, 8th) row 2 (2, 3, 4) times—22 (22, 24, 26) sts. Work even until piece measures 18"/45.5cm from beg, end with a WS row.

Cap shaping
Bind off 1 st at beg of next 2 rows.

Dec row (RS) K2, k2tog, work to last 4 sts, SKP, k2. Work 3 rows even. Rep dec row—16 (16, 18, 20) sts. Work 1 (1, 3, 3) rows even. Bind off 5 sts at beg of next 2 rows. Bind off rem 6 (6, 8, 10) sts.

FINISHING
Block pieces to measurements. Sew shoulder seams.

Neckband
With RS facing, circular needle and 3 strands of yarn held tog, beg at first bound-off st of front neck, pick up and k37 (37, 39, 39) sts evenly around neck edge, then cast on 12 sts—49 (49, 51, 51) sts at end. Work in k1, p1 rib for 5 rows. Dec 1 st each side on next row, work 1 row even, then rep dec every row 8 times more. Bind off rem 31 (31, 33, 33) sts. Sew cast-on sts to neck on the inside. Set in sleeves. Sew side and sleeve seams. ●

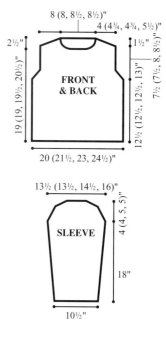

Noted for her modern method of shaping knits, designer Rebecca Moses combines keen color and distinct proportion in this oversized tunic with drop shoulders, extra-long foldback sleeves and scoop neck. The sweater is knit with a soft mohair in fast 3x3 ribs; finishing is minimal. Shown in size 36. The Ribbed Tunic first appeared in the Fall '89 issue of *Vogue Knitting*.

Ribbed Tunic

SIZES
To fit 32 (34, 36, 38, 40)"/81 (86, 91, 96, 101)cm bust. Directions are for smallest size with larger sizes in parentheses. If there is only one figure it applies to all sizes.

KNITTED MEASUREMENTS
● Bust 37½ (40, 42, 44½, 47)"/93 (99, 105, 111, 117)cm.
● Length 29 (30, 30, 30½, 31)"/73 (76, 76, 77.5, 79)cm.
● Upper arm 20 (21, 21, 22, 22)"/50 (53, 53, 56, 56)cm.

MATERIALS
Original Yarn
● 14 (14, 15, 16, 17) 1¾oz/50g balls (each approx 80yd/73m) of Lang Yarns/Joseph Galler, Inc. *Forever* (mohair/viscose/wool⑤) in #6328 light rust
Substitute Yarn
● 7 (7, 8, 8, 9) 1¾oz/50g balls (each approx 160yd/147m) of Cleckheaton *Flowerdale Mohair 8 ply* by Plymouth Yarn (mohair/wool/nylon③) in #24 twig
● One pair size 9 (5.5mm) needles OR SIZE TO OBTAIN GAUGE
● Size 9 (5.5mm) circular needle, 24"/60cm long
Note
The original yarn used for this sweater is no longer available. A comparable substitute has been made, which is available at the time of printing. Check gauge of substitute yarns very carefully before beginning.

GAUGE
20 sts and 18 rows to 4"/10cm over rib pat using size 9 (5.5mm) needles. FOR PERFECT FIT, TAKE TIME TO CHECK GAUGE.
Note
To work gauge swatch, cast on 21 sts. Work in rib pat for 18 rows. Bind off in rib. Pull swatch lengthwise so that ribs pull in. Piece should measure 4¼"/10.5cm wide by 4"/10cm long.

STITCH GLOSSARY
Rib Pat (multiple of 6 sts + 3 extra)
Row 1 (RS) K3, *p3, k3; rep from * to end.
Row 2 K the knit sts and p the purl sts. Rep rows 1 and 2 for rib pat.
Note
While knitting piece, pull lengthwise every few inches so rib sts pull in, to obtain more accurate measurements.

BACK
With straight needles, cast on 93 (99, 105, 111, 117) sts. Work in rib pat for 19 (19½, 19½, 19½, 20)"/48 (49.5, 49.5, 49.5, 51)cm. Place a marker at each side of last row to mark beg of armhole. Cont in rib until armhole measures 9 (9½, 9½, 10, 10)"/23 (24, 24, 25.5, 25.5)cm above markers, end with a WS row.

Neck shaping
Next row (RS) Work 29 (31, 34, 37, 39) sts, join 2nd ball of yarn and bind off 35 (37, 37, 37, 39) sts, work to end. Working both sides at once, dec 1 st at each neck edge *every* row 4 times. Bind off rem 25 (27, 30, 33, 35) sts each side for shoulders.

FRONT
Work as for back until armhole measures 7 (7½, 7½, 8, 8)"/18 (19, 19, 20.5, 20.5)cm above markers, end with a WS row.

Neck shaping
Next row (RS) Work 32 (34, 37, 40, 42) sts, join 2nd ball of yarn and bind off 29 (31, 31, 31, 33) sts, work to end. Working both sides at once, bind off from each neck edge 2 sts once, then dec 1 st every other row 5 times. Bind off rem 25 (27, 30, 33, 35) sts each side.

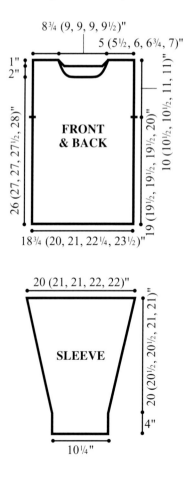

8¾ (9, 9, 9, 9½)"
5 (5½, 6, 6¾, 7)"
1"
2"
26 (27, 27, 27½, 28)"
10 (10½, 10½, 11, 11)"
19 (19½, 19½, 19½, 20)"
FRONT & BACK
18¾ (20, 21, 22¼, 23½)"

20 (21, 21, 22, 22)"
SLEEVE
20 (20½, 20½, 21, 21)"
4"
10¼"

SLEEVES

With straight needles, cast on 51 sts. Work in rib pat for 4"/10cm. Cont in rib, inc 1 st each side (working inc sts into rib) [every 4th row once, every 2nd row once] 5 (10, 10, 15, 15) times, every 4th row 14 (7, 7, 0, 0) times—99 (105, 105, 111, 111) sts. Work even until piece measures 24 (24^1/$_2$, 24^1/$_2$, 25, 25)"/60 (61, 61, 62.5, 62.5)cm from beg. Bind off in rib.

FINISHING

Block pieces. DO NOT PRESS. Sew shoulder seams.

Edging

With WS facing and circular needle, pick up and k 1 st in every st and 2 sts in every 3 rows around neck edge. Bind off all sts from WS. Sew top of sleeves to front and back between markers. Sew side and sleeve seams, sewing last 4"/10cm of sleeve invisibly on WS (cuff foldback). •

Bold split-collar styling and a full spectrum of intense color make this oversized V-neck pullover unique. Beefy, space-dyed chenille knit in reverse stockinette creates a woven look. A Vogue Original. Shown in size Medium. The Split-Collar V-Neck Pullover first appeared in the Winter '97 issue of *Vogue Knitting*.

Split-Collar V-Neck Pullover

SIZES
To fit Small (Medium, Large). Directions are for smallest size with larger sizes in parentheses. If there is only one figure it applies to all sizes.

KNITTED MEASUREMENTS
● Bust 37 (41, 44¹/2)"/94 (104, 113)cm.
● Length 28¹/2 (29, 30)"/72.5 (73.5, 76)cm.
● Upper arm 19 (19, 20)"/48 (48, 50)cm.

MATERIALS
● 7 (8, 10) 3¹/2oz/100g balls (each approx 66yd/60m) of Trendsetter Yarns *Brava* (acrylic/nylon®) in #1076 multi
● One pair size 11 (8mm) needles OR SIZE TO OBTAIN GAUGE
● Size 10 (6mm) circular needle, 24"/60cm long
● Stitch marker

GAUGE
9 sts and 12 rows to 4"/10cm over rev St st using size 11 (8mm) needles. FOR PERFECT FIT, TAKE TIME TO CHECK GAUGE.

BACK
With size 11 (8mm) needles, cast on 50 (54, 60) sts. Work in rev St st (p on RS, k on WS) for 7¹/2 (8, 8¹/2)"/19 (20.5, 21.5)cm. Dec 1 st each side on next row and rep dec every 6th row 3 (3, 4) times more—42 (46, 50) sts. Work even until piece measures 18 (18¹/2, 19)"/46 (47, 48.5)cm from beg, end with a WS row.

Armhole shaping
Bind off 3 sts at beg of next 2 rows— 36 (40, 44) sts. Work even until armhole measures 8¹/2 (8¹/2, 9)"/21.5 (21.5, 22.5)cm.

Neck and shoulder shaping
Next row Work 14 (16, 18) sts, join 2nd ball of yarn and bind off center 8 sts, work to end. Working both sides at once, bind off from each neck edge 3 sts once, 2 sts once, 1 st once, AT SAME TIME, when armhole measures 9¹/2 (9¹/2, 10)"/24 (24, 25)cm, bind off from each shoulder edge 4 (5, 6) sts twice.

FRONT
Work as for back until armhole measures 2¹/2 (2¹/2, 3)"/6.5 (6.5, 7.5)cm, end with a WS row.

Neck and shoulder shaping
Next row Work 17 (19, 21) sts, join 2nd ball of yarn and bind off center 2 sts, work to end. Working both sides at once, shape V-neck as foll:
Next row Knit.
Next row (RS) Work to last 3 sts of left front, p2tog, p1; on right front, p1, p2tog, p to end. Rep last 2 rows 8 times more, AT SAME TIME, when armhole measures 9¹/2 (9¹/2, 10)"/24 (24, 25)cm, shape shoulder as for back.

SLEEVES
With size 11 (8mm) needles, cast on 23 (23, 25) sts. Work in rev St st, inc 1 st each side every 6th row 5 times, then every 4th row 5 times—43 (43, 45) sts. Work even until piece measures 19"/48cm from beg. Bind off all sts.

FINISHING
Sew shoulder seams.

Collar
With RS facing and circular needle, beg at right front V-neck, pick up and k 17 sts along right neck edge, 29 sts across back neck and 17 sts along left front neck—63 sts. Join and place marker at end of rnd for center of V-neck.
Rnd 1 *K1, p1; rep from * to last st, k1. Work in k1, p1 rib as established for 8 rnds. Turn.
Next row *P1, k1; rep from * to last st, p1. Turn. Work back and forth in rib as established until collar measures 8"/20.5cm. Bind off loosely in rib. With center of bound-off sts of sleeve at shoulder seam, set in sleeves, sewing last 1¹/4"/3cm at top of sleeve to bound-off armhole sts. Sew side and sleeve seams. ●

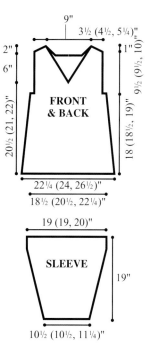

This cardigan combines the generous warmth of outerwear with modern proportions. Slightly oversized and worked in easy garter stitch, it features drop shoulders, briefly ribbed edges and a wide, round neck. Designed by Michele Rose. Shown in size 34. The Garter-Stitch Cardigan first appeared in the Fall '90 issue of *Vogue Knitting*.

Garter-Stitch Cardigan

SIZES
To fit 30 (32, 34, 36, 38, 40)"/76 (81, 86, 91, 96, 101)cm bust. Directions are for smallest size with larger sizes in parentheses. If there is only one figure it applies to all sizes.

KNITTED MEASUREMENTS
● Bust (buttoned) 40^1/$_4$ (42^1/$_4$, 44^1/$_4$, 46^1/$_4$, 48^1/$_4$, 50^1/$_4$)"/100 (105, 111, 117, 120, 126)cm.
● Length 21^1/$_2$ (22, 22, 22^1/$_2$, 23^1/$_2$, 24)"/54 (55.5, 55.5, 57, 59.5, 60.5)cm.
● Upper arm 19 (20, 20, 21, 21, 22)"/47 (50, 50, 53, 53, 55)cm.

MATERIALS
Original Yarn
● 8 (9, 9, 10, 10, 11) 1^3/$_4$oz/50g balls (each approx 107yd/97m) of Patons *Fashion Mohair* (mohair/wool/nylon⑤) in #2811 yellow
Substitute Yarn
● 10 (11, 11, 12, 12, 13) 1^1/$_2$oz/40g balls (each approx 90yd/82m) of Classic Elite *La Gran Mohair* (mohair/wool/nylon⑤) in #6516 ecru
● One pair each sizes 7 and 9 (4.5 and 5.5mm) needles OR SIZE TO OBTAIN GAUGE
● Six ^{7}/$_8$"/22mm buttons
● Stitch markers
Note
The original yarn used for this sweater is no longer available. A comparable substitute has been made, which is available at the time of printing. Check gauge of substitute yarns very carefully before beginning.

GAUGE
14 sts and 25 rows to 4"/10cm over garter st using size 9 (5.5mm) needles. FOR PERFECT FIT, TAKE TIME TO CHECK GAUGE.

BACK
With smaller needles, cast on 70 (73, 77, 81, 84, 88) sts. Work in k1, p1 rib for 1^1/$_4$"/3cm. Change to larger needles. Work in garter st (k every row) until piece measures 12 (12, 12, 12, 13, 13)"/30.5 (30.5, 30.5, 30.5, 33, 33)cm from beg. Place marker each side of last row for beg of armhole. Work even in garter st until armhole measures 8^1/$_2$ (9, 9, 9^1/$_2$, 9^1/$_2$, 10)"/21 (22.5, 22.5, 24, 24, 25)cm above markers.

Neck shaping
Next row (RS) Work 24 (25, 26, 28, 29, 31) sts, join 2nd ball of yarn and bind off 22 (23, 25, 25, 26, 26) sts, work to end. Working both sides at once, bind off from each neck edge 4 sts once, 3 sts once. Bind off rem 17 (18, 19, 21, 22, 24) sts each side.

LEFT FRONT
With smaller needles, cast on 33 (35, 37, 39, 40, 42) sts. Rib as for back. Change to larger needles. Work in garter st, placing armhole marker at side edge (beg of RS row) as for back, until armhole measures 6^1/$_2$ (7, 7, 7^1/$_2$, 7^1/$_2$, 8)"/16 (17.5, 17.5, 19, 19, 20)cm above marker, end with a RS row.

Neck shaping
Next row (WS) Bind off 6 (7, 8, 8, 8, 8) sts (neck edge), work to end. Cont to

bind off from neck edge 4 sts once, 2 sts once, dec 1 st every other row 4 times. When same length as back, bind off rem 17 (18, 19, 21, 22, 24) sts.

RIGHT FRONT
Work as for left front, placing armhole marker at end of a WS row and working neck shaping at beg of RS rows.

SLEEVES
With smaller needles, cast on 36 (38, 38, 38, 40, 41) sts. Work in k1, p1 rib for 1^1/$_4$"/3cm. Change to larger needles. Work in garter st inc 1 st each side every 6th row 6 (8, 8, 16, 11, 15) times, every 8th row 9 (8, 8, 2, 6, 3) times—66 (70, 70, 74, 74, 77) sts. Work even until piece measures 19^1/$_2$ (20, 20, 20, 20^1/$_2$, 20^1/$_2$)"/48.5 (50, 50, 50, 51, 51)cm from beg. Bind off.

FINISHING
Block pieces. Sew shoulder seams.

Left front band
With RS facing and smaller needles, pick up and k83 (85, 85, 87, 91, 93) sts along straight edge of left front. Work in k1, p1 rib for 1^1/$_4$"/3cm. Bind off in rib. Place markers on band for 5 buttons, with the first ^{3}/$_4$"/2cm from lower edge, the last 4"/10cm from first neck dec and 3 others evenly between.

Right front band
Work as for left front band, working buttonholes opposite markers after ^{1}/$_2$"/1.5cm has been worked by binding off 3 sts for each buttonhole. On foll row, cast on 3 sts over bound-off sts.

Neckband

With RS facing and smaller needles, pick up and k103 (105, 109, 109, 111, 111) sts around neck edge, including tops of front bands. Work in k1, p1 rib for 1¼"/3cm, working a buttonhole 2 sts in from right front edge after ¼"/.5cm. Bind off in rib. Sew top of sleeves to front and back between markers. Sew side and sleeve seams. Sew on buttons. •

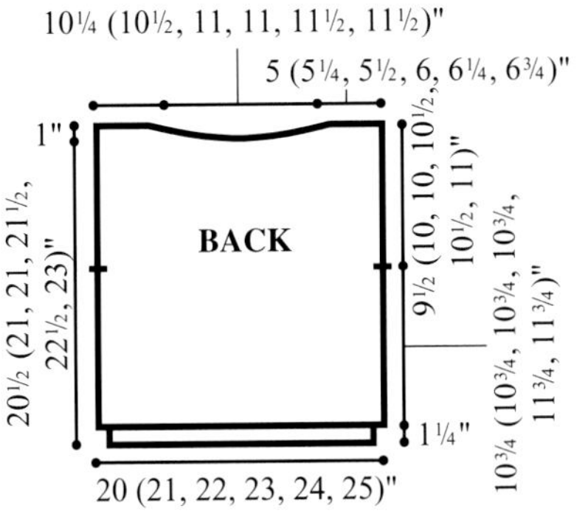

10¼ (10½, 11, 11, 11½, 11½)"
5 (5¼, 5½, 6, 6¼, 6¾)"
1"
BACK
20½ (21, 21, 21½, 22½, 23)"
9½ (10, 10, 10½, 10½, 11)"
10¾ (10¾, 10¾, 10¾, 11¾, 11¾)"
1¼"
20 (21, 22, 23, 24, 25)"

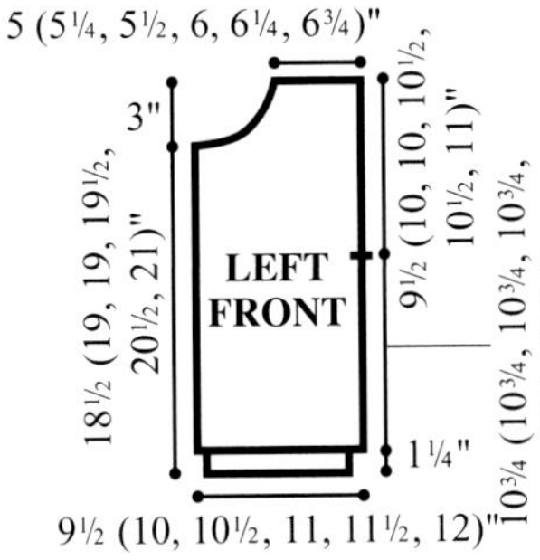

5 (5¼, 5½, 6, 6¼, 6¾)"
3"
LEFT FRONT
18½ (19, 19, 19½, 20½, 21)"
9½ (10, 10, 10½, 10½, 11)"
10¾ (10¾, 10¾, 10¾, 11¾, 11¾)"
1¼"
9½ (10, 10½, 11, 11½, 12)"

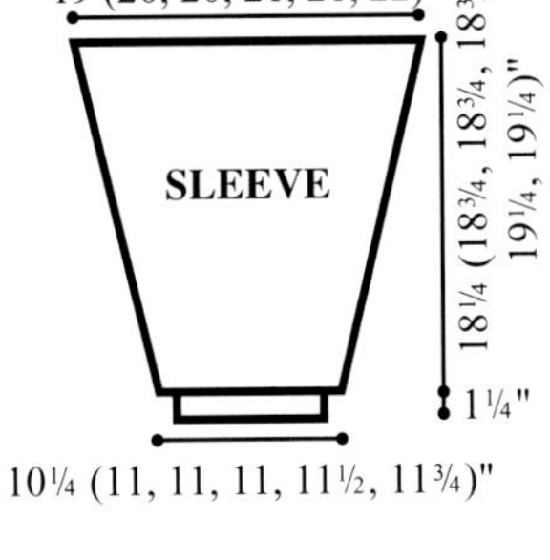

19 (20, 20, 21, 21, 22)"
SLEEVE
18¼ (18¾, 18¾, 18¾, 19¼, 19¼)"
1¼"
10¼ (11, 11, 11, 11½, 11¾)"

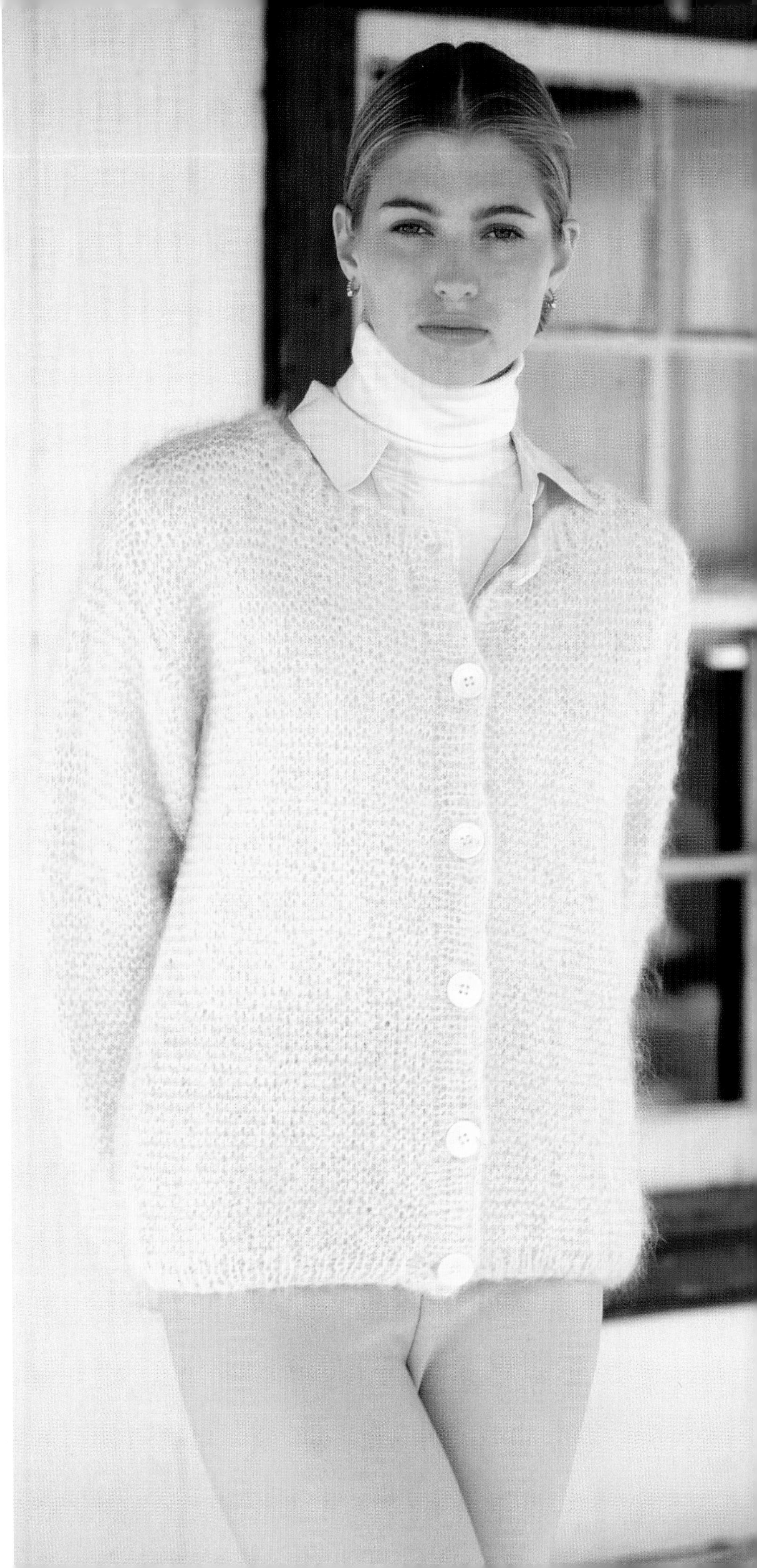

This oversized pullover tunic pairs optimal warmth with plenty of freedom of movement. Knit with square armholes for easy maneuvering, the sweater features a garter-stitch lower edge and rolled neck and cuffs. Super quick to knit using big needles and a medley of yarns. A Vogue Original. Shown in size Medium. The Rollneck Pullover first appeared in the Winter '94/95 issue of *Vogue Knitting*.

Rollneck Pullover

SIZES
To fit Small (Medium, Large). Directions are for smallest size with larger sizes in parentheses. If there is only one figure it applies to all sizes.

FINISHED MEASUREMENTS
● Bust 38 (42, 45)"/89 (106.5, 114.5)cm.
● Width at lower edge 45 (48, 52)"/114.5 (122, 132)cm.
● Length 23¹/₂ (24¹/₂, 25¹/₂)"/60 (62.5, 65)cm.
● Upper arm 17 (18, 19)"/43.5 (46, 48.5)cm.

MATERIALS
Original Yarn
● 8 (8, 9) 1³/₄oz/50g balls (each approx 148yd/135m) of Anny Blatt *Sweet Mohair* (kid mohair/wool/polyamid④) in #33 slate blue (A)
● 9 (9, 10) 1³/₄oz/50g balls (each approx 42yd/38m) of Anny Blatt *Amboise* (mohair/wool④) in #123 blue (B)
● 2 1³/₄oz/50g balls (each approx 190yd/175m) of Anny Blatt *Gyps'Anny* (viscose/metallized polyester②) in #16 silver (C) and #34 dark silver (D)
Substitute Yarn
● 12 (12, 14) 1³/₄oz/50g balls (each approx 98yd/90m) of Filatura Di Crosa/Stacy Charles *Mohair Lungo* (mohair/wool⑤) in #602 light blue (A)
● 7 (7, 8) 1³/₄oz/50g balls (each approx 55yd/50m) of Ad Hoc/Stacy Charles *Gemini* (mohair/wool/viscose⑥) in #156 blue (B)

● 3 1³/₄oz/50g balls (each approx 164yd/150m) of Filatura Di Crosa/Stacy Charles *No Smoking* (viscose/polyester③) in #101 silver (C) and #129 blue (D)
● One pair size 35 (19mm) needles OR SIZE TO OBTAIN GAUGE

Note
The original yarns used for this sweater are no longer available. Comparable substitutions have been made, which are available at the time of printing. Check gauge of substitute yarns very carefully before beginning.

GAUGE
6 sts and 8 rows to 5"/12.5cm over St st with 3 strands of A and 1 strand each of B, C and D held tog using size 35 (19mm) needles.
FOR PERFECT FIT, TAKE THE TIME TO CHECK GAUGE.

Notes
1 Sweater is worked with 6 strands of yarn held tog as foll: 3 strands A, 1 strand each of B, C and D.
2 For ease in working, keep C and D in separate plastic bags.

BACK
With yarns as noted, cast on 27 (29, 31) sts. K 2 rows. Beg with a purl row, work in St st (k on RS, p on WS), dec 1 st each side every 14th row twice—23 (25, 27) sts. Work even until piece measures 15 (15¹/₂, 16)"/38 (39.5, 41)cm from beg, end with a WS row.

Armhole shaping
Bind off 2 sts at beg of next 2 rows— 19 (21, 23) sts. Work even until armhole measures 8¹/₂ (9, 9¹/₂)"/21.5 (23, 24.5)cm. Bind off all sts.

FRONT
Work as for back until armhole measures 8 (8¹/₂, 9)"/20.5 (21.5, 23)cm, end with a WS row.

Neck shaping
Next row (RS) K6 (7, 8) sts, turn work and bind off same 6 (7, 8) sts. With RS facing, join yarn and bind off center 7 sts, k to end. Bind off rem 6 (7, 8) sts.

SLEEVES
With yarns as noted, cast on 16 (17, 18) sts. Beg with a purl row, work in St st, inc 1 st each side every 14th row

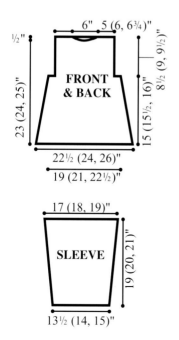

twice—20 (21, 22) sts. Work even until piece measures 19 (20, 21)"/48.5 (51, 53.5)cm from beg. Bind off all sts.

FINISHING
Sew left shoulder seam.

Highneck
With RS facing and yarns as noted, pick up and k8 sts along back neck, 9 sts along front neck—17 sts. P 1 row. Cont in St st, inc 1 st each side every other row 3 times—23 sts. Work even until highneck measures 8"/20.5cm. Bind off loosely. Sew right shoulder, including highneck. Sew top of sleeve to straight edge of armhole. Sew bound-off sts of body to side of sleeves. Sew side and sleeve seams. ●

This loose-fitting, split-color pullover with drop shoulders and distinct garter-stitch edge is knit in two easy pieces, then stitched together. Designed by Barbara Nudelman and Susan Prince for Stitchworx. The Split-Color Pullover first appeared in the Fall/Winter '84 issue of *Vogue Knitting*.

Split-Color Pullover

SIZES
To fit 32 (34, 36, 38)"/81 (86, 91, 96)cm bust. Directions are for smallest size with larger sizes in parentheses. If there is only one set of figures it applies to all sizes.

KNITTED MEASUREMENTS
● Bust 36 (38, 40, 42)"/90 (96, 100, 104)cm.
● Length 20"/50.5cm.
● Upper arm 24"/60cm.

MATERIALS
Original Yarn
● 5 (6, 6, 7) 1³/₄oz/50g balls (each approx 70yd/64m) of Emu/Merino *Finlandia* (wool⑤) in #5033 gold (A)
● 5 (6, 6, 7) balls in #5074 grey (B)
Substitute Yarn
● 2 (2, 2, 2) 8oz/250g hanks (each approx 310yd/286m) of Wool Pak Yarns NZ/Baabaajoes Wool Company *14 Ply* (wool④) in mist (A) and oatmeal (B)
● One pair each sizes 8 and 9 (5 and 5.5mm) needles OR SIZE TO OBTAIN GAUGE
● Stitch markers
Note
The original yarn used for this sweater is no longer available. A comparable substitute has been made, which is available at the time of printing. Check gauge of substitute yarns very carefully before beginning.

GAUGE
16 sts and 20 rows to 4"/10cm over St st using size 9 (5.5mm) needles. FOR PERFECT FIT, TAKE TIME TO CHECK GAUGE.

Note
Sweater is designed with A sections on left side and B sections on right side.

BACK
Section A
With smaller needles and A, cast on 36 (38, 40, 42) sts. Work in garter st (k every row) for 1¹/₂"/4cm, end with a WS row. Change to larger needles and St st (k on RS, p on WS) as foll:
Row 1 (RS) Knit.
Row 2 (WS) K1 (selvage st), purl to last st, k1 (selvage st). Rep rows 1 and 2 until back section A measures 8"/20.5cm from beg, or desired length to underarm, end with a RS row. Mark end of last row for armhole. Work even until armhole measures 12"/30cm, end with a WS row. Bind off all sts.

Section B
With B, work as for back section A, placing armhole marker at beg instead of end of row.

FRONT
Work as for back sections.

SLEEVES
(Note: Make one sleeve in color A and one sleeve in color B.) With smaller needles, cast on 34 (36, 36, 38) sts. Work in garter st for 1"/2.5cm, end with a WS row. Change to larger needles and St st. Inc 1 st each end of every other row 31 (30, 30, 29) times—96 sts. Work even in St st until sleeve measures 16"/40.5cm from beg, or desired sleeve length, end with a WS row. Bind off all sts.

FINISHING
Block pieces to measurements. With WS of pieces tog, sew back section A and B tog at center as foll: With side A facing, back st using color B and yarn needle. (Note: Be sure to work very loosely.) Beg at approx ¹/₈"/3mm down from neck edge and bring needle through both sections inside selvage st, *then insert needle back ¹/₈"/3mm behind where needle came through and bring the needle out ¹/₈"/3mm in front of where needle came through; rep from * along center front of section A. With side B of same piece facing and color A, rep back st as for A section.
Sew front sections A and B as for back sections. Sew front to back at shoulders 5¹/₂ (5¹/₂, 6, 6¹/₂)"/14 (14, 15, 16.5)cm from each side edge. Sew sleeves to front and back between markers. Sew side and sleeve seams. Press seams lightly on WS with warm iron and damp cloth. ●

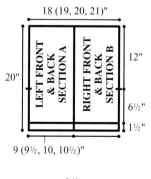

18 (19, 20, 21)"

LEFT FRONT & BACK SECTION A

RIGHT FRONT & BACK SECTION B

20"

12"

6¹/₂"

1¹/₂"

9 (9¹/₂, 10, 10¹/₂)"

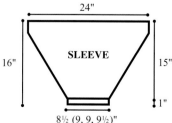

24"

SLEEVE

16"

15"

1"

8¹/₂ (9, 9, 9¹/₂)"

CAREFREE CARDIGANS

The ever versatile cardigan— a must for every wardrobe

A year-round favorite, this long-sleeved button-front cardigan has comfortable raglan sleeves and a flattering crew neck. Designed by Teva Durham. Shown in size Medium. The Button-Front Cardigan first appeared in the Fall '97 issue of *Vogue Knitting*.

Button-Front Cardigan

SIZES
To fit X-Small (Small, Medium, Large). Directions are for smallest size with larger sizes in parentheses. If there is only one figure it applies to all sizes.

KNITTED MEASUREMENTS
● Bust (buttoned) 32 (35½, 39, 42½)"/81 (90, 99, 108)cm.
● Length (including ½ of top of sleeve cap width) 20½ (22, 23, 24½)"/52 (56, 58.5, 62)cm.
● Upper arm 14 (15, 16, 17½)"/35.5 (38.5, 40.5, 44.5)cm.

MATERIALS
● 6 (7, 7, 8) 3½oz/100g hanks (each approx 138yd/100m) of Manos Del Uruguay/Simpson Southwick *700 Tex* (wool⑤) in #28 cinnamon
● One each sizes 9 and 10 (5.5 and 6mm) circular needles, 36"/90cm long OR SIZE TO OBTAIN GAUGE
● Stitch holders
● Seven ⅝"/16mm buttons

GAUGE
14 sts and 19 rows to 4"/10cm over St st, using size 10 (6mm) needle. FOR PERFECT FIT, TAKE TIME TO CHECK GAUGE.

Note
With hand-dyed yarns it is advisable to blend the yarns from several skeins by alternating 2 rows with one ball and 2 rows with another throughout to avoid obvious color changes.

STITCH GLOSSARY
Twisted Rib (over odd number of sts)
Row 1 (RS) K1, k1 through back loop (tbl), *p1 tbl, k1 tbl; rep from * to last st, k1.
Row 2 K1, p1 tbl, *k1 tbl, p1 tbl; rep from * to last st, k1.

BODY
With smaller needle, cast on 133 (145, 157, 169) sts. Work back and forth in Twisted Rib for ¾"/2cm, end with a WS row.
Buttonhole row (RS) Rib 4, yo, k2tog tbl, work to end. Work even until piece measures 2¾ (3, 3½, 3½)"/7 (7.5, 9, 9)cm, end with a WS row. Change to larger needle.
Next row (RS) Rib 7 and place these sts on holder for front band, k to last 7 sts, dec 10 sts evenly across, place last 7 sts on holder—109 (121, 133, 145) sts. Work even in St st until piece measures 12 (12¾, 13½, 14)"/30.5 (32.5, 34, 35.5)cm from beg, end with a WS row.

Divide for underarms
Next row (RS) Work 24 (27, 29, 32) sts (right front), bind off 6 (6, 8, 8) sts (underarm), work until there are 49 (55, 59, 65) sts for back, join 2nd ball of yarn and bind off 6 (6, 8, 8) sts (underarm), work rem 24 (27, 29, 32) sts (left front). Work on sts of back only, placing right and left front sts on holder.

BACK
P 1 row on WS.

Next (dec) row (RS) K2, ssk, k to last 4 sts, k2tog, k2.
Next row Purl. Cont to rep last 2 rows 9 (11, 13, 15) times more—29 (29, 31, 33) sts.

Neck shaping
Next row (RS) K2, ssk, k6, place next 9 (11, 11, 13) sts on holder (for neck), join 2nd ball of yarn, k6, k2tog, k2. Working both sides at once, cont with raglan decs at side edges, AT SAME TIME, dec 1 st at each neck edge *every* row 3 times. Bind off rem 4 sts each side.

LEFT FRONT
P 1 row on WS.
Next row (RS) K2, ssk, k to end. Cont to work raglan decs at armhole edge as for back, AT SAME TIME, after 10 (12, 12, 14) decs have been worked, end with RS row and work as foll:

Neck shaping
Next row (WS) Bind off 3 (4, 4, 5) sts, work to end. Cont with armhole decs, AT SAME TIME, dec 1 st from neck edge on next row, then *every* row 4 (4, 0, 0) times, every other row 0 (0, 4, 4) times. Bind off rem 3 sts.

RIGHT FRONT
Join yarn at underarm and work as for left front, reversing shaping by working k2tog, k2 at end of RS rows, and binding off for neck at beg of RS row.

SLEEVES

With smaller needle, cast on 29 (29, 33, 39) sts. Work back and forth in Twisted Rib for 2¾ (3, 3½, 3⅓)"/7 (7.5, 9, 9)cm, dec 4 sts evenly on last WS row—25 (25, 29, 35) sts. Change to larger needle. Work in St st, inc 1 st each side every 6th row 1 (9, 6, 2) times, every 8th row 11 (5, 8, 11) times—49 (53, 57, 61) sts. Work even until piece measures 23¾ (24, 26, 26)"/60.5 (61, 66, 66)cm from beg, end with a WS row.

Raglan cap shaping

Bind off 3 (3, 4, 4) sts at beg of next 2 rows.
Next row (RS) K2, ssk, k to last 4 sts, k2tog, K2.
Next row (WS) P2, p2tog, p to last 4 sts, p2tog tbl, p2. Rep last 2 rows 2 (2, 3, 3) times more, then cont to work decs on RS rows only 10 (12, 13, 15) times—11 (11, 15, 15) sts. Work 4 rows even. Bind off.

FINISHING

Bands

With RS facing and smaller needle, cont rib over 7 sts of left front band until band fits along front edge to neck when slightly stretched. Place sts on holder. Sew band in place. Place markers for 6 buttons evenly spaced along band, with the first opposite buttonhole at lower edge, the last 2"/5cm from neck edge and 4 others spaced evenly between. Work right front band to correspond, working buttonholes opposite markers. Block pieces. Sew raglan sleeves to armholes, matching last 4 rows at top of sleeves to bound-off sts at top of back; on fronts sew last 4 rows of sleeve over raglan points down neck edge. Sew sleeve seams.

Collar

With RS facing and smaller needle, work in rib pat over 7 sts on holder, pick up and k14 (16, 16, 18) sts along neck edge to sts on back holder, k9 (11, 11, 13) sts from back neck holder, pick up and k14 (16, 16, 18) sts along neck edge to holder, work sts from left band as foll: * p1 tbl, k1 tbl; rep from * to last st, k1. Work 1 row in rib pat over all sts. Cont rib for 4 rows more, working buttonhole on next rib row. Bind off in rib. Sew on buttons. •

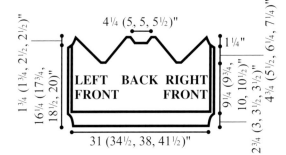

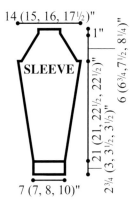

Seed-Stitch Striped Cardigan

V-neck perfection in a loose-fitting cardigan with vertical, seed-stitched stripes, drop shoulders and set-in pockets. Designed by Christian de Falbe. Shown in size 34. The Seed-Stitch Striped Cardigan first appeared in the Fall/Winter '87 issue of *Vogue Knitting*.

Seed-Stitch Striped Cardigan

Note
The original yarn used for this sweater is no longer available. A comparable substitute has been made, which is available at the time of printing. Check gauge of substitute yarns very carefully before beginning.

SIZES
To fit 30 (32, 34, 36, 38, 40)"/ 76 (81, 86, 91, 96, 101)cm bust. Directions are for smallest size with larger sizes in parentheses. If there is only one set of figures it applies to all sizes.

KNITTED MEASUREMENTS
- Bust (buttoned) 36 (38, 40, 42½, 44½, 46)"/91 (95, 100.5, 107, 111.5, 116.5)cm.
- Length 26 (26½, 27, 27½, 28, 28½)"/66 (67, 68, 69.5, 71, 72)cm.
- Upper arm 19 (19, 20, 20, 21, 21)"/48 (48, 50, 50, 53, 53)cm.

MATERIALS
Original Yarn
- 11 (12, 12, 13, 13, 14) 1¾oz/50g balls (each approx 132yd/120m) of Christian de Falbe/Silk City *Chandos* (wool③) in walnut
Substitute Yarn
- 21 (22, 22, 24, 24, 26) .88oz/25g hanks (each approx 72yd/67m) of Rowan/Westminster Fibers *Lightweight DK* (wool②) in #82 natural
- One pair each sizes 3 and 5 (3.25 and 3.75mm) needles OR SIZE TO OBTAIN GAUGE
- Size 3 (3.25mm) circular needle, 36"/90cm long
- Stitch holders and markers
- Six ⅝"/15mm buttons

GAUGE
23 sts and 30 rows to 4"/10cm over St st using size 5 (3.5mm) needles. FOR PERFECT FIT, TAKE TIME TO CHECK GAUGE.

STITCH GLOSSARY
Seed St (over 3 sts)
Row 1 K1, p1, k1. Rep row 1 for seed st.

BACK
With smaller needles, cast on 92 (96, 100, 104, 108, 112, 116) sts. Work in k1, p1 rib for 2"/5cm, inc 13 (13, 15, 15, 17, 17) sts evenly across last row—105 (109, 115, 123, 129, 133) sts. Change to larger needles.
Beg pat: Row 1 (RS) Work 13 (13, 16, 16, 19, 19) sts in St st (k on RS, p on WS), [3 sts in seed st, 16 (17, 17, 19, 19, 20) sts in St st] 4 times, 3 sts in seed st, 13 (13, 16, 16, 19, 19) sts in St st. Cont in pats until piece measures 16½ (17, 17, 17½, 17½, 18)"/42 (43, 43, 44.5, 44.5, 45.5)cm from beg. Place markers each side of last row for beg of armhole. Work even until armhole measures 9½ (9½, 10, 10, 10½, 10½)"/24 (24, 25, 25, 26.5, 26.5)cm. Bind off.

POCKET LININGS (make 2)
With larger needles, cast on 39 (39, 39, 43, 43, 47) sts. Work in St st for 5"/12.5cm. Place sts on a holder.

LEFT FRONT
With smaller needles, cast on 44 (46, 49, 52, 55, 59) sts. Work in k1, p1 rib for 2"/5cm, inc 5 (6, 6, 6, 6, 5) sts evenly across last row—49 (52, 55, 58, 61, 64) sts. Change to larger needles.
Beg pat: Row 1 (RS) Work 3 (3, 6, 5, 8, 7) sts in St st, 3 sts in seed st, [7 (7, 7, 8, 8, 9) sts in St st, 3 sts in seed st] 4 times, 3 (6, 6, 6, 6, 6) sts in St st. Cont in pats until piece measures 6"/15cm from beg, end with a WS row.

Pocket rib and joining lining
Next row (RS) Work 6 (6, 9, 8, 11, 10) sts in St st, place marker, work in k1, p1 rib over next 37 (37, 37, 41, 41, 45) sts, place marker, work in St st to end. Cont to work sts between markers in rib and rem sts in St st until rib measures ¾"/2cm, end with a WS row.
Next row (RS) K to first marker, bind off next 37 (37, 37, 41, 41, 45) sts knitwise, k to end.
Next row P to 1 st before bound-off sts, with RS of 1 pocket lining facing WS of work, p next st on needle tog with first st on holder, p across sts on holder to last st, p last st on holder tog with next st on needle, p to end. Cont in pat on all sts as foll:
Beg pat: Next row (RS) Work 13 (13, 16, 16, 19, 19) sts in St st, 3 sts in seed st, 16 (17, 17, 19, 19, 20) sts in St st, 3 sts in seed st, 14 (16, 16, 17, 17, 19) sts in St st. Cont in pat until piece measures 14 (14½, 15, 15½, 16, 16½)"/36 (37, 38, 39.5, 41, 42)cm from beg, end with a WS row.

Neck shaping
Work to last 2 sts, dec 1 st (neck edge). Cont to dec 1 st at neck edge every 4th row 6 (9, 12, 9, 9, 15) times more, then

every 6th row 10 (8, 6, 8, 8, 4) times—
32 (34, 36, 40, 43, 44) sts. Work even
until same length as back. Bind off.

RIGHT FRONT

Work as for left front, reversing all
shaping and placement of pats, as foll:
Beg pat: Row 1 (RS) Work 3 (6, 6, 6, 6,
6) sts in St st, [3 sts in seed st, 7 (7, 7,
8, 8, 9) sts in St st] 4 times, 3 sts in
seed st, 3 (3, 6, 5, 8, 7) sts in St st.

SLEEVES

With smaller needles, cast on 47 (47,
47, 47, 51, 51) sts. Work in k1, p1 rib for
3"/7.5cm, inc 10 (10, 10, 10, 12, 12) sts
evenly across last row—57 (57, 57, 57,
63, 63) sts. Change to larger needles.
(Note: Work first 3 inc sts each side into
seed st, then next 7 (7, 7, 7, 8, 8) sts in
St st, next 3 sts in seed st and rem sts
in St st. When sleeve measures 9"/23cm
from beg, discontinue the first, 3rd, 5th
and 7th sets of seed st and work these
sts in St st.)

Beg pat: Row 1 (RS) Work 7 (7, 7, 7,
8, 8) sts in St st, [3 sts in seed st, 7 (7,
7, 7, 8, 8) sts in St st] 5 times. Work 1
row even. Cont in pat, inc 1 st each
end of next row and rep inc every 4th
row 25 (25, 28, 28, 28, 28) times more.
Cont in pat on 109 (109, 115, 115, 121,
121) sts as foll:

Next row Work 13 (13, 16, 16, 15, 15)
sts in St st, [3 sts in seed st, 17 (17,
17, 17, 19, 19) sts in St st] 4 times, 3
sts in seed st, 13 (13, 16, 16, 15, 15)
sts in St st. Cont in pat until piece
measures 18 (18, 18½, 18½, 19,
19)"/45 (45, 46, 46, 47.5, 47.5)cm from
beg. Bind off.

FINISHING

Block pieces. Sew shoulder seams.
Sew top of sleeve to front and back
armholes between markers. Sew side
and sleeve seams.

Neck and front band

With RS facing and circular needle,
beg at lower right front edge, pick up
and k170 (173, 176, 179, 182, 185) sts
along right front edge to shoulder, 41
(41, 43, 43, 43, 45) sts along back
neck, 170 (173, 176, 179, 182, 185) sts
along left front edge—381 (387, 395,
401, 407, 415) sts. Work back and
forth as with straight needles in k1, p1
rib for 3 rows. Place markers on right
front for 6 buttonholes, first marker
½"/1.5cm from lower edge, last marker
at first neck dec, 4 spaced evenly
between. Rib next row, working
buttonholes at each marker as foll: yo,
k2tog for each buttonhole. Rib until
band measures 1"/2.5cm. Bind off in
rib. Sew on buttons. •

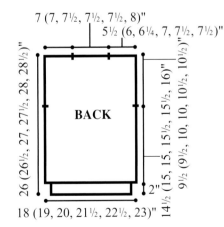

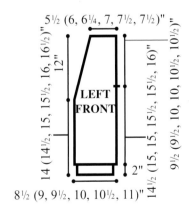

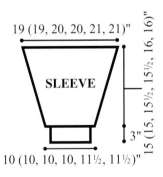

This softly textured double-breasted cropped jacket is standard-fitting and features set-in three-quarter sleeves and a Peter Pan collar. A Vogue Original. Shown in size Small. The Double-Breasted Jacket first appeared in the Winter '95/96 issue of *Vogue Knitting*.

Double-Breasted Jacket

SIZES
To fit Small (Medium, Large, X-Large). Directions are for smallest size with larger sizes in parentheses. If there is only one figure it applies to all sizes.

KNITTED MEASUREMENTS
● Bust (buttoned) 36 (39, 42, 45)"/91.5 (99, 106.5, 114)cm.
● Length 19$\frac{1}{2}$ (20, 20$\frac{1}{2}$, 21)"/49.5 (51, 52, 53.5)cm.
● Upper arm 13 (14, 15, 16)"/33 (35.5, 38, 40.5)cm.

MATERIALS
Original Yarn
● 10 (11, 11, 12) 1$\frac{3}{4}$oz/50g balls (each approx 99yd/90m) of Lang/Berroco *Rivoli* (polymide/mohair/acrylic④) in #8960 red
Substitute Yarn
● 14 (15, 15, 16) 1$\frac{3}{4}$oz/50g balls (each approx 75yd/70m) of Stahl Wolle/Tahki Imports *Sansibar* (wool/acrylic/mohair/polyamide⑤) in #2065 red
● One pair each sizes 5 and 7 (3.75 and 4.5mm) needles OR SIZE TO OBTAIN GAUGE
● Eight $\frac{3}{8}$"/10mm ball buttons
Note
The original yarn used for this sweater is no longer available. A comparable substitute has been made, which is available at the time of printing. Check gauge of substitute yarns very carefully before beginning.

GAUGE
17 sts and 25 rows to 4"/10cm over St st using size 7 (4.5mm) needles.
FOR PERFECT FIT, TAKE TIME TO CHECK GAUGE.

BACK
With smaller needles, cast on 82 (86, 94, 98) sts. Work in k2, p2 rib for 1"/2.5cm, end with a RS row. Change to larger needles. P next row on WS, dec 5 (3, 5, 3) sts evenly across—77 (83, 89, 95) sts. Cont in St st until piece measures 11"/28cm from beg, end with a WS row.

Armhole shaping
Bind off 3 sts at beg of next 2 rows, 2 sts at beg of next 4 (4, 6, 6) rows, dec 1 st each side every other row 3 (4, 3, 3) times—57 (61, 65, 71) sts. Work even until armhole measures 7$\frac{1}{2}$ (8, 8$\frac{1}{2}$, 9)"/19 (20.5, 21.5, 23)cm, end with a WS row.

Shoulder and neck shaping
Bind off 6 (6, 7, 8) sts at beg of next 2 rows, 6 (7, 7, 8) sts at beg of next 4 rows, AT SAME TIME, join 2nd ball of yarn and bind off center 9 (9, 11, 11) sts for neck and working both sides at once, bind off from each neck edge 3 sts twice.

LEFT FRONT
With smaller needles, cast on 53 (55, 57, 61) sts. Work in rib as foll:
Row 1 (RS) P2 (0, 2, 2), *k2, p2; rep from * to last 3 sts, p1, k2 (selvage sts).
Row 2 Sl 2 purlwise, k1, rib to end.
Rep last 2 rows for 1"/2.5cm, end with

a RS row. Change to larger needles.
Next row (WS) Work 3 selvage sts, p across, dec 6 (5, 4, 5) sts evenly—47 (50, 53, 56) sts. Cont to work 3 selvage sts, cont in St st until same length as back to armhole. Shape armhole at side edge (beg of RS rows) as for back—37 (39, 41, 44) sts. Work even until armhole measures 6 (6$\frac{1}{2}$, 7, 7$\frac{1}{2}$)"/15 (16.5, 17.5, 19)cm, end with a RS row.

Neck shaping
Next row (WS) Bind off 9 sts knitwise (neck edge), work to end. Cont to bind off from neck edge 4 (4, 5, 5) sts once, 3 sts once, 2 sts once, 1 st once. When same length as back to shoulder, shape shoulder at side edge as for back.

RIGHT FRONT
Work as for left front, reversing shaping and working 3 sts at front edge as foll:
Row 1 (RS) Wyib, sl 2 purlwise, p1, rib to end.
Row 2 (WS) Rib to last 3 sts, k1, p2.
When piece measures 3"/7.5cm from beg, work buttonhole row on RS row as foll: Work 3 sts, k2tog, yo, k8, k2tog, yo, work to end. Make 3 more sets of buttonholes at 4$\frac{1}{2}$ (4$\frac{3}{4}$, 5, 5$\frac{1}{4}$)"/11.5 (12, 12.5, 13.5)cm intervals.

SLEEVES
With smaller needles, cast on 38 (38, 42, 42) sts. Work in k2, p2 rib for 1"/2.5cm. Change to larger needles. P next row on WS, inc 1 (3, 0, 2) sts—39 (41, 42, 44) sts. Cont in St st, inc 1 st each side every 8th (8th, 6th, 6th) row 8 (9, 11, 12) times—55 (59, 64, 68) sts.

Work even until piece measures 13 (13½, 13½, 14)"/33 (34.5, 34.5, 35.5) cm from beg.

Cap shaping
Bind off 3 sts at beg of next 2 rows, 2 sts at beg of next 2 (2, 4, 4) rows, dec 1 st each side every other row 5 (7, 7, 9) times, every 4th row twice, bind off 2 sts at beg of next 4 rows, 3 sts at beg of next 2 rows. Bind off rem 17 (17, 18, 18) sts.

FINISHING
Block pieces to measurements. Sew shoulder seams.

Collar
With RS facing and larger needles, beg 2"/5cm in from right front neck edge, pick up and k55 (55, 59, 59) sts evenly around neck, ending 2"/5cm in from left front neck.

Row 1 (RS) K1, M1, p1, k to last 2 sts, p1, M1, k1. Place 4 markers after the 15th st from beg, then every 9 (9, 10, 10) sts 3 times.

Row 2 Sl 2 purlwise, k1, p to last 3 sts, k1, p2.

Row 3 Wyib, sl 2 purlwise, p1, *k to 1 st before marker, M1, k2, M1; rep from * 3 times more, work to last 3 sts, p1, k2. Rep last 2 rows 5 times more—105 (105, 109, 109) sts. Work 3 rows even. Bind off purlwise on RS. Set in sleeves. Sew side and sleeve seams. Sew on buttons. •

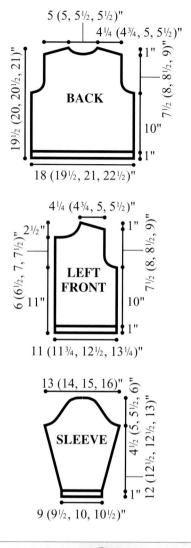

Cabled Twin Set

Adrienne Vittadini abbreviates the twin set using cables to emphasize a body-hugging design. The standard-fitting cardigan has set-in sleeves and a round neck; the sleeveless shell is close-fitting with rolled edges. Shown in size Small. The Cabled Twin Set first appeared in the Winter '94/95 issue of *Vogue Knitting*.

Cabled Twin Set

SIZES

To fit X-Small (Small, Medium, Large). Directions are for smallest size with larger sizes in parentheses. If there is only one figure it applies to all sizes.

KNITTED MEASUREMENTS

CARDIGAN:

- Bust (buttoned) 34 (37, 39, 40)"/86.5 (94, 99, 101.5)cm.
- Length 18 (18½, 19, 20)"/46 (47, 48.5, 51)cm.
- Upper arm 14 (15, 15, 16)"/36 (38, 38, 41)cm.

TANK:

- Bust 32 (34, 36, 38)"/81.5 (86.5, 91.5, 96.5)cm.
- Length 18 (18½, 19, 19½)"/46 (47, 48.5, 49.5)cm.

MATERIALS

CARDIGAN:

Original Yarn

- 9 (10, 11, 11) 1¾oz/50g balls (each approx 90yd/82m) of Reynolds/JCA *Frivoli* (mohair⑤) in #49 pink

Substitute Yarn

- 9 (10, 11, 11) 1½oz/40g balls (each approx 90yd/81m) Classic Elite *La Gran Mohair* (mohair/wool/nylon⑤) in #6565 pomegranate
- Stitch markers
- Cable needle (cn)
- Seven ⅝"/15mm buttons

TANK:
Original Yarn
- 3 (3, 4, 4) balls in #49 pink

Substitute Yarn
- 3 (3, 4, 4) balls in #6565 pomegranate

BOTH:
- One pair each sizes 7 and 9 (4.5 and 5.5mm) needles OR SIZE TO OBTAIN GAUGE
- Stitch markers

Note

The original yarn used for this sweater is no longer available. A comparable substitute has been made, which is available at the time of printing. Check gauge of substitute yarns very carefully before beginning.

GAUGE

- 15 sts and 20 rows to 4"/10cm over rev St st using size 9 (5.5mm) needles.
- 18 sts and 20 rows to 4"/10cm over cable pat using size 9 (5.5mm) needles. FOR PERFECT FIT, TAKE TIME TO CHECK GAUGES.

STITCH GLOSSARY

Cable Pat (multiple of 10 sts plus 6 extra)

Row 1 (RS) K6, *p4, k6; rep from *.
Row 2 P6, *k4, p6; rep from *.
Row 3 Sl 3 sts to cable needle (cn) and hold to *front* of work, k3; k3 from cn (cable twist complete), *p4, work cable twist; rep from *.
Rows 4-8 K the knit sts and p the purl sts. Rep rows 3-8 for cable pat.

CARDIGAN

BACK

With smaller needles, cast on 70 (74, 78, 82) sts.
Row 1 (WS) *K2, p2; rep from *, end k2.
Row 2 (RS) *P2, k2; rep from *, end p2.

Cont in k2, p2 rib until piece measures 2"/5cm from beg, ending with a WS row and inc 6 (8, 8, 8) sts across last row—76 (82, 86, 90) sts. Change to larger needles.
Beg pat: Next row P5 (3, 5, 2), place marker (pm), work row 1 of cable pat on next 66 (76, 76, 86) sts, pm, p5 (3, 5, 2). Working sts before and after markers in rev St st (p on RS, k on WS), cont in cable pat until piece measures 11 (11, 11½, 12)"/28 (28, 29.5, 30.5)cm from beg, end with a WS row.

Armhole shaping

Dec 1 st each side every other row 8 (8, 9, 9) times—60 (66, 68, 72) sts. Work even until armhole measures 7 (7½, 7½, 8)"/18 (19, 19, 20.5)cm. Bind off all sts.

LEFT FRONT

With smaller needles, cast on 34 (38, 38, 38) sts. Work in k2, p2 rib as for back, ending with a WS row and inc 3 (3, 5, 5) sts across last row—37 (41, 43, 43) sts. Change to larger needles.
Beg pat: Next row (RS) P5 (3, 5, 2) pm, work cable pat on next 26 (36, 36, 36) sts, pm, p6 (2, 2, 5). Cont in cable pat, working sts before and after markers in rev St st, until piece measures same as back to armhole, end with a WS row.

Armhole shaping

Next row (RS) Dec 1 st, work to end—36 (40, 42, 42) sts. Cont to dec 1 st at armhole edge every other row 7 (7, 8, 8) times more—29 (33, 34, 34) sts. Work even until piece measures 15 (15½, 16, 17)"/38 (39.5, 41, 43.5)cm from beg, end with a RS row.

Neck shaping

Next row (WS) Cont pat, bind off 5 sts at beg of row, work to end. Bind off 4 (5, 6, 5) sts from neck edge once, dec 1 st at neck edge every other row 3 (5, 5, 4) times. When armhole measures same as back, bind off rem 17 (18, 18, 20) sts.

RIGHT FRONT

Work as for left front. Reverse pat placement as foll:

Next row (RS) P6 (2, 2, 5) sts, pm, work cable pat over next 26 (36, 36, 36) sts, pm, p5 (3, 5, 2). Reverse armhole shaping by dec at end of RS rows. Work neck shaping at beg of RS rows.

SLEEVES

With smaller needles, cast on 26 (26, 30, 30) sts. Work in k2, p2 rib as for back until piece measures 5½"/14cm from beg, ending with a WS row and inc 4 sts across last row—30 (30, 34, 34) sts.

Beg pat: Next row P2 (2, 4, 4), work cable pat on next 26 sts, p2 (2, 4, 4). Cont in cable pat, AT SAME TIME, inc 1 st each side (working inc sts into cable pat) every 4th row 12 (19, 10, 14) times, every 6th row 5 (0, 7, 5) times—64 (68, 68, 72) sts. Work even until sleeve measures 22 (22½, 23, 23½)"/56 (57.5, 58.5, 60)cm from beg, end with a WS row.

Cap shaping

Dec 1 st each side every other row 8 (8, 9, 9) times—48 (52, 50, 54) sts. Bind off 4 (4, 5, 5) sts at beg of next 8 (8, 6, 6) rows. Bind off rem 16 (20, 20, 24) sts.

FINISHING

Block pieces lightly. Sew shoulder seams.

Buttonband

With RS facing and smaller needles, beg at neck edge and pick up and k81 (83, 85, 91) sts along left front.
Row 1 (WS) *K2, p2; rep from *, end k2, p1.
Row 2 K1, p2; *k2, p2; rep from * to end. Rep rows 1-2 until band measures 1½"/4cm. Bind off in rib. Place 6 markers on band, the first 1"/2.5cm from lower edge, the last 2"/5cm from beg of neck shaping and 4 others spaced evenly between.

Buttonhole band

With RS facing and smaller needles, beg at lower edge and pick up and k81 (83, 85, 91), sts along right front.
Row 1 (WS) P1, k2, *p2, k2; rep from *.
Row 2 *P2, k2; rep from *, end p2, k1. Rep row 1 and work buttonhole on this row opposite each marker as foll: yo,

work 2 tog. Work row 2, then rep rows 1-2 until band measures same as buttonband. Bind off in rib.

Neckband

With RS facing and smaller needles, pick up and k86 (90, 94, 94) sts evenly around neck edge and top of bands.
Row 1 (WS) *P2, k2; rep from *, end p2.
Row 2 *K2, p2; rep from *, end k2. Rep row 1, working 7th buttonhole by yo, work 2 tog directly above other buttonholes. Work row 2, then rep rows 1-2 until neckband measures 1½"/4cm. Bind off in rib. Set in sleeves. Sew side and sleeve seams. Sew on buttons.

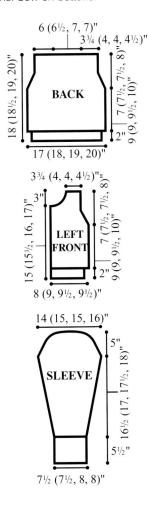

6 (6½, 7, 7)"
3¾ (4, 4, 4½)"
18 (18½, 19, 20)"
BACK
7 (7½, 7½, 8)"
7 (7½, 9½, 10)"
2"
17 (18, 19, 20)"

3¾ (4, 4, 4½)"
3"
15 (15½, 16, 17)"
LEFT FRONT
7 (7½, 7½, 8)"
7 (9, 9½, 10)"
2"
8 (9, 9½, 9½)"

14 (15, 15, 16)"
5"
SLEEVE
16½ (17, 17½, 18)"
5½"
7½ (7½, 8, 8)"

TANK

(Note: Armhole and neck edges will curl.)
BACK
With smaller needles, cast on 56 (60, 62, 66) sts.

Row 1 *K2, p2; rep from *, end k0 (0, 2, 2).
Row 2 P0 (0, 2, 2), *k2, p2; rep from * to end. Rep last 2 rows once. Change to larger needles.
Next row (RS) Purl. Cont in rev St st (p on RS, k on WS) until piece measures 9½ (10, 10, 10½)"/24.5 (25.5, 25.5, 27) from beg, end with a RS row.

Armhole shaping

Next (dec) row (WS) K3, ssk, work to last 5 sts, k2tog, k3—54 (58, 60, 64) sts. Work 1 row even. Rep dec row every other row 9 (10, 9, 10) times more—36 (38, 42, 44) sts. Work even until armhole measures 8 (8, 8½, 8½)"/20.5 (20.5, 21.5, 21.5)cm, end with a WS row.

Shoulder shaping

Bind off 6 (7, 8, 9) sts at beg of next 2 rows. Bind off rem 24 (24, 26, 26) sts.

FRONT

Work as for back until armhole measures 4 (4, 4½, 4½)"/10.5 (10.5, 11.5, 11.5)cm, end with a RS row. Place markers on either side of center 12 sts.

Neck and shoulder shaping

Next row (WS) Work to marker, join 2nd ball of yarn and bind off center 12 sts, work to end. Working both sides at once, work 1 row even.
Next row (WS) Work to last 5 sts, k2tog, k3; on 2nd side, k3, ssk, work to end. In same way, dec 1 st at each neck edge every other row 3 (3, 4, 4) times more, every 4th row twice. Work even until armhole measures same as back, end with a WS row. Bind off 6 (7, 8, 9) sts at beg of next 2 rows.

FINISHING

Sew side and shoulder seams. •

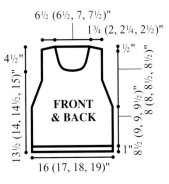

6½ (6½, 7, 7½)"
1¾ (2, 2¼, 2½)"
4½"
½"
8 (8, 8½, 8½)"
13½ (14, 14½, 15)"
FRONT & BACK
8½ (9, 9, 9½)"
1"
16 (17, 18, 19)"

This elegant, sheer button-front top is close-fitting with three-quarter set-in sleeves and self finishing. A Vogue Original. Shown in size Small. The Close-Fitting Cardigan first appeared in the Spring/Summer '96 issue of *Vogue Knitting*.

Close-Fitting Cardigan

SIZES
To fit Small (Medium, Large, X-Large). Directions are for smallest size with larger sizes in parentheses. If there is only one figure it applies to all sizes.

FINISHED MEASUREMENTS
● Bust (buttoned) 36 (39, 42, 45)"/91.5 (99, 106.5, 114)cm.
● Length 19½ (20, 20½, 21)"/49.5 (51, 52, 53.5)cm.
● Upper arm 13 (14, 14½, 15)"/33 (35.5, 37, 39.5)cm.

MATERIALS
Original Yarn
● 4 (5, 5, 6) spools (each approx 100yd/90m) of Tahki ¼" *Rayon Ribbon* (rayon⑥) in #750 ecru
Substitute Yarn
● 4 (5, 5, 6) spools (each approx 100yd/90m) of Judi & Co ¼" *Rayon Ribbon* (rayon⑥) in ecru
● One pair size 13 (9mm) needles OR SIZE TO OBTAIN GAUGE
● Four ⅞"/25mm buttons
Note
The original yarn used for this sweater is no longer available. A comparable substitute has been made, which is available at the time of printing. Check gauge of substitute yarns very carefully before beginning.

GAUGE
12 sts and 18 rows to 4"/10cm over St st using size 13 (9mm) needles.
FOR PERFECT FIT, TAKE TIME TO CHECK GAUGE.

BACK
With size 13 (9mm) needles, cast on 55 (59, 63, 68) sts. Work in St st for 11"/28cm, end with a WS row.

Armhole shaping
Bind off 2 sts at beg of next 4 (4, 4, 6) rows, dec 1 st each side every other row 3 (4, 4, 3) times—41 (43, 47, 50) sts. Work even until armhole measures 7½ (8, 8½, 9)"/19 (20.5, 21.5, 23)cm, end with a WS row.

Shoulder and neck shaping
Bind off 6 (7, 7, 8) sts at beg of next 2 rows, 7 (7, 8, 8) sts at beg of next 2 rows, AT SAME TIME, bind off center 7 (7, 9, 10) sts for neck and working both sides at once, bind off from each neck edge 4 sts once.

LEFT FRONT
With size 13 (9mm) needles, cast on 29 (31, 33, 36) sts. Work in St st until same length as back to armhole. Shape armhole at side edge (beg of RS rows) as for back—22 (23, 25, 27) sts. Work even until armhole measures 6 (6½, 7, 7½)"/15 (16.5, 17.5, 19)cm, end with a RS row.

Neck shaping
Next row (WS) Bind off 3 (3, 3, 4) sts (neck edge), work to end. Cont to bind off from neck edge 2 sts twice, 1 st 2 (2, 3, 3) times, AT SAME TIME, when same length as back to shoulder, shape shoulder at side edge as for back. Place markers on front edge for 4 buttons, the first ¾"/2cm from lower edge, the last

½"/.5cm below first neck dec, and two others spaced evenly between.

RIGHT FRONT
Work as for left front, reversing shaping and working buttonholes opposite markers as foll:
Buttonhole row (RS) K3, k2tog, yo, k to end.

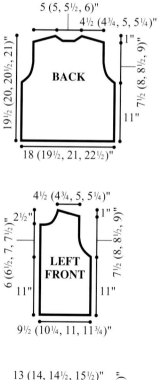

SLEEVES

With size 13 (9mm) needles, cast on 19 (20, 22, 23) sts. Work in St st, inc 1 st each side every 4th row 3 (5, 5, 7) times, every 6th row 7 (6, 6, 5) times—39 (42, 44, 47) sts. Work even until piece measures 13 (13$\frac{1}{2}$, 13$\frac{1}{2}$, 14)"/33 (34.5, 34.5, 35.5)cm from beg.

Cap shaping

Bind off 3 sts at beg of next 2 rows, 2 sts at beg of next 6 rows, dec 1 st each side every other row 2 (3, 4, 5) times, every 4th row twice. Bind off rem 13 (14, 14, 15) sts.

FINISHING

Pin pieces to measurements and block with steam iron to set gauge. Sew shoulder seams. Set in sleeves. Sew side and sleeve seams. Sew on buttons. •

This barely-there cardigan features an easy openwork stitch pattern and seed-stitch bands—it's perfect for layering over figure-skimming camisoles or tank tops. Designed by Gail Diven. Shown in size Small. The Openwork Cardigan first appeared in the Spring/Summer '98 issue of *Vogue Knitting*.

Openwork Cardigan

SIZES
To fit X-Small (Small, Medium, Large). Directions are for smallest size with larger sizes in parentheses. If there is only one figure it applies to all sizes.

KNITTED MEASUREMENTS
● Bust 33$\frac{1}{2}$ (35$\frac{1}{2}$, 37, 38$\frac{1}{2}$)"/ 85 (90, 94, 98)cm.
● Length 16$\frac{3}{4}$ (17$\frac{3}{4}$, 18$\frac{1}{4}$, 19$\frac{1}{4}$)"/42.5 (45, 46, 48.5)cm.
● Upper arm 13$\frac{3}{4}$ (14$\frac{1}{4}$, 15, 16)"/35 (36, 38, 40.5)cm.

MATERIALS
● 3 (3, 4, 4) 4$\frac{1}{2}$oz/125g hanks (each approx 256yd/233m) of Classic Elite *Provence* (cotton③) in #2601 white
● Size 7 (4.5mm) needles OR SIZE TO OBTAIN GAUGE
● Stitch holders

GAUGE
18 sts and 24 rows to 4"/10cm over lace pat st using size 7 (4.5mm) needles. FOR PERFECT FIT, TAKE TIME TO CHECK GAUGE.

Notes
1 For accurate pattern matching, count rows (the number of lace ladder sts) and match at seams and neck edges.
2 Before or after shaping, work extra sts outside lace pat in garter st.

STITCH GLOSSARY
Seed Stitch (even number of sts)
Row 1 (RS) *K1, p1; rep from * to end.
Row 2 *P1, k1; rep from * to end. Rep these 2 rows for seed st.

Lace Pattern Stitch (multiple of 4 sts plus 2 selvage sts)
Row 1 (RS) K1 (selvage st), *k2tog, yo twice, SKP (sl 1, k1, psso); rep from *, end k1 (selvage st).
Row 2 K1, *k1, k1 and p1 into double yo, k1; rep from *, end k1. Rep rows 1 and 2 for lace pat st.

BACK
Cast on 74 (78, 82, 86) sts. Work 6 rows in seed st. Then work in lace pat st until piece measures 9$\frac{1}{2}$ (10, 10, 10$\frac{1}{2}$)"/24 (25.5, 25.5, 26.5)cm from beg, end with a WS row.

Armhole shaping
Bind off 4 (4, 5, 5) sts at beg of next 2 rows. Bind off 1 st at beg of 6 rows—60 (64, 66, 70) sts. Work even until armhole measures 6 (6$\frac{1}{2}$, 7, 7$\frac{1}{2}$)"/15.5 (16.5, 17.5, 19)cm.

Neck and shoulder shaping
Next row (RS) Work 24 (25, 26, 27) sts, join 2nd ball of yarn and bind off center 12 (14, 14, 16) sts, work to end. Working both sides at once, bind off 5 sts from each neck edge once. When armhole measures 7 (7$\frac{1}{2}$, 8, 8$\frac{1}{2}$)"/17.5 (19, 20.5, 21.5)cm, shape shoulders by binding off 10 sts from each shoulder edge 1 (2, 1, 0) times, 9 (0, 11, 11) sts 1 (0, 1, 2) times.

LEFT FRONT
Cast on 42 (46, 50, 54) sts. Work 6 rows seed st.
Next row (RS) K1, rep from * of row 1 of lace pat st 9 (10, 11, 12) times, work 5 sts in seed st (front band). Cont to work in this way until same length as back to armhole.

Armhole shaping
Next row (RS) Bind off 4 (4, 5, 5) sts (armhole edge), work to end. Bind off 1 st from armhole edge 3 times—35 (39, 42, 46) sts. Work even until armhole measures 3$\frac{1}{2}$ (4, 4$\frac{1}{2}$, 5)"/9 (10, 11.5, 12.5)cm, end with a WS row.

Neck shaping
Next row (RS) Work pat to last 5 sts, place these 5 sts for front band on a holder. Cont in pat, bind off from neck edge 3 (3, 3, 4) sts 2 (3, 3, 3) times, 2 sts 1 (1, 2, 2) times, 1 st 3 times—19 (20, 21, 22) sts. When same length as back to shoulder, shape shoulder at side edge (beg of RS rows) as for back.

RIGHT FRONT
Work as for left front, reversing front band and all shaping.

SLEEVES
(Note: Work inc sts in garter st, until a full 4 sts for pat rep is increased for pat.)
Cast on 42 sts. Work 6 rows in seed st. Then work in lace pat st, inc 1 st each side on 3rd row then every 6th row 9 (10, 12, 14) times more—62 (64, 68, 72) sts. Work even until piece measures 17$\frac{1}{2}$ (17$\frac{1}{2}$, 18, 18)"/44.5 (44.5, 45.5, 45.5)cm from beg.

Cap shaping
Bind off 4 (4, 5, 5) sts at beg of next 2 rows, 2 sts at beg of next 4 (4, 2, 2) rows. Bind off 1 st at beg of next 10 (10, 12, 12) rows. Bind off rem 36 (38, 42, 46) sts.

FINISHING
Block pieces to measurements. Sew shoulder seams.

Neckband

With RS facing, beg at right front neck, k5 sts from holder, pick up and k64 (70, 74, 82) sts evenly around neck edge, k5 sts from left front holder—74 (80, 84, 92) sts. Work in seed st for 5 rows. Bind off in pat. ●

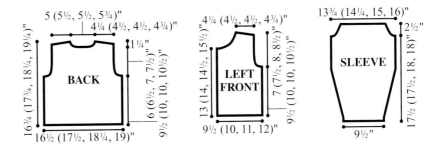

BACK

5 (5½, 5½, 5¾)"
4¼ (4½, 4½, 4¾)"
1¼"
16¾ (17¾, 18¼, 19¼)"
6 (6½, 7, 7½)"
9½ (10, 10, 10½)"
16½ (17½, 18¼, 19)"

LEFT FRONT

4¼ (4½, 4½, 4¾)"
13 (14, 14½, 15½)"
7 (7½, 8, 8½)"
9½ (10, 10, 10½)"
9½ (10, 11, 12)"

SLEEVE

13¾ (14¼, 15, 16)"
2½"
17½ (17½, 18, 18)"
9½"

An updated version of a perennial classic. This standard-fitting, button-front ribbed cardigan has vents at the sides and cuffs. Tweedy angora-blend yarn adds a luxurious twist. Shown in size Medium. The Side-Slit Cardigan first appeared in the Winter '97 issue of *Vogue Knitting*.

Side-Slit Cardigan

SIZES
To fit X-Small (Small, Medium, Large, X-Large). Directions are for smallest size with larger sizes in parentheses. If there is only one figure it applies to all sizes.

KNITTED MEASUREMENTS
● Bust (buttoned) 33½ (35, 37, 39¼, 40½)"/84 (87, 92, 98.5, 102.5)cm.
● Waist 32 (33, 35, 37¾, 39½)"/80 (83, 87, 94.5, 97.5)cm.
● Length 23 (23¼, 23½, 23¾, 24¼)"/58.5 (59, 59.5, 60, 61.5)cm.
● Upper arm 13 (13¼, 13½, 14½, 15½)"/33 (33.5, 34, 37, 39.5)cm.

MATERIALS
● 7 (8, 8, 9, 10) 1¾oz/50g balls (each approx 140yd/135m) of Tahki Yarns *Sable* (wool/angora④) in #1617 grey
● One pair each sizes 5 and 8 (3.75 and 5mm) needles OR SIZE TO OBTAIN GAUGE
● Stitch holders
● Seven ⅞"/20mm buttons
Note
The original color used for this sweater is no longer available. A comparable color substitute has been made, which is available at the time of printing.

GAUGE
19 sts and 26 rows to 4"/10cm over pat st using size 8 (5mm) needles.
FOR PERFECT FIT, TAKE TIME TO CHECK GAUGE.

STITCH GLOSSARY
Pattern Stitch (multiple of 2 sts plus 1)
Row 1 (RS) K1, *p1, k1; rep from * to end.
Row 2 Purl. Rep these 2 rows for pat st.

BACK
With larger needles, cast on 79 (81, 85, 89, 93) sts. Work in pat st for 4"/10cm. Dec 1 st each side on next (RS) row and rep dec every 8th row 3 times more—71 (73, 77, 81, 85) sts. Work even until piece measures 9¼"/23.5cm from beg. Inc 1 st each side of next (RS) row and rep inc every 10th row 3 times more—79 (81, 85, 89, 93) sts. Work even until piece measures 15"/38cm from beg.

Armhole shaping
Bind off 5 (5, 5, 6, 6) sts at beg of next 2 rows. Dec 1 st each side every other row 3 (3, 4, 4, 5) times—63 (65, 67, 69, 71) sts. Work even until armhole measures 7 (7¼, 7½, 7¾, 8¼)"/18 (18.5, 19, 19.5, 21)cm.

Shoulder shaping
Bind off 6 sts at beg of next 6 (6, 4, 4, 2) rows, 7 sts at beg of next 0 (0, 2, 2, 4) rows. Bind off rem 27 (29, 29, 31, 31) sts for back neck.

LEFT FRONT
With larger needles, cast on 43 (45, 47, 51, 53) sts. Working the first 36 (38, 40 44, 46) sts in pat st and the last 7 sts in k1, p1 rib (for front band), work side seam shaping at beg of RS rows as on back. There are 39 (41, 43, 47, 49) sts at waist and 43 (45, 47, 51, 53) sts at bust. Work even until piece measures 15"/38cm from beg.

Armhole shaping
Next row (RS) Bind off 5 (5, 5, 6, 6) sts, work to end. Dec 1 st at armhole edge every other row 3 (3, 4, 4, 5) times—35 (37, 38, 41, 42) sts. Work even until armhole measures 5¼ (5½, 5¾, 6, 6½)"/13.5 (14, 14.5, 15.5, 16.5)cm, end with a RS row.

Neck and shoulder shaping
Next row (WS) Sl first 7 sts to a holder, bind off 2 (2, 2, 3, 3) sts, work to end. Cont to shape neck, binding off 2 sts every other row 4 (5, 5, 6, 6) times. When same length as back to shoulder, bind off 6 sts from shoulder edge 3 (3, 2, 2, 1) times, 7 sts 0 (0, 1, 1, 2) times.

RIGHT FRONT
Work as for left front, reversing shaping and working 7 buttonholes, the first one 2"/5cm from lower edge, the last one ½"/1.25cm from top edge, and the others spaced evenly between as foll:
Buttonhole row (WS) Rib 3 sts, yo, k2tog, work to end.

SLEEVES
(Note: Sleeve length is planned for sleeve to be slightly long with slit, or to be folded back in a split cuff.) With larger needles, cast on 39 (39, 39, 41, 41) sts. Work even in pat st for 2½"/6.5cm. Inc 1 st each side of next RS row and rep inc every 8th (8th, 6th, 6th, 6th) row 10 (11, 12, 13, 15) times more—61 (63, 65, 69, 73) sts. Work even until piece measures 18½"/47cm from beg.

Cap shaping

Bind off 5 (5, 5, 6, 6) sts at beg of next 2 rows. Dec 1 st each side every other row 15 (16, 17, 18, 20) times. Bind off 5 sts at beg of next 2 rows. Bind off rem 11 sts.

FINISHING

Block pieces to measurements. Sew shoulder seams. With smaller needles, pick up and k92 (92, 92, 100, 100) sts evenly around neck edge, including sts from holders. P 1 row on WS, then p 1 row, k 1 row, p 1 row. Bind off. Roll edge to inside and sew. Leaving 3"/7.5cm free at lower edge, sew side seams. Leaving 2¼"/5.75cm free at cuff edge, sew sleeve seams. Set sleeves into armholes. Sew on buttons. •

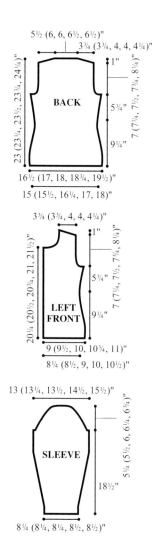

Stylish box pleats add drama to a roomy, oversized jacket with square armholes, a modified shawl collar and seed-stitch borders. Designed by Melissa Leapman. Shown in size Medium. The Pleated Jacket first appeared in the Fall '93 issue of *Vogue Knitting*.

Pleated Jacket

SIZES
To fit Small (Medium, Large). Directions are for smallest size with larger sizes in parentheses. If there is only one figure it applies to all sizes.

KNITTED MEASUREMENTS
● Bust (buttoned) 40½ (43¾, 47)"/103 (111, 119)cm.
● Length 27½ (29, 30½)"/70 (74, 77.5)cm.
● Sleeve 19 (20, 21)"/48 (51, 53.5)cm.

MATERIALS
Original Yarn
● 14 (15, 16) 1¾oz/50g balls (each approx 108yd/98m) of Crystal Palace *Romance* (wool/viscose③) in #41 burgundy (A)
● 14 (15, 16) 1¾oz/50g balls (each approx 93yd/85m) of Crystal Palace *Velourine* (cotton/viscose③) in #553 burgundy (B)
Substitute Yarn
● 13 (13, 14) 1¾oz/50g balls (each approx 124yd/115m) of Rowan/Westminster Fibers *Designer DK* (wool③) in #637 burgundy (A)
● 8 (8, 9) 1¾oz/50g balls (each approx 173yd/160m) of Rowan/Westminster Fibers *Fine Cotton Chenille* (cotton/polyester③) in #407 ruby (B)
● One pair size 10 (6mm) needles OR SIZE TO OBTAIN GAUGE
● Size 10 (6mm) double pointed needles (dpn)
● Stitch markers
● Eight ¾"/20mm buttons

Note
The original yarns used for this sweater are no longer available. Comparable substitutes have been made which are available at the time of printing. Check gauge of substitute yarns very carefully before beginning.

GAUGE
14 sts and 22 rows to 4"/10cm over St st using size 10 (6mm) needles and 1 strand each of A and B held tog. FOR PERFECT FIT, TAKE TIME TO CHECK GAUGE.

Note
One strand each of A and B are held tog throughout.

BACK
With size 10 (6mm) needles and 1 strand each of A and B, cast on 132 (136, 140) sts.
Row 1 (RS) [P1, k1] 8 (9, 10) times; sl 1, **[k1, p1] twice, p1, [k1, p1] 5 times, p1, [p1, k1] twice, sl 1, *[k1, p1] 8 times, k1, sl 1. ** Rep from ** to ** once. Rep from ** to *, end [k1, p1] 8 (9, 10) times.
Row 2 (WS) [P1, k1] 10 (11, 12) times; p1, sl 1, **[p1, k1] 5 times, sl 1, *[p1, k1] 13 times, p1, sl 1. ** Rep from ** to **. Rep from ** to *, end [p1, k1] 10 (11, 12) times, p1. Rep last 2 rows once.
Next row (RS) K16 (18, 20), *sl 1, k4, p1, k10, p1, k4, sl 1, k17; rep from * twice, end last rep k16 (18, 20).
Next row (WS) P21 (23, 25), *sl 1, p10, sl 1, p27; rep from * twice, end last rep p21 (23, 25). Rep last 2 rows until piece

measures 16 (17, 18)"/41 (43, 46)cm from beg, end with a WS row.

Form pleats
First pleat (RS) K12 (14, 16), *sl 5 sts to dpn, sl next 5 sts to 2nd dpn, turn dpn's WS tog and hold in *front* of next 5 sts, insert RH needle through next st of 3 thicknesses and k3tog; rep across rem 4 sts on dpn. Sl 5 sts to dpn, sl next 5 sts to 2nd dpn, turn dpn's RS tog and hold in *back* of next 5 sts, insert RH needle through next st of 3 thicknesses and k3tog, rep across rem 4 sts on dpn, k9.*
2nd and 3rd pleats Rep from * to * across, end k12 (14, 16)—72 (76, 80) sts. Work even in St st (k on RS, p on WS) until piece measures 18 (19, 20)"/46 (48, 51)cm from beg, end with a WS row.

Armhole shaping
Bind off 6 sts at beg of next 2 rows—60 (64, 68) sts. Work even until armhole measures 9½ (10, 10½)"/24 (25.5, 27)cm. Bind off all sts.

LEFT FRONT
With size 10 (6mm) needles and 1 strand each of A and B, cast on 38 (42, 46) sts.
Row 1 (RS) *K1, p1; rep from * across row.
Row 2 K the purl sts and p the knit sts. Rep row 2 twice.
Next row (RS) K31 (35, 39) sts, place marker (pm), p1, [k1, p1] 3 times (for 7-st border).
Next row (WS) [P1, k1] 3 times, k1, p to end. Work even in pat as established until piece measures 18 (19, 20)"/46 (48, 51)cm from beg, end

...ith a WS row.

Armhole shaping

Next row (RS) Bind off 6 sts, work to end—32 (36, 40) sts. Work even until piece measures 23½ (25, 26½)"/60 (63.5, 67)cm from beg, end with a RS row.

Neck shaping

Next row (WS) Bind off 7 sts, work to end. Dec 1 st at neck edge every row 0 (0, 2) times, then every other row 6 (9, 10) times—19 (20, 21) sts. Work even until armhole measures 9½ (10, 10½)"/24 (25.5, 27)cm. Bind off all sts. Place markers for 8 buttons, with first and last 1"/2.5cm from lower edge and beg of neck shaping and others evenly between.

RIGHT FRONT

Work as for left front, reversing shaping by working armhole shaping at beg of a WS row and beg neck shaping on a RS row. Work buttonholes in 7-st border opposite markers as foll: work 2 sts, bind off 3 sts, work to end. On next row, cast on 3 sts over bound-off sts.

SLEEVES

With size 10 (6mm) needles and 1 strand each of A and B, cast on 31 (34, 37) sts.
Row 1 (RS) *K1, p1; rep from *, end k1 (0, 1).
Row 2 K the purl sts and p the knit sts. Rep row 2 until piece measures 3"/7.5cm, end with a WS row. Change to St st and inc 1 st each side every 4th row 15 (12, 10) times, then every 6th row 3 (6, 8) times—67 (70, 73) sts. Work even until piece measures 19 (20, 21)"/48 (51, 53.5)cm from beg. Bind off.

FINISHING

Block pieces. Sew shoulder seams.

Collar

With size 10 needles (6mm) and 1 strand each of A and B, cast on 21 (24, 27) sts.
Row 1 *K1, p1; rep from *, end k1 (0, 1).
Row 2 Cast on 3 sts and working them into pat, k the purl sts and p the knit sts. Rep last row 13 times—63 (66, 69) sts. Work even in pat as established for 2"/5cm.

Beg short row shaping: Next row Work to last 3 sts, wyib sl next st purl-wise, wyif sl st back to LH needle (1 st wrapped), turn (3 sts on RH needle).
Next row Work 57 (60, 63) sts, wrap next st as before, turn (3 sts on RH needle).
Next row Work 54 (57, 60) sts, wrap next st as before, turn (6 sts on RH needle).
Next row Work 51 (54, 57) sts, wrap next st as before, turn (6 sts on RH needle). Cont to work short rows as established, working 3 sts less each row until 21 (24, 27) sts rem. Cut yarn. Join yarn at one edge and bind off 63 (66, 69) sts, working wrap and next st tog across. Sew cast-on edge of collar to neck. Sew top of sleeves to armhole. Sew bound-off sts of armhole to side edges of sleeves. Sew side and sleeve seams. Sew on buttons. •

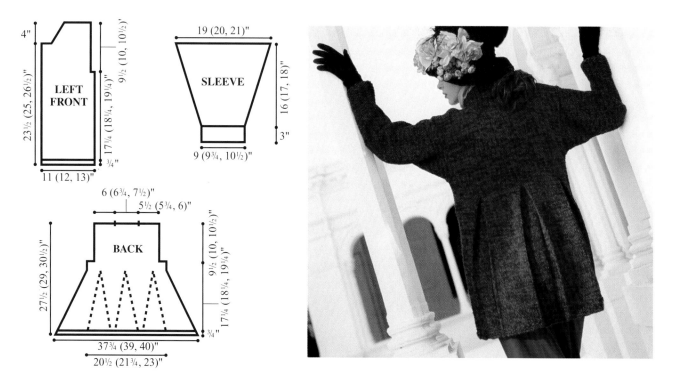

Fringed Scarf Coat

Marc Jacobs for Perry Ellis whips up a three-quarter-length jacket with oversized ease. Patch pockets, an attached fringed scarf and garter-stitch borders add textural interest. Shown in size Medium-Large. The Fringed Scarf Coat first appeared in the Fall '90 issue of *Vogue Knitting*.

Fringed Scarf Coat

SIZES
To fit Small (Medium-Large, X-Large). Directions are for smallest size with larger sizes in parentheses. If there is only one figure it applies to all sizes.

KNITTED MEASUREMENTS
● Bust (buttoned) 50 (54, 58)"/124.5 (138.5, 144.5)cm.
● Length 30 (32, 33)"/76 (81.5, 83.5)cm.
● Upper arm 21 (22, 23)"/53 (56, 58)cm.

MATERIALS
Original Yarn
● 27 (29, 31) 1³/₄oz/50g balls (each approx 92yd/84m) of Bernat®/Spinrite *Rusticale* (wool/mohair④) in #14042 winter white
Substitute Yarn
● 13 (14, 15) 3¹/₂oz/100g skeins (each approx 200yds/182m) of Berella® *Muskoka* by Spinrite (wool④) in #9821 cream
● One pair size 9 (5.5mm) needles OR SIZE TO OBTAIN GAUGE
● Size 9 (5.5mm) circular needle, 36"/90cm long (Optional: Used for ease in working back after sleeves have been cast on.)
● Size G (4.5mm) crochet hook
● Stitch holders
● One 1"/25mm button

Note
The original yarn used for this sweater is no longer available. A comparable substitute has been made, which is available at the time of printing. Check gauge of substitute yarns very carefully before beginning.

GAUGE
18 sts and 22 rows to 4"/10cm over St st using size 9 (5.5mm) needles.
FOR PERFECT FIT, TAKE TIME TO CHECK GAUGE.

BACK
With size 9 (5.5mm) needles, cast on 102 (112, 120) sts. Work in garter st (k every row) for 3"/7.5cm, inc 10 sts evenly across last row—112 (122, 130) sts. Work in St st (k on RS, p on WS) until piece measures 19¹/₂ (21, 21¹/₂)"/49.5 (53.5, 54.5)cm from beg.

Sleeve shaping
Cast on 52 sts at beg of next 2 rows for sleeves—216 (226, 234) sts. Work even until piece measures 10¹/₂ (11, 11¹/₂)"/26.5 (28, 29)cm above sleeve cast-on. Bind off all sts.

LEFT FRONT
(Note: Short rows are worked to keep front bands from pulling in. There are 12 rows in garter st band for every 10 rows of St st.) With size 9 (5.5mm) needles, cast on 57 (60, 65) sts. Work in garter st (k every row) for 3"/7.5cm, inc 5 (6, 6) sts evenly across last row—62 (66, 71) sts.
Next row (RS) Work 50 (54, 59) sts in St st, 12 sts in garter st (front edge). Keeping 12 sts at front edge in garter st and rem sts in St st, work short rows as foll:

Short row (WS) K12, wrap next st, turn work, k to end. Cont to rep short row (counting over St st rows) *every 4th row once, every 6th row once; rep from * until piece measures same length as back to sleeve shaping, end with a WS row.

Sleeve shaping
Cast on 52 sts at beg of next (RS) row—114 (118, 123) sts. Work even until piece measures 8¹/₂ (9, 9¹/₂)"/21.5 (23, 24)cm above sleeve cast-on, end with a RS row.

Neck shaping
Bind off 15 (15, 16) sts (neck edge), work to end. Cont to bind off from neck edge 2 sts 3 (2, 3) times. Dec 1 st at neck edge every other row 1 (2, 1) times. When same length as back, bind off rem 92 (97, 100) sts.

RIGHT FRONT
Work as for left front, reversing all shaping and placement of garter st band and working a buttonhole in band ³/₄"/2cm before first neck bind-off as foll:
Buttonhole row (RS) K5, bind off 4, work to end. On next row, cast on 4 sts over bound-off sts.

SCARF
With size 9 (5.5mm) needles, cast on 42 sts. Work in garter st for 3"/7.5cm, inc 4 sts evenly across last row—46 sts.
Next row (RS) K12 sts in garter st, 27 sts in St st and 7 sts in garter st. Cont in garter st and St st as established, working short rows at each garter st edge as for fronts, until piece measures 87"/220.5cm from beg, dec 4 sts evenly across last row—42 sts. Work in garter st for 3"/7.5cm. Bind off.

POCKETS (make 2)

With size 9 (5.5mm) needles, cast on 27 sts. Work in St st for 4"/10cm. Work in garter st for 3"/7.5cm. Bind off.

FINISHING

Block pieces. Sew shoulder seams and top of sleeve seams.

Sleeve cuff

With RS facing and size 9 (5.5mm) needles, pick up and k103 (108, 113) sts along lower edge of each sleeve. Work in garter st for 3"/7.5cm. Bind off. Sew side seams, leaving 3"/7.5cm garter st borders unsewn. Sew underarm sleeve seams including sleeve cuff. Sew pockets on fronts, 4½"/11.5cm from lower edge and 3½"/9cm from side seam. Sew on button. Fold scarf in half and mark center on 7-st garter edge. Mark center back neck. Match center points of scarf and coat and sew along back neck.

Fringe

Add fringe to short ends of scarf as foll: Cut strands of yarn 12"/31cm long. With WS of scarf facing, crochet hook and 2 strands of yarn (folded in half), insert hook from front to back through piece and over folded yarn. Pull yarn through. Draw ends through and tighten. Trim yarn. •

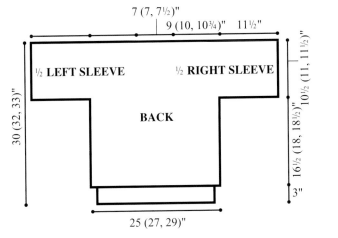

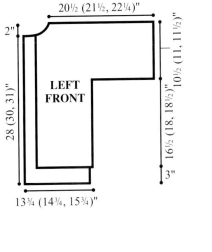

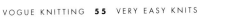

Raglan sleeves and a modified funnel neck put a chic spin on the simple cardigan jacket. The yarn is a thick, extra-lush chenille for high style and incredible comfort. Designed by Rosemary Drysdale. Shown in size Small. The Raglan Jacket first appeared in the Winter '98/99 issue of *Vogue Knitting*.

Raglan Jacket

SIZES

To fit Small (Medium/Large, X-Large). Directions are for smallest size with larger sizes in parentheses. If there is only one figure it applies to all sizes.

KNITTED MEASUREMENTS

● Bust (buttoned) 42 (46, 50)"/106.5 (116.5, 127)cm.
● Length 23½ (24, 24½)"/59.5 (61, 62)cm.
● Upper arm 16½ (18½, 20½)"/42 (47, 52)cm.

MATERIALS

● 9 (10, 11) 3½oz/100g balls (each approx 72yd/66m) of Trendsetter Yarns *Cenci* (viscose/acrylic®) in #11 beige
● One pair each sizes 10½ and 13 (7 and 9mm) needles OR SIZE TO OBTAIN GAUGE
● Stitch holders
● Six ¾"/20mm buttons

GAUGE

8 sts and 15 rows to 4"/10cm over St st using size 10½ (7mm) needles. FOR PERFECT FIT, TAKE TIME TO CHECK GAUGE.

Note
To keep knitting from biasing, be sure to pull yarn from the center of the ball.

BACK

With larger needles, cast on 43 (47, 51) sts. Change to smaller needles and work in St st until piece measures 12 (12½, 13)"/30.5 (31.5, 33)cm from beg, end with a WS row.

Raglan armhole shaping

[Dec 1 st each side on next row. Work 3 rows even. Dec 1 st each side on next row. Work 1 row even] 5 (4, 3) times. [Dec 1 st each side on next row. Work 1 row even] 3 (7, 11) times. Place rem 17 sts on a holder for back neck.

LEFT FRONT

With larger needles, cast on 24 (26, 28) sts. Change to smaller needles and work in St st until same length as back to armhole.

Raglan armhole and neck shaping

Shape armhole at side edge (beg of RS rows) as for back, AT SAME TIME, when there are 13 sts, end with a RS row and work as foll:
Next row (WS) Bind off 5 sts (neck edge), work to end. Cont armhole shaping, dec 1 st at neck edge at beg of next WS row. After all decs have been worked, place rem 5 sts on a holder. Place markers on front edge for 6 buttons, with the first ¾"/2cm from lower edge, the last 3½"/9cm from neck, and 4 others spaced evenly between.

RIGHT FRONT

Work as for left front, reversing shaping and working buttonholes opposite markers as foll:

Buttonhole row (RS) K3, yo, k2tog, work to end.

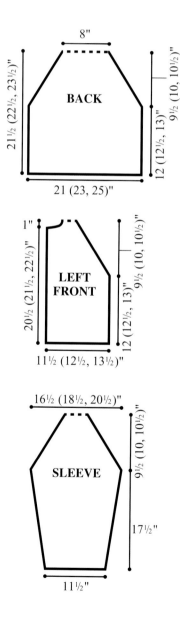

SLEEVES

With larger needles, cast on 24 sts. Change to smaller needles and work in St st, inc 1 st each side every 12th (8th, 6th) row 5 (7, 9) times—34 (38, 42) sts. Work even until piece measures 17$\frac{1}{2}$"/44.5cm from beg, end with a WS row.

Raglan cap shaping

Work same as back armhole shaping. Bind off rem 8 sts.

FINISHING

Block pieces to measurements. Sew raglan sleeve caps to raglan armholes. Sew side and sleeve seams.

Neckband

With RS facing and smaller needles, beg at right front neck, pick up and k60 sts evenly around neck edge, including sts from holders. P 1 row. **Next row (RS)** K12, [k2tog] twice, k6, [k2tog] twice, k8, [k2tog] twice, k6, [k2tog] twice, k12—52 sts. P 1 row. **Next row** K11, [k2tog] twice, k4, [k2tog] twice, k6, [k2tog] twice, k4, [k2tog] twice, k11—44 sts. Work even in St st for 5 rows. Bind off knitwise on RS. Sew on buttons. •

Kid mohair combines with a stylish zipper front and hood to create a seasonless sweater right in step with 21st-century style. Designed by Gitta Schrade. Shown in size Medium. The Hooded Zip Cardigan first appeared in the Winter '98/99 issue of *Vogue Knitting*.

Hooded Zip Cardigan

SIZES
To fit Small (Medium, Large, X-Large, XX-Large). Directions are for smallest size with larger sizes in parentheses. If there is only one figure it applies to all sizes.

KNITTED MEASUREMENTS
● Bust (closed) 38 (40, 42, 44, 46)"/96.5 (101.5, 106.5, 111.5, 117)cm.
● Length 24¹/₂ (25, 25¹/₂, 25¹/₂, 26)"/62 (63.5, 64.5, 64.5, 66)cm.
● Upper arm 17 (18, 19, 19, 20)"/43 (45.5, 48, 48, 51)cm.

MATERIALS
● 9 (10, 11, 12, 13) 1³/₄oz/50g balls (each approx 109yd/100m) of Anny Blatt *Kid Mohair* (wool/mohair/polyamide⑤) in #298 camel
● One pair each sizes 5 and 7 (3.75 and 4.5mm) needles OR SIZE TO OBTAIN GAUGE
● Stitch holders
● Separating zipper 22 (23, 23, 23, 24)"/56 (58, 58, 58, 61)cm long
● Matching sewing thread
● One zipper pull by Wolf—Nothing But Cutlery

GAUGE
16 sts and 22 rows to 4"/10cm over St st using size 7 (4.5mm) needles. FOR PERFECT FIT, TAKE TIME TO CHECK GAUGE.

BACK
With smaller needles, cast on 76 (80, 84, 88, 92) sts. Work in k1, p1 rib for 1¹/₂"/4cm. Change to larger needles and cont in St st until piece measures 15"/38cm from beg. End with a WS row.

Armhole shaping
Bind off 2 sts at beg of next 2 rows. Dec 1 st each side every other row 2 (2, 3, 3, 4) times—68 (72, 74, 78, 80) sts. Work even until armhole measures 8¹/₂ (9, 9¹/₂, 9¹/₂, 10)"/21.5 (23, 24, 24, 25.5)cm, end with a WS row.

Neck and shoulder shaping
Bind off 7 (8, 8, 8, 9) sts at beg of next 4 rows, 7 (7, 8, 9, 8) sts at beg of next 2 rows, AT SAME TIME, bind off center 14 (14, 14, 16, 16) sts for neck and working both sides at once, bind off 3 sts from each neck edge twice.

LEFT FRONT
With smaller needles, cast on 38 (40, 42, 44, 46) sts. Work in k1, p1 rib for 1¹/₂"/4cm. Change to larger needles.
Next row (RS) Knit.
Next row (WS) K1 (selvage st); p to end. Rep these 2 rows until piece measures 3³/₄"/9.5cm from beg, end with a WS row.

Beg pocket
Next row (RS) K12 (14, 16, 18, 20), sl rem 26 sts to a holder and separately cast on 26 sts for lining to replace these sts. Work even on these sts until pieces measure 10¹/₄"/26cm from beg, end with a WS row.
Next row (RS) K17 (19, 21, 23, 25), bind off rem 21 sts. Leave these sts on a spare needle. Rejoin yarn to work 26 sts on holder from RS. Work 2 rows in St st. Dec 1 st at beg of next (RS) row then rep dec every 4th row 4 times more—21 sts. Work even until piece measures 10¹/₄"/26cm from beg and there are same number of rows as in pocket lining.
Next row (WS) P21, then p the 17 (19, 21, 23, 25) sts from spare needle. Work even until piece measures 15"/38cm from beg.

Armhole shaping
Work armhole shaping at side seam edge (beg of RS rows) as for back—34 (36, 37, 39, 40) sts. Work even until armhole measures 7¹/₂ (8, 8¹/₂, 8¹/₂, 9)"/19 (20.5, 21.5, 21.5, 23)cm, end with a RS row.

Neck and shoulder shaping
Next row (WS) Bind off 5 (5, 5, 6, 6) sts for neck, p to end. Cont to bind off 2 sts from neck edge every other row 4 times and AT SAME TIME, when armhole measures same as back, bind off 7 (8, 8, 8, 9) sts from shoulder edge twice and 7 (7, 8, 9, 8) sts once.

RIGHT FRONT
Work as for left front, reversing all shaping and beg pocket as foll:
Next row (WS) P12 (14, 16, 18, 20), sl rem 26 sts to a holder and separately cast on 26 sts for lining.

SLEEVES
With smaller needles, cast on 40 (42, 44, 44, 44) sts. Work in k1, p1 rib for

1¹/₂"/4cm. Change to larger needles
and cont in St st, inc 1 st each side
every 4th row 10 (8, 13, 13, 14) times,
then every 6th row 4 (7, 3, 3, 4)
times—68 (72, 76, 76, 80) sts. Work
even until piece measures 17 (17¹/₄,
17¹/₂, 17¹/₂, 17¹/₂)"/43 (44, 44.5, 44.5,
44.5)cm from beg.

Cap shaping
Bind off 2 sts at beg of next 6 rows.
Dec 1 st each side of next 10 rows.
Bind off rem 36 (40, 44, 44, 48) sts.

HOOD
Left half
With larger needles, cast on 52 (52,
52, 56, 56) sts.
Row 1 (RS) Knit.
Row 2 K3, p to end. Rep these
2 rows until piece measures
13"/33cm from beg.
Next row (RS) Bind off 8 sts, k to end.
Work 1 row even. Rep last 2 rows twice
more. Then, bind off 7 (7, 7, 8, 8) sts
from same edge every RS row 4 times.

Right half
Work as for left half, reversing shaping
by having 3 garter sts at beg of RS
rows and binding off at beg of WS rows.

FINISHING
Block pieces to measurements.

Pocket edging
With smaller needles, pick up and k34
sts from RS on pocket edge. Work in
k1, p1 rib for 1¹/₂"/4cm. Bind off in rib.
Sew pocket linings and pocket edge in
place. Sew shoulder seams. Sew two
halves of hood tog along back and top
seam. Sew cast-on edge of hood
around neck edge. Sew sleeves into
armholes. Sew side and sleeve seams.
Pin and baste zipper in place. Sew
zipper in place leaving selvage st free.
Whipstitch zipper in place on WS. •

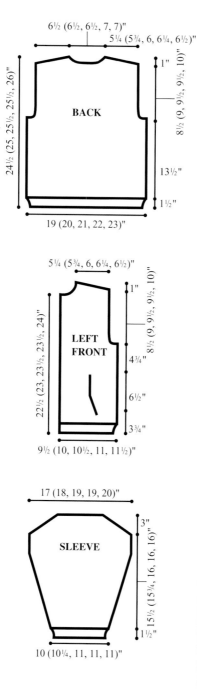

BACK

6¹/₂ (6¹/₂, 6¹/₂, 7, 7)"

5¹/₄ (5³/₄, 6, 6¹/₄, 6¹/₂)"

1"

8¹/₂ (9, 9¹/₂, 9¹/₂, 10)"

13¹/₂"

1¹/₂"

24¹/₂ (25, 25¹/₂, 25¹/₂, 26)"

19 (20, 21, 22, 23)"

LEFT FRONT

5¹/₄ (5³/₄, 6, 6¹/₄, 6¹/₂)"

1"

8¹/₂ (9, 9¹/₂, 9¹/₂, 10)"

4³/₄"

6¹/₂"

3³/₄"

22¹/₂ (23, 23¹/₂, 23¹/₂, 24)"

9¹/₂ (10, 10¹/₂, 11, 11¹/₂)"

SLEEVE

17 (18, 19, 19, 20)"

3"

15¹/₂ (15³/₄, 16, 16, 16)"

1¹/₂"

10 (10¹/₄, 11, 11, 11)"

Hooded Poncho

Marc Jacobs for Perry Ellis uses bold cables and a brightly-colored tweedy wool to create a dramatic hooded poncho. Knit in reverse stockinette, it features ribbed edges and cabled front pockets. The Hooded Poncho first appeared in the Fall '89 issue of *Vogue Knitting*.

Hooded Poncho

SIZES
One size fits all.

KNITTED MEASUREMENTS
● Length 33¹/₂"/85cm.

MATERIALS
● 18 3¹/₂oz/100g balls (each approx 110yd/100m) of Tahki Yarns *Soho Bulky Tweed* (wool⑤) in #320 red
● One pair each sizes 8 and 10 (5 and 6mm) needles OR SIZE TO OBTAIN GAUGE
● One each sizes 8 and 10 (5 and 6mm) circular needles, 29"/80cm long
● Stitch holders and markers
● Cable needle (cn)
● Seven ³/₄"/20mm buttons

Note
The original color used for this sweater is no longer available. A comparable color substitute has been made, which is available at the time of printing.

GAUGE
● 14 sts and 20 rows to 4"/10cm over rev St st using size 10 (6mm) needles.
● 8 sts to 1³/₄"/4.5cm over cable pat using size 10 (6mm) needles.
FOR PERFECT FIT, TAKE TIME TO CHECK GAUGES.

STITCH GLOSSARY
Cable Pat (over 8 sts)
Row 1 (RS) Knit.
Row 2 Purl.
Row 3 Sl 4 sts to cn and hold to *front*, k4, sl sts from cn to left needle and [k4, turn, p4, turn, k4] on these sts.
Rows 4-10 Work in St st. Rep rows 1-10 for cable pat.

BACK
With smaller circular needle, cast on 199 sts. Work back and forth as with straight needles in k1, p1 rib for 1¹/₂"/4cm. Change to larger circular needle. Sl first 7 sts to holder. Cut yarn, rejoin and k next (WS) row to last 7 sts, dec 41 sts evenly across, sl last 7 sts to holder—144 sts on needle. Cont in rev St st (p on RS, k on WS) until piece measures 32¹/₂"/82.5cm from beg, end with a WS row.

Neck shaping
Next row (RS) P54, join 2nd ball of yarn and bind off 36 sts, p to end. Working both sides at once, dec 1 st at each neck edge *every* row 3 times. Work 1 row even. Bind off rem 51 sts each side for shoulders. (Note: Work rem pieces on straight needles.)

POCKET LININGS (make 2)
With larger needles, cast on 20 sts. Work in St st for 6"/15cm. Place sts on holder.

LEFT FRONT
With smaller needles, cast on 105 sts. Work in k1, p1 rib for 1¹/₂"/4cm. Change to larger needles. Sl first 7 sts to a holder. Cut yarn, rejoin and k next (WS) row to last 7 sts, dec 19 sts evenly across, sl last 7 sts to holder—72 sts on needle.
Beg rev St st and cable pat: Row 1 (RS) P48, work cable pat over 8 sts, p16. Cont in pat until piece measures 15¹/₂"/39.5cm from beg, end with a WS row.

Pocket joining
Next row (RS) P39, sl next 20 sts to holder for pocket. Sl sts of one pocket lining from holder to LH needle, work pat across sts of lining, p to end. Cont in pat until piece measures 27¹/₂"/70cm from beg, end with a cable row 10, dec 2 sts across 8 cable sts on last row—70 sts. Work in rev St st on all sts until piece measures 32"/81cm from beg, end with a RS row.

Neck shaping
Next row (WS) Bind off 12 sts (neck edge), work to end. Cont to dec 1 st at neck edge *every* row 7 times. Bind off rem 51 sts for shoulder.

RIGHT FRONT
Work as for left front, reversing neck shaping by binding at beg of RS row and reversing pocket placement. Reverse placement of cable pat as foll:
Next row (RS) P16, work cable pat over 8 sts, p48.

HOOD
With smaller needles, cast on 55 sts. Work in k1, p1 rib for 3 rows.
Next (eyelet) row Rib 2, [yo, k2tog, rib 5] 7 times, yo, k2tog, rib 2. Rib until band measures 1¹/₂"/4cm. Change to larger needles. K next row on WS to last 7 sts, dec 2 sts, sl last 7 sts to a holder—46 sts on needle. Cont in rev St st, inc 1 st at end of RS rows as foll: [every 2nd row once, every 4th row once] 5 times—56 sts. Work even until piece measures 9"/23cm from beg, end with a WS row. Dec 1 st at same edge on next row and rep dec every other row 22 times more—33 sts. Work even, if necessary, until piece measures 18"/46cm from beg. Mark piece for center of hood. Work 2nd half of hood as foll: Inc 1 st at same edge on next row, then every other row 22

times more—56 sts. Work even until piece measures 9"/23cm from center. Work 6 rows even, then dec 1 st at same edge [every 2nd row once, every 4th row once] 5 times—46 sts. Work even for 3 rows, inc 2 sts on last (WS) row—48 sts. Change to smaller needles. Cast on 7 sts at beg of next row and rib on 55 sts for 1½"/4cm, working eyelet row same as first half. Bind off in rib.

FINISHING
Sew shoulder seams.

Pocket edging
Sl sts from pocket holders to smaller needles and work in k1, p1 rib for 1½"/4cm, inc 7 sts evenly across first row—27 sts. Bind off in rib. Sew pocket linings to WS of fronts. Sew sides of rib to fronts.

Side edging
With RS facing and smaller needles, pick up and k130 sts along each side edge of back. Work in k1, p1 rib for 1½"/4cm. Bind off in rib. Sew sides of rib to 7 sts on holder at lower edge rib. Place marker on each band for a button, 14"/35.5cm from lower edge. Work rib along side edges of each front same as for back, working a buttonhole on 4th row opposite marker by binding off 3 sts. On next row, cast on 3 sts over bound-off sts.

Hood edging
With RS facing and smaller needles, pick up and k141 sts along straight edge of hood. Work in k1, p1 rib for 1½"/4cm. Bind off in rib. Sew sides of band to 7 sts on holders at each end. Fold hood in half at center and sew back seam. Sew edge of eyelet rib around front and back neck.

Left front edging
With RS facing and smaller needles, beg at neck edge, pick up and k127 sts along 1½"/4cm of eyelet rib, then along left front edge to lower edge. Work in k1, p1 rib for 1½"/4cm. Bind off in rib. Sew sides of rib to 7 sts on holder at lower edge rib. Place markers on band for 5 buttons, the first 13"/33cm from lower edge, the last at first neck dec, 3 others evenly between.

Right front edging
With RS facing and smaller needles, beg at lower edge, work same as left front edging, working buttonholes opposite markers on 4th row same as on front side edging.

Cord
With 2 strands of yarn, make a twisted cord 48"/122cm long as foll: Cut strands 3 times the desired length. Knot them together 1"/2.5cm from each end. Insert a pencil or knitting needle through one end. Place other end over a doorknob. Turn strands until they are tightly twisted. Hold the strands taut and fold the piece in half. Allow cord to twist onto itself. Thread through eyelet rnd on neckband to tie at center front.

Tassels (make 2)
Wrap yarn around cardboard 4"/10cm long. Thread strand of yarn through cardboard and tie at top, leaving a long end. Cut lower edge. Wrap long end around 1"/2.5cm down from upper edge and insert into top. Attach to each end of twisted cord. Sew on buttons. ●

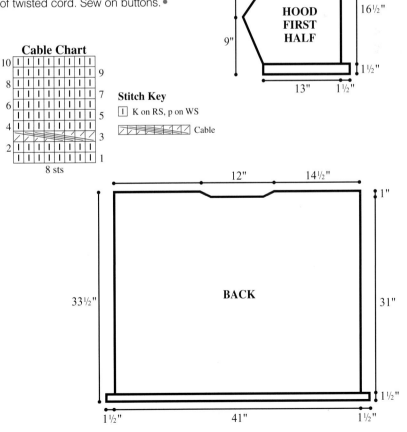

Cable Chart

Stitch Key
- ☐ K on RS, p on WS
- ▨ Cable

8 sts

Simple
cables and
striking
stitch patterns
add new
dimension

Turtleneck Pullover

The compelling charm of clever stitchery—alternating cables and ribs give this turtle-neck pullover maximum impact. Standard-fitting, it features drop shoulders and roomy front patch pockets. Designed by Michele Rose. Shown in size 34. The Turtleneck Pullover first appeared in the Winter '91/92 issue of *Vogue Knitting*.

SIZES

To fit 32 (34, 36, 38)"/81 (86, 91, 96)cm bust. Directions are for smallest size with larger sizes in parentheses. If there is only one figure it applies to all sizes.

KNITTED MEASUREMENTS

● Bust 34 (36, 38, 40)"/86.5 (91.5, 96.5, 101.5)cm.
● Length 28 (28, 29, 29)"/71 (71, 73.5, 73.5)cm.
● Upper arm 18 (18¾, 19½, 20½)"/45.5 (47.5, 49.5, 52)cm.

MATERIALS

● 14 (15, 15, 16) 1¾oz/50g balls (each approx 127yd/115m) of Rowan/Westminster Fibers *Designer DK* (wool③) in #693 tan
● One pair each sizes 3 and 5 (3.25 and 3.75mm) needles OR SIZE TO OBTAIN GAUGE
● Size 3 (3.25mm) circular needle, 16"/40cm long
● Cable needle (cn)
● Stitch markers

Note

The original color used for this sweater is no longer available. A comparable color substitute has been made, which is available at the time of printing.

GAUGE

● 25 sts and 32 rows to 4"/10cm over St st using size 5 (3.75mm) needles.
● 42 sts to 6"/15cm over rib pat using size 5 (3.75mm) needles.
● 20 sts to 2"/5cm over cable pat

using size 5 (3.75mm) needles.
FOR PERFECT FIT, TAKE TIME TO CHECK GAUGES.

STITCH GLOSSARY

4-st Front Cable
Sl 2 sts to cn and hold to *front*, k2, k2 from cn.

4-st Back Cable
Sl 2 sts to cn and hold to *back*, k2, k2 from cn.

Rib Pat (multiple of 11 sts)
Row 1 *K1, p1, k5, p1, k1, p2; rep from * to end.
Row 2 K the knit sts and p the purl sts.
Rep rows 1 and 2 for rib pat.

Cable Pat (over 20 sts)
Row 1 P2, k4, 4-st back cable, 4-st front cable, k4, p2.
Rows 2, 4, 6 K2, p16, k2.
Row 3 P2, k2, 4-st back cable, k4, 4-st front cable, k2, p2.
Row 5 P2, 4-st back cable, k8, 4-st front cable, p2.
Rep rows 1-6 for cable pat.

BACK

With smaller needles, cast on 126 (130, 138, 142) sts. Work in garter st (k every row) for 6 rows.
Next row (RS) *K2, p2; rep from *, end k2.
Next row *P2, k2; rep from *, end p2. Rep last 2 rows twice more, inc 0 (2, 0, 2) sts on last WS row—126 (132, 138, 144) sts. Change to larger needles.
Beg pats: Row 1 (RS) K22 (25, 28, 31), place marker (pm), work row 1 of

cable pat over 20 sts, pm, 11-st rep of rib pat 4 times, end last rep k1, pm, cable pat over 20 sts, pm, k22 (25, 28, 31). Cont in pats as established working sts outside markers in St st (k on RS, p on WS) until piece measures 27¼ (27¼, 28¼, 28¼)"/69 (69, 71.5, 71.5)cm from beg.

Shoulder and neck shaping

Bind off 14 (15, 16, 17) sts at beg of next 4 rows (shoulder edges), 13 (14, 15, 16) sts at beg of next 2 rows, AT SAME TIME, bind off center 32 sts and working both sides at once with separate balls of yarn, bind off from each neck edge 3 sts once, 2 sts once, 1 st every other row once.

FRONT

Work as for back until piece measures 25 (25, 26, 26)"/63.5 (63.5, 66, 66)cm from beg, end with a WS row.

Neck and shoulder shaping

Next row (RS) Cont in pats, work 53 (56, 59, 62) sts, join 2nd ball of yarn and bind off center 20 sts, work to end. Working both sides at once, bind off from each neck edge 6 sts once, 3 sts once, 2 sts once, then 1 st every other row once. When piece measures same length as back to shoulder, shape shoulder as for back.

SLEEVES

With smaller needles, cast on 46 (46, 50, 50) sts. Work 6 rows in garter st. Work in k2, p2 rib for 6 rows, inc 1 (1, 3, 3) sts evenly across last WS row—

47 (47, 53, 53) sts. Change to larger needles.

Beg pats: Row 1 (RS) K4 (4, 0, 0), p1 (1, 0, 0), k1 (1, 0, 0), p2 (2, 0, 0), work 11-st rep of rib pat 3 (3, 4, 4) times, end k1, p1, k4 (4, 5, 5), p0 (0, 1, 1), k0 (0, 1, 1), AT SAME TIME, inc 1 st each side (working inc sts into rib pat) every other row 5 (11, 11, 15) times, every 4th row 34 (31, 31, 30) times—125 (131, 137, 143) sts. Work even until piece measures 20"/51cm from beg. Bind off in rib.

LEFT POCKET

With larger needles, cast on 42 (44, 46, 48) sts.

Beg rib pat: Row 1 (RS) K0 (0, 0, 2), p0 (0, 1, 1), k0 (0, 1, 1), p0 (2, 2, 2), work 11-st rep of rib pat 3 times, end k1, p1, k5, p1, k1. Cont in pat as established until piece measures 5"/12.5cm from beg. Change to smaller needles and work k2, p2 rib for 6 rows. Work 6 rows in garter st. Bind off.

RIGHT POCKET

Work as for left pocket rev pat placement.

FINISHING

Block pieces. Sew shoulder seams.

Turtleneck

With RS facing and circular needle, pick up and k124 sts evenly around neck edge. Join. Work in k2, p2 rib for 6¼"/16cm. Bind off loosely in rib.

Pocket placement

Sew lower edge of pockets on last row of k2, p2 rib on front, then sew inner side edges even with edges of front rib panel. Place markers on front and back for armholes 9 (9½, 10, 10½)"/23 (24, 25.5, 26.5)cm down from shoulders. Sew top of sleeves between markers. Sew side and sleeve seams. Sew outer edge of pocket over seam. •

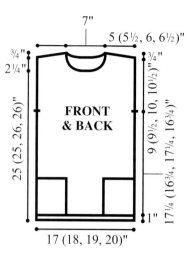

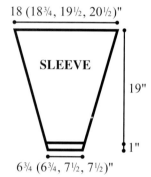

Button-Placket Tunic

This oversized, round-neck tunic with drop shoulders and seed-stitch edges is the sort of weekend classic that looks right year after year. A few modern details—side slits, double-buttoned front placket and mock back placket add contemporary appeal. Designed by Anne Mieke Louwerens. Shown in size 36. The Button-Placket Tunic first appeared in the Holiday '87 issue of *Vogue Knitting*.

Button-Placket Tunic

SIZES
To fit 32 (34, 36, 38, 40)"/81 (86, 91, 96, 101)cm bust. Directions are for smallest size with larger sizes in parentheses. If there is only one figure it applies to all sizes.

KNITTED MEASUREMENTS
● Bust 43 (45, 48, 50, 52)"/107 (113, 119, 125, 129)cm.
● Length 27³/₄ (28¹/₄, 28³/₄, 29¹/₄, 29³/₄)"/70 (71.5, 73, 74, 75)cm.
● Upper arm 18 (19, 19, 20, 20)"/45 (48, 48, 50, 50)cm.

MATERIALS
Original Yarn
● 16 (17, 17, 18, 19) 1³/₄oz/50g balls (each approx 85yd/77m) of Classic Elite *Cambridge* (cotton/wool④) in #3916 ecru
Substitute Yarn
● 8 (8, 8, 9, 9) 3¹/₂oz/100g skeins (each approx 185yd/170m) of Reynolds/JCA *Saucy* (cotton③) in #817 ecru
● One pair each sizes 6 and 7 (4 and 4.5mm) needles OR SIZE TO OBTAIN GAUGE
● Stitch markers and holders
● Twelve ⁷/₈"/20mm buttons
Note
The original yarn used for this sweater is no longer available. A comparable substitute has been made, which is available at the time of printing. Check gauge of substitute yarns very carefully before beginning.

GAUGE
20 sts and 28 rows to 4"/10cm over St st using size 7 (4.5mm) needles. FOR PERFECT FIT, TAKE TIME TO CHECK GAUGE.

STITCH GLOSSARY
Seed St
Row 1 *K1, p1; rep from *, end k1.
Row 2 K the purl sts and p the knit sts. Rep row 2 for seed st.

BACK
With smaller needles, cast on 95 (101, 107, 113, 117) sts. Work in seed st for ³/₄"/2cm. Change to larger needles.
Next row (RS) Work seed st over first 5 sts, place marker (pm); k to last 5 sts, inc 12 sts across, pm; work 5 sts seed st—107 (113, 119, 125, 129) sts. Cont to work first and last 5 sts in seed st and rem sts in St st (k on RS, p on WS), sl markers, until piece measures 9¹/₂ (9¹/₂, 10, 10, 10¹/₂)"/24 (24, 25.5, 25.5, 26.5)cm from beg. Remove markers, end seed st and cont in St st on all sts until piece measures 12¹/₂ (12¹/₂, 13, 13, 13¹/₂)"/32 (32, 33.5, 33.5, 34.5)cm from beg, end with a WS row.

Placket
Next row (RS) K44 (47, 50, 53, 55), pm, work center 19 sts in seed st, pm, k to end. Cont to work center 19 sts in seed st and rem sts in St st until piece measures 26¹/₂ (27, 27¹/₂, 28, 28¹/₂)"/67 (68.5, 70, 71, 72)cm from beg.

Neck shaping
Next row (RS) Work 37 (39, 42, 44, 46) sts, join 2nd ball of yarn and bind off center 33 (35, 35, 37, 37) sts, work to end. Working both sides at once, dec 1 st at each neck edge every other row twice. Work even until piece measures 27³/₄ (28¹/₄, 28³/₄, 29¹/₄, 29³/₄)"/70 (71.5, 73, 74, 75)cm from beg. Bind off rem 35 (37, 40, 42, 44) sts each side.

FRONT
Work as for back until same length as back to placket, end with a WS row.

Placket shaping
Next row: Left half (RS) K44 (47, 50, 53, 55), place rem sts on holder, cast on 19 sts. Cont to work seed st over 19 cast-on sts and St st on rem sts, until piece measures 25¹/₄ (25³/₄, 26¹/₄, 26³/₄, 27¹/₄)"/64 (65.5, 67, 68, 69)cm from beg, end with a RS row.

Neck shaping
Bind off 12 sts at beg of next WS (neck edge) row, work to end. Work 3 rows even. Place rem 7 sts of placket on a holder, bind off from neck edge 4 sts once, 2 (3, 3, 4, 4) sts once. Dec 1 st at neck edge every other row 3 times. When same length as back, bind off sts for shoulders.
Right half From RS, work seed st across first 19 sts on holder, work in St st to end. Cont to work as for left half until placket measures 2¹/₂"/6.5cm, end with a WS row.
Next (buttonhole) row (RS) Work 3 sts, bind off 3 sts, work to last 6 sts of placket, bind off 3 sts, work to end. On next row, cast on 3 sts over bound-off sts. Place markers on left placket for 5 sets of buttons with the first set opposite buttonholes just made, the last set ¹/₂"/1.5cm from

upper edge, and 3 sets evenly between. Complete as for left half, reversing shaping by working neck decs at beg of RS rows, and working buttonholes opposite markers.

SLEEVES

With smaller needles, cast on 41 (45, 45, 47, 47) sts. Work in seed st for $^3/_4$"/2cm. Change to larger needles. Work in St st, inc 1 st each end every 4th row 24 (25, 25, 26, 26) times—89 (95, 95, 99, 99) sts. Work even until piece measures 15$^1/_2$ (16, 16, 16$^1/_2$, 16$^1/_2$)"/39 (40, 40, 41, 41)cm from beg. Bind off.

FINISHING

Block pieces. Sew shoulder seams. Sew cast-on edge of left placket band under right placket.

Neckband

With RS facing and smaller needles, work seed st across 7 sts of right front placket holder, pick up and k10 (12, 12, 14, 14) sts along right front neck, 39 (41, 41, 43, 43) sts along back neck, 10 (12, 12, 14, 14) sts along left front neck, work seed st across 7 sts of left front placket holder— 73 (79, 79, 85, 85) sts. Work in seed st for $^3/_4$"/2cm. Bind off. Place markers 9 (9$^1/_2$, 9$^1/_2$, 10, 10)"/22.5 (24, 24, 25, 25)cm down from shoulders on front and back for armholes. Sew top of sleeves between markers. Sew side seams leaving seed st side edges unsewn. Sew sleeve seams. Sew 10 buttons on left front placket. Sew rem 2 buttons at lower corners of back placket. •

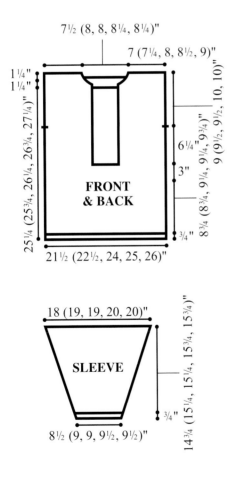

An easy, textured stitch pattern and ribbed bands give this standard-fitting V-neck vest lots of surface interest. It's a versatile wardrobe builder that moves effortlessly from home to office. Designed by Carol Covington. Shown in size 34. The Textured-Stitch Vest first appeared in the Winter Special '89/90 issue of Vogue Knitting.

Textured-Stitch Vest

SIZES
To fit 30 (32, 34, 36, 38, 40)"/76 (81, 86, 91, 96, 101)cm bust. Directions are for smallest size with larger sizes in parentheses. If there is only one figure it applies to all sizes.

KNITTED MEASUREMENTS
● Bust 33 (35, 37, 39, 41, 43)"/83 (87, 93, 97, 103, 107)cm.
● Length 21½ (22, 22½, 23, 23½, 24)"/54.5 (56, 57, 58, 59.5, 61)cm.

MATERIALS
Original Yarn
● 6 (6, 7, 7, 8, 8) 1¾oz/50g balls (each approx 110yd/100m) of Bernat®/Spinrite *Ultrawash Worsted* (wool④) in #12526 burgundy
Substitute Yarn
● 4 (4, 4, 5, 5, 6) 3½oz/100g skeins (each approx 200yds/182m) of Berella® *Muskoka* by Spinrite (wool④) in #9840 wine
● One pair each size 5 and 7 (4 and 4.5mm) needles OR SIZE TO OBTAIN GAUGE
● Size 6 (4mm) circular needle, 16"/40cm long
Note
The original yarn used for this sweater is no longer available. A comparable substitute has been made, which is available at the time of printing. Check gauge of substitute yarns very carefully before beginning.

GAUGE
20 sts and 26 rows to 4"/10cm over textured st using size 7 (4.5mm) needles.

FOR PERFECT FIT, TAKE TIME TO CHECK GAUGE.

STITCH GLOSSARY
Textured St (over an odd # of sts)
Row 1 (RS) Knit.
Rows 2 and 4 Purl.
Row 3 K1, *p1, k1; rep from * to end.
Rep rows 1-4 for textured st.

BACK
With smaller needles, cast on 83 (87, 93, 97, 103, 107) sts. Work in k1, p1 rib for 2"/5cm. Change to larger needles and work in textured st until piece measures 11½ (12, 12, 12½, 12½, 13)"/29 (30.5, 30.5, 31.5, 31.5, 33)cm from beg.

Armhole shaping
Bind off 4 (4, 5, 5, 5, 5) sts at beg of next 2 rows, 2 sts at beg of next 2 (2, 2, 4, 4, 4) rows. Dec 1 st each side every other row 3 (4, 4, 3, 3, 4) times—65 (67, 71, 73, 79, 81) sts. Work even until armhole measures 9 (9, 9½, 9½, 10, 10)"/23 (23, 24, 24, 25.5, 25.5)cm.

Shoulder shaping
Bind off 5 (6, 6, 6, 7, 7) sts at beg of next 4 rows, 6 (5, 6, 7, 7, 7) sts at beg of next 2 rows. Bind off rem 33 (33, 35, 35, 37, 39) sts.

FRONT
Work as for back until same length as back to armhole.

Armhole and neck shaping
Work armhole shaping as for back, AT SAME TIME, when armhole measures 1½"/4cm, join 2nd ball of yarn and bind off center st on next (RS) row.

Working both sides at once, dec 1 st at each neck edge [every 4th row once, every other row once] 7 (7, 7, 7, 8, 9) times, every 4th row 2 (2, 3, 3, 2, 1) times, AT SAME TIME, when same length as back to shoulder, shape shoulder as for back.

FINISHING
Block pieces. Sew shoulder and side seams.

V-neckband
With RS facing and circular needle, pick up and k27 (27, 29, 29, 31, 31) sts along back neck, 56 (56, 59, 59, 62, 62) sts along left front neck edge, 1 st in center bound-off st and mark this st, 56 (56, 59, 59, 62, 62) sts along right front neck edge—140 (140, 148, 148, 156, 156) sts. Join and work in k1, p1 rib as foll:
Rnd 1 Rib to 2 sts before center st, ssk, k center st, k2tog, beg with k1, rib to end of rnd. Rep last rnd, keeping to rib pat until band measures 1"/2.5cm. Bind off in rib.

Armhole bands
With RS facing and circular needle, pick up and k110 (110, 116, 116, 122, 122) sts around each armhole edge. Join and work in k1, p1 rib for 1"/2.5cm. Bind off in rib. ●

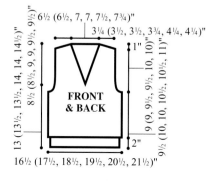

6½ (6½, 7, 7, 7½, 7¾)"
3¼ (3½, 3½, 3¾, 4¼, 4¼)"
1"
8½ (8½, 9, 9, 9½, 9½)"
9½ (9½, 14, 14, 14½)"
13 (13½, 13½, 14, 14, 14½)"
9 (9, 9½, 9½, 10, 10)"
9½ (10, 10, 10½, 10½, 11)"
2"
FRONT & BACK
16½ (17½, 18½, 19½, 20½, 21½)"

Casual charm with oversized appeal—ultra-soft mohair makes this pullover extra warm and cozy. Knit with wide ribs for captivating dimension, the sweater features drop shoulders and a wide cowl neck for dramatic effect. Designed by Norah Gaughan. Shown in size Medium. The Wide-Rib Pullover first appeared in the Winter '92/93 issue of *Vogue Knitting*.

Wide-Rib Pullover

SIZES
To fit Small (Medium, Large). Directions are for smallest size with larger sizes in parentheses. If there is only one figure it applies to all sizes.

KNITTED MEASUREMENTS
● Bust 43 (48, 53)"/109 (122, 134.5)cm.
● Length 27 (28, 29)"/68.5 (71, 73.5)cm.
● Upper arm 19 (20, 21)"/48.5 (51, 53.5)cm.

MATERIALS
● 10 (11, 12) 1¾oz/50g balls (each approx 98yd/90m) of Filatura Di Crosa/Stacy Charles *Mohair Lungo* (mohair/wool⑤) in #607 blue (MC)
● 9 (10, 11) 1½oz/40g balls (each approx 131yd/120m) of Filatura Di Crosa/Stacy Charles *No Smoking* (viscose/polyester③) in #136 blue (CC)
● One pair each sizes 9 and 10½ (5.5 and 6.5mm) needles OR SIZE TO OBTAIN GAUGE
● Size 9 (5.5mm) circular needle, 24"/60cm long

Note
The original colors used for this sweater are no longer available. Comparable color substitutes have been made, which are available at the time of printing.

GAUGE
14 sts and 17 rows to 4"/10cm over 4/4 rib using size 10½ (6.5mm) needles. FOR PERFECT FIT, TAKE TIME TO CHECK GAUGE.

STITCH GLOSSARY
4/4 Rib (multiple of 8 sts + 4 extra)
Row 1 (RS) K4, *p4, k4; rep from *.
Row 2 (WS) P4, *k4, p4; rep from *.
Rep rows 1 and 2 for 4/4 rib.
Note
One strand of MC and CC are held together throughout.

BACK
With smaller needles, cast on 74 (82, 90) sts. Work in k2, p2 rib for 3"/7.5cm, end with a RS row. Change to larger needles. P 1 row, inc 1 st each side—76 (84, 92) sts. Work in 4/4 rib until piece measures 26 (27, 28)"/66 (68.5, 71)cm from beg, end with a WS row.

Neck shaping
Next row (RS) Work 27 (30, 32) sts, join 2nd ball of yarn and bind off center 22 (24, 28) sts, work to end. Working both sides at once, bind off from each neck edge 6 sts twice. Bind off rem 15 (18, 20) sts each side for shoulder.

FRONT
Work as for back until piece measures 25 (26, 27)"/63.5 (66, 68.5)cm from beg, end with a WS row.

Neck shaping
Next row (RS) Work 31 (34, 36) sts, join 2nd ball of yarn and bind off center 14 (16, 20) sts, work to end. Working both

sides at once, bind off from each neck edge 4 sts 4 times. When same length as back to shoulder, bind off rem sts for shoulders.

SLEEVES
With smaller needles, cast on 34 (34, 38) sts. Work in k2, p2 rib for 3"/7.5cm, end with a RS row. Change to larger needles. P 1 row, inc 6 (8, 8) sts evenly across—40 (42, 46) sts.
Next row (RS) K2 (3, 1), p4, work in 4/4 rib, end p4, k2 (3, 1). Cont to work in 4/4 rib as established, inc 1 st each side (working inc sts in 4/4 rib) every 4th row 13 (14, 14) times—66 (70, 74) sts. Work even until piece measures 16 (17, 18)"/40.5 (43, 45.5)cm from beg. Bind off.

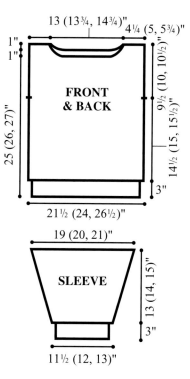

FRONT & BACK

13 (13¾, 14¾)"
4¼ (5, 5¾)"
1"
1"
25 (26, 27)"
9½ (10, 10½)"
14½ (15, 15½)"
3"
21½ (24, 26½)"

19 (20, 21)"
SLEEVE
13 (14, 15)"
3"
11½ (12, 13)"

FINISHING
Block pieces. Sew shoulder seams.

Cowl neck
With RS facing and circular needle, pick up and k92 (96, 104) sts evenly around neck edge. Join and work in k2, p2 rib for 13 (14, 14)"/33 (35.5, 35.5)cm. Bind off loosely. Place markers 9$\frac{1}{2}$ (10, 10$\frac{1}{2}$)"/24 (25.5, 26.5)cm down from shoulders on front and back for armholes. Sew top of sleeves between markers. Sew side and sleeve seams. •

How the West was dressed! Contrast cable fringe trim gives a versatile pullover cowgirl-style. It's oversized with drop shoulders and a high funnel neck. Designed by Kathy Donovan. Shown in size Large. The Fringed Pullover first appeared in the Fall '92 issue of *Vogue Knitting*.

Fringed Pullover

SIZES
To fit Small (Medium, Large, X-Large). Directions are given for smallest size with larger sizes in parentheses. If there is only one figure it applies to all sizes.

KNITTED MEASUREMENTS
● Bust 44¹/₂ (47, 49, 51¹/₂)"/113 (119.5, 124.5, 131)cm.
● Length without fringe 25 (25, 26, 27)"/63.5 (63.5, 66, 68.5)cm.
● Upper arm 18 (20, 20, 22)"/45.5 (51, 51, 56)cm.

MATERIALS
Original Yarn
● 8 (9, 9, 10) 3¹/₂oz/100g balls (each approx 110yd/100m) of Crystal Palace *Boss Tweed* (wool ④) in #143 brown tweed (MC)
● 3 balls in #180 oatmeal tweed (CC)
Substitute Yarn
● 13 (15, 15, 17) 1³/₄oz/50g skeins (each approx 68yd/63m) of Tahki Yarns *Cottage Chunky Knit* (wool ⑤) in #583 tan (MC)
● 5 skeins in #585 grey (CC)
● One pair each sizes 10 and 10¹/₂ (6 and 6.5mm) needles OR SIZE TO OBTAIN GAUGE
● Size 10 (6mm) circular needle, 24"/60cm long
● Cable needle (cn)
Note
The original yarns used for this sweater are no longer available. Comparable substitutes have been made, which are available at the time of printing. Check gauge of substitute yarns very carefully before beginning.

GAUGE
13 sts and 18 rows to 4"/10cm over St st using size 10¹/₂ (6.5mm) needles. FOR PERFECT FIT, TAKE TIME TO CHECK GAUGE.

STITCH GLOSSARY
6-st Front Cable
Sl 3 sts to cn and hold to *front*, k3, k3 from cn.
6-st Back Cable
Sl 3 sts to cn and hold to *back*, k3, k3 from cn.

BACK
With larger needles and MC, cast on 74 (78, 82, 86) sts. Work in St st (k on RS, p on WS) until piece measures 23¹/₂ (23¹/₂, 24¹/₂, 25¹/₂)"/60 (60, 62, 65)cm from beg, end with a WS row.

Neck shaping
Next row (RS) K21 (23, 25, 27) sts, join 2nd ball of yarn and bind off 32 sts, work to end. Working both sides at once, dec 1 st from each neck edge every other row twice.

Shoulder shaping
Bind off 10 (11, 12, 13) sts at beg of next 2 rows, then 9 (10, 11, 12) sts at beg of next 2 rows.

FRONT
Work as for back until piece measures 20¹/₂ (20¹/₂, 21¹/₂, 22¹/₂)"/52 (52, 55.5, 57)cm from beg, end with a WS row.

Neck shaping
Next row (RS) K28 (30, 32, 34) sts, join 2nd ball of yarn and bind off 18 sts, work to end. Working both sides at once, dec

1 st from each neck edge every other row 9 times, AT SAME TIME, when same length as back to shoulder, shape shoulder as for back.

SLEEVES
With larger needles and MC, cast on 34 sts. Work in St st, inc 1 st each side (working inc sts into St st) every 4th row 3 (10, 10, 19) times, then every 6th row 10 (6, 6, 0) times—60 (66, 66, 72) sts. Work even until piece measures 17 (18, 18, 18)"/43 (45.5, 45.5, 45.5)cm from beg. Bind off.

FINISHING
Block pieces. Sew shoulder seams.

Neckband
With RS facing, circular needle, and MC, pick up and k84 sts along neck edge. Join. Work in k2, p2 rib for 3¹/₂"/9cm.
Dec row *K2, p2tog; rep from *—63 sts. Work in k2, p1 rib for 2"/5cm more. Bind off loosely in rib. Fold neckband to WS at dec row. Sew in place. Place markers 9 (10, 10, 11)"/23 (25.5, 25.5, 28)cm down from shoulders on front and back for armholes. Sew top of sleeves between markers. Sew side and sleeve seams.

Contrast cable fringe
With smaller needles and CC, cast on 12 sts.
Row 1 (RS) K3, work 9 sts of chart pat. Cont to work in pat as established, keeping first 3 sts in St st until piece measures 38¹/₂"/98cm from beg, end with a WS row.
Next row K3, bind off 9 sts. Unravel first 3 sts every row. Cut loops of each row to make fringe. Sew short ends of cable

together. Tack in place around neck. Rep
contrast cable fringe for lower edge,
working until piece measures 46½ (49,
51, 53½)"/118 (124.5, 129.5, 136)cm
from beg. Sew along lower edge of
sweater front and back.

Sleeve cable trim
With smaller needles and CC, cast on 9
sts. Work 9 sts of chart pat for 13"/33cm.
Bind off. Sew short ends together and
sew around lower edge of sleeve. •

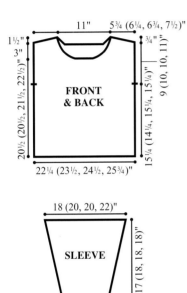

11"   5¾ (6¼, 6¾, 7½)"
1½"   ¾"
3"

**FRONT
& BACK**

20½ (20½, 21½, 22½)"   15¼ (14¼, 15¼, 15¼)"   9 (10, 10, 11)"

22¼ (23½, 24½, 25¾)"

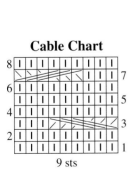

18 (20, 20, 22)"

SLEEVE

17 (18, 18, 18)"

10"

Cable Chart

8 | I | I | I | I | I | I | I | I | I
7
6 | I | I | I | I | I | I | I | I | I
5
4 | I | I | I | I | I | I | I | I | I
3
2 | I | I | I | I | I | I | I | I | I
1

9 sts

Stitch Key

I   K on RS, p on WS

⟋⟍   6-st Back Cable

⟋⟍   6-st Front Cable

This unstructured, oversized moss-stitch pullover with drop shoulders is knit in a rich, neutral chenille for plush texture. The sweater features a back-buttoned highneck and rolled, stockinette-stitch edges. Designed by Norah Gaughan. Shown in size Medium. The Moss-Stitch Pullover first appeared in the Fall '92 issue of *Vogue Knitting*.

Moss-Stitch Pullover

SIZES
To fit Small (Medium, Large). Directions are for smallest size with larger sizes in parentheses. If there is only one figure it applies to all sizes.

KNITTED MEASUREMENTS
● Bust 40 (45, 50)"/101.5 (114.5, 127)cm.
● Length 26¹/₂ (27¹/₂, 28¹/₂)"/67.5 (70, 72.5)cm.
● Upper arm 17¹/₂ (18¹/₂, 20¹/₂)"/ 44.5 (47, 52)cm.

MATERIALS
● 7 (8, 10) 3¹/₂oz/100g balls (each approx 154yd/140m) of Rowan/ Westminster Fibers *Cotton Chenille* (cotton⑤) in #351 raisin
● One pair each sizes 6 and 7 (4 and 4.5mm) needles OR SIZE TO OBTAIN GAUGE
● Sizes 6 and 7 (4 and 4.5mm) circular needles, 16"/40cm long
● Stitch marker
● One ³/₄"/20mm button

GAUGE
14 sts and 24 rows to 4"/10cm over moss st using size 7 (4.5mm) needles. FOR PERFECT FIT, TAKE TIME TO CHECK GAUGE.

STITCH GLOSSARY
Moss St (over an even # of sts)
Row 1 (RS) *K1, p1; rep from *.
Rows 2 and 4 (WS) Knit the k sts and purl the p sts.
Row 3 *P1, k1; rep from *. Rep rows 1-4 for moss st.

Slip St Pat (over 5 sts)
Row 1 (RS) P1, sl 1, k1, sl 1, p1.
Row 2 (WS) K1, p3, k1. Rep rows 1 and 2 for slip st pat.

BACK
With smaller needles, cast on 73 (81, 91) sts. Work in St st (k on RS, p on WS) for 1"/2.5cm, end with a WS row. Change to larger needles.
Beg pats: Row 1 (RS) Work moss st over 16 (18, 22) sts, slip st pat over 5 sts, moss st 31 (35, 37) sts, slip st pat over 5 sts, moss st over 16 (18, 22) sts. Cont in pats as established until piece measures 25¹/₂ (26¹/₂, 27¹/₂)"/65 (67.5, 70)cm from beg, end with a WS row.

Neck shaping
Next row (RS) Work 32 (35, 39) sts, join 2nd ball of yarn and bind off 9 (11, 13) sts, work to end. Working both sides at once, bind off from each neck edge 4 sts twice. Work even until piece measures 26¹/₂ (27¹/₂, 28¹/₂)"/67.5 (70, 72.5)cm from beg. Bind off rem 24 (27, 31) sts each side for shoulders.

FRONT
Work as for back until piece measures 24 (25, 26)"/61 (63.5, 66)cm from beg, end with a WS row.

Neck shaping
Next row (RS) Work 33 (36, 40) sts, join 2nd ball of yarn and bind off 7 (9, 11) sts, work to end. Working both sides at once, bind off from each neck edge 3 sts once, 2 sts twice, dec 1 st every other row twice. When same length as

back to shoulder, bind off rem 24 (27, 31) sts each side for shoulders.

SLEEVES
With smaller needles, cast on 34 (36, 38) sts. Work in St st for 1"/2.5cm, end with a WS row. Change to larger needles.
Beg pats: Row 1 (RS) Work moss st over 4 (4, 5) sts, slip st pat over 5 sts, moss st over 16 (18, 18) sts, slip st pat over 5 sts, moss st over 4 (4, 5) sts. Cont in pats as established, inc 1 each side (working inc sts into moss st) every 4th row 0 (0, 3) times, every 6th row 12 (14, 15) times, then every 8th row 3 (2, 0) times—64 (68, 74) sts. Work even until piece measures 17¹/₂ (18, 18¹/₂)"/44.5 (45.5, 47)cm from beg, end with a WS row. Bind off.

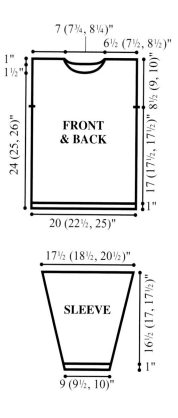

Schematic measurements
7 (7³/₄, 8¹/₄)"
6¹/₂ (7¹/₂, 8¹/₂)"
1"
1¹/₂"
24 (25, 26)"
8¹/₂ (9, 10)"
17 (17¹/₂, 17¹/₂)"
FRONT & BACK
20 (22¹/₂, 25)"
1"

17¹/₂ (18¹/₂, 20¹/₂)"
SLEEVE
16¹/₂ (17, 17¹/₂)"
1"
9 (9¹/₂, 10)"

FINISHING
Block pieces. Sew shoulder seams.

Mock turtleneck
With RS facing and larger circular needle, beg at center back, pick up and k60 (64, 68) sts evenly around neck edge. Join and place marker. Work moss st for 2"/5cm, sl marker every rnd. Working back and forth without joining, cont in moss st pat for 4 rows. Change to smaller needles and St st.
Next row (RS) K1, yo, (buttonhole) work to end. Cont in St st for 1"/2.5cm. Bind off loosely. Place markers 8½ (9, 10)"/21.5 (23, 25.5)cm down from shoulders on front and back for armholes. Sew top of sleeves between markers. Sew side and sleeve seams, leaving St st areas free. Sew on button opposite buttonhole. ●

Drop-Shoulder Tunic

Textural stitches give this terrific-looking, loose-fitting tunic with rolled collar and drop shoulders lots of surface dimension, while super-bright yarn adds dramatic color. Designed by Heather McLean. Shown in size Medium. The Drop-Shoulder Tunic first appeared in the Winter '96/97 issue of Vogue Knitting.

SIZES
To fit Small (Medium, Large). Directions are for smallest size with larger sizes in parentheses. If there is only one figure it applies to all sizes.

KNITTED MEASUREMENTS
● Bust 44 (46, 48)"/112 (117, 122)cm.
● Length 27¹/₂"/70cm.
● Upper arm 22¹/₂ (24, 24)"/ 57 (61, 61)cm.

MATERIALS
Original Yarn
● 10 (10, 11) 3¹/₂oz/100g skeins (each approx 230yd/207m) of Colinette DK (wool) in #16 blue parrot
Substitute Yarn
● 8 (8, 8) 4oz/125g hanks (each approx 313yd/288m) of Cherry Tree Hill Yarn DK (silk/merino③) in Green Mountain Madness
● One pair each size 4 and 5 (3.5 and 3.75mm) needles OR SIZE TO OBTAIN GAUGE
● Stitch holders
Note
The original yarn used for this sweater is no longer available.* A comparable substitute has been made, which is available at the time of printing. Check gauge of substitute yarns very carefully before beginning.
*Original yarn is available in the United Kingdom at the time of printing.

GAUGE
23 sts and 30 rows to 4"/10cm over main stitch pat, using size 4 (3.5mm) needles. FOR PERFECT FIT, TAKE TIME TO CHECK GAUGE

STITCH GLOSSARY
Double Seed Stitch
Row 1 *K1, p1, rep from * to end.
Rows 2 & 4 K the knit sts, p the purl sts.
Row 3 *P1, k1, rep from * to end. Rep Rows 1-4 for pat.

Main Stitch Pattern (multiple of 7 sts)
Row 1 (RS) *K5, p2, rep from * to end.
Row 2 & all even rows K the knit sts, p the purl sts.
Row 3 K4, p2, *k5, p2, rep from * to last st, k1.
Row 5 K3, p2, *k5, p2, rep from * to last 2 sts, k2.
Row 7 K2, p2, *k5, p2, rep from * to last 3 sts, k3.
Row 9 K1, p2, *k5, p2, rep from * to last 4 sts, k4.
Row 11 P1, k2, *p5, k2, rep from * to last 4 sts, p4.
Row 13 P2, k2, *p5, k2, rep from * to last 3 sts, p3.
Row 15 P3, k2, *p5, k2, rep from * to last 2 sts, p2.
Row 17 P4, k2, *p5, k2, rep from * to last st, p1.
Row 19 *P5, k2, rep from * to end.
Row 20 K the knit sts, p the purl sts. Rep rows 1-20 for main stitch pat.

BACK
With smaller needles, cast on 126 (133, 140) sts. Work in double seed stitch for 2¹/₂"/6.5cm. Change to larger needles. Work in main stitch pat for 180 rows.

Neck shaping
Next row (RS) Working in main stitch, pat 50 (52, 54) sts, join 2nd ball of yarn, pat next 26 (29, 32) sts and place on holder, pat 50 (52, 54) sts. Working both sides at once, cont in main stitch pat dec 1 st at each neck edge every row 9 times. Bind off rem 41 (43, 45) sts each side.

FRONT
Work as for back until 164 rows of main stitch pat have been completed.

Neck shaping
Next row (RS) Working in main stitch, pat 54 (56, 58) sts, join 2nd ball of yarn, pat next 18 (21, 24) sts and place on holder, pat 54 (56, 58) sts. Working both sides at once, cont in main stitch pat dec 1 st at each neck edge every row 6 times, then every other row 7 times. Work 4 rows even. Bind off rem 41 (43, 45) sts each side.

SLEEVES
With smaller needles, cast on 50 sts. Work in k1, p1 rib for 2¹/₂"/6.5cm, inc 20 sts evenly across last row—70 sts. Change to larger needles. Work in main stitch pat, inc 1 st each side every 3 rows 8 times, then every 4 rows 22 (26, 26) times working added sts into main stitch pat—130 (138, 138) sts. Cont until 128 rows of main stitch pat have been completed or until desired length. Bind off loosely.

FINISHING
Block pieces to measurements. Sew left shoulder seam.

Neckband

With RS facing and smaller needles, pick up and k 10 sts along right back neck edge, 26 (29, 32) sts from center back holder, 10 sts along left back neck edge, 15 sts along left front neck edge, 18 (21, 24) sts from center front holder, 15 sts along right front neck edge—94 (100, 106) sts. Work 15 rows in k1, p1 rib, then 10 rows St st. Bind off loosely. Sew right shoulder seam including neckband. Set in sleeves. Sew side sleeve and seams leaving 2¹/₂"/6.5cm seed stitch welt open at side seams. •

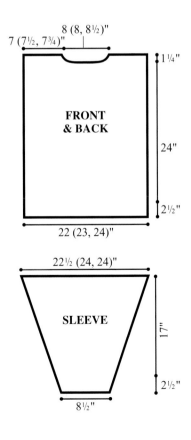

8 (8, 8¹/₂)"

7 (7¹/₂, 7³/₄)"

1¹/₄"

FRONT & BACK

24"

2¹/₂"

22 (23, 24)"

22¹/₂ (24, 24)"

SLEEVE

17"

2¹/₂"

8¹/₂"

A casual classic from designer Calvin Klein. This oversized pullover with drop shoulders and crew neck is worked in a distinctive broken-cable pattern. Shown in size 36. The Broken-Cable Pullover first appeared in the Spring/Summer '86 issue of *Vogue Knitting*.

Broken-Cable Pullover

SIZES

To fit 32 (34, 36, 38)"/81 (86, 91, 96)cm bust. Directions are for smallest size with larger sizes in parentheses. If there is only one set of figures it applies to all sizes.

KNITTED MEASUREMENTS

● Bust 38 (40, 42, 43)"/96 (100, 104, 108)cm.
● Length 24 (24½, 25, 25½)"/60.5 (62, 63.5, 64.5)cm.
● Upper arm 17 (18, 18, 19)"/43 (46, 46, 48)cm.

MATERIALS

Original Yarn

● 13 (14, 14, 15) 1¾oz/50g balls (each approx 100yd/90m) of Joseph Galler *Bamboo* (silk④) in #514 grey

Substitute Yarn

● 16 (17, 17, 18) 1¾oz/50g spools (each approx 85yd/78m) of Skacel Collection *Hillary* (rayon④) in #4 gold
● One pair each sizes 5 and 8 (3.75 and 5mm) needles OR SIZE TO OBTAIN GAUGE
● Cable needle (cn)

Note

The original yarn used for this sweater is no longer available. A comparable substitute has been made, which is available at the time of printing. Check gauge of substitute yarns very carefully before beginning.

GAUGE

20 sts and 26 rows to 4"/10cm over St st using size 8 (5mm) needles.
FOR PERFECT FIT, TAKE TIME TO CHECK GAUGE.

BACK

With smaller needles, cast on 96 (100, 104, 108) sts. Work in k2, p2 rib for 2"/5cm. Change to larger needles.
Beg broken cable pat: Rows 1-12
Work in St st (k on RS, p on WS).
Row 13 (RS) K24 (26, 28, 30), sl next 6 sts to cable needle (cn) and hold to *front*, k6, k6 from cn—front cable made, k24, work front cable over 12 sts, k24 (26, 28, 30).
Rows 14-24 Work in St st.
Row 25 K6 (8, 10, 12), sl next 6 sts to cn and hold to *back*, k6, k6 from cn—back cable made, *k24, work back cable over 12 sts; rep from * once more, end k6 (8, 10, 12). Rep rows 2-25 for broken cable pat until piece measures 24 (24½, 25, 25½)"/60.5 (62, 63.5, 64.5)cm from beg, end with a WS row. Bind off all sts.

FRONT

Work as for back until piece measures 21 (21½, 22, 22½)"/52.5 (54, 55.5, 56.5)cm.

Neck shaping

Next row (RS) Work across 40 (42, 44, 46) sts, join 2nd ball of yarn and bind off center 16 sts, work to end. Working both sides at once, bind off 3 sts from each neck edge once, 2 sts 3 (4, 4, 5) times, then dec 1 st every other row 3 (2, 2, 2) times. When same length as

back, bind off rem 28 (29, 31, 31) sts each side for shoulders.

SLEEVES

(Note: Work all inc sts into pat.) With smaller needles, cast on 50 (52, 52, 56) sts. Work in k2, p2 rib for 1½"/4cm, inc 1 st each side of last row—52 (54, 54, 58) sts. Change to larger needles. Work 8 rows even. Inc 1 st each side of next row, then every 6th row 16 (17, 17, 18) times, AT SAME TIME, work broken cable pat as foll:
Rows 1-12 Work in St st.
Row 13 K21 (22, 22, 24), work front cable over 12 sts, k21 (22, 22, 24).
Rows 14-24 Work in St st.

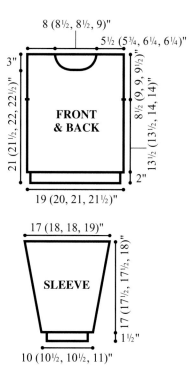

8 (8½, 8½, 9)"

5½ (5¾, 6¼, 6¼)"

3"

21 (21½, 22, 22½)"

8½ (9, 9, 9½)"

FRONT & BACK

13½ (13½, 14, 14)"

2"

19 (20, 21, 21½)"

17 (18, 18, 19)"

SLEEVE

17 (17½, 17½, 18)"

1½"

10 (10½, 10½, 11)"

Row 25 K5 (6, 6, 8), work back cable over 12 sts, k24, work back cable, k5 (6, 6, 8). Rep rows 2-25 and when reaching next row 13, work as foll: k25 (26, 26, 28), work front cable over 12 sts, k25 (26, 26, 28). After all inc, there are 86 (90, 90, 96) sts. Work even until piece measures 18$\frac{1}{2}$ (19, 19, 19$\frac{1}{2}$)"/47 (47.5, 47.5, 49)cm from beg. Bind off all sts.

FINISHING

Block pieces to measurements. Sew left shoulder seam.

Neckband

With RS facing and smaller needle, pick up and k40 (42, 42, 46) sts along back neck, 20 (21, 21, 23) sts along left front neck edge, 16 sts along front bind-off and 20 (21, 21, 23) sts along right front neck edge—96 (100, 100, 108) sts. Work in k2, p2 rib for 1"/2.5cm. Bind off in rib. Sew right shoulder seam, including neckband. Place markers 8$\frac{1}{2}$ (9, 9, 9$\frac{1}{2}$)"/21.5 (23, 23, 24)cm down from shoulders on front and back for armholes. Sew top of sleeves between markers. Sew side and sleeve seams. •

In this simple rollneck tunic, handpainted yarn creates a kaleidescope of color. Garter-stitch detailing along the bust and lower edge add surface interest and subtle shaping. A Vogue Original. Shown in size Medium. The Rollneck Tunic first appeared in the Spring/Summer '98 issue of *Vogue Knitting*.

Rollneck Tunic

SIZES

To fit X-Small (Small, Medium, Large, X-Large). Directions are for smallest size with larger sizes in parentheses. If there is only one figure it applies to all sizes.

KNITTED MEASUREMENTS

- Bust 33 (35, 37, 40, 42)"/83 (88, 92, 100, 105)cm.
- Length 28 (28½, 29, 29½, 30)"/71 (72, 73.5, 75, 76)cm.
- Upper arm 12½ (13, 13, 14, 15)"/32 (33, 33, 35.5, 38)cm.

MATERIALS

- 11 (12, 13, 14, 15) 1¾oz/50g balls (each approx 107yd/96m) of Brown Sheep Co. *Kaleidescope* (cotton/wool④) in Anaheim
- One pair size 6 (4mm) needles OR SIZE TO OBTAIN GAUGE
- Size 6 (4mm) circular needle, 16"/40cm long

GAUGE

20 sts and 28 rows to 4"/10cm over St st using size 6 (4mm) needles.
FOR PERFECT FIT, TAKE TIME TO CHECK GAUGE.

BACK

With size 6 (4mm) needles, cast on 89 (96, 100, 110, 115) sts. Work in garter st (k every row) for 4"/10cm. Cont in St st (k on RS, p on WS) dec 1 st each side on every 30th (26th, 26th, 20th, 20th) row 3 (4, 4, 5, 5) times—83 (88, 92, 100, 105) sts. Work even until piece measures 20 (20, 20½, 20½, 20½)"/50.5 (50.5, 52, 52, 52)cm from beg, end with a WS row.

Armhole shaping

Cont in garter st, bind off 3 (3, 3, 4, 5) sts at beg of next 2 rows, dec 1 st each side every other row 2 (3, 3, 4, 4) times—73 (76, 80, 84, 87) sts. Cont in garter st until armhole measures 4"/10cm. Then cont in St st until armhole measures 7 (7½, 7½, 8, 8½)"/18 (19, 19, 20.5, 21.5)cm, end with a WS row.

Neck and shoulder shaping

Bind off 6 (6, 6, 7, 7) sts at beg of next 6 (4, 2, 4, 2) rows, 0 (7, 7, 8, 8) sts at beg of next 0 (2, 4, 2, 4) rows, AT SAME TIME, join 2nd ball of yarn and bind off center 17 (18, 20, 20, 21) sts for neck Working both sides at once, bind off from each neck edge 5 sts twice.

FRONT

Work as for back until armhole measures 5 (5½, 5½, 6, 6½)"/13 (14, 14, 15.5, 16.5)cm, end with a WS row.

Neck and shoulder shaping

Next row (RS) Work 32 (33, 34, 36, 37) sts, join 2nd ball of yarn and bind off center 9 (10, 12, 12, 13) sts, work to end. Working both sides at once, bind off from each neck edge 3 sts twice, 2 sts twice, dec 1 st every other row 4 times, AT SAME TIME, when same length as back to shoulder, shape shoulder as for back.

SLEEVES

With size 6 (4mm) needles, cast on 43 (45, 45, 46, 47) sts. Work in garter st for 4"/10cm. Cont in St st, inc 1 st each side every 8th row 10 (10, 10, 9, 3) times, every 6th row 0 (0, 0, 3, 11) times—63 (65, 65, 70, 75) sts. Work even until

piece measures 17 (17½, 17½, 18, 18)"/43 (44, 44, 45.5, 45.5)cm from beg.

Cap shaping

Bind off 3 sts at beg of next 2 rows, 2 sts at beg of next 6 rows, dec 1 st each side every other row 10 (12, 12, 13, 15) times, bind off 3 sts at beg of next 2 rows, 2 sts at beg of next 2 rows. Bind off rem 15 (13, 13, 16, 17) sts.

FINISHING

Sew shoulder seams.

Collar

With RS facing and circular needle, pick up and k88 (90, 94, 94, 96) sts evenly around neck edge. Join and work in St st (k every rnd) for 6"/15cm. Bind off loosely. Collar will roll naturally to RS. Set in sleeves. Sew side and sleeve seams. •

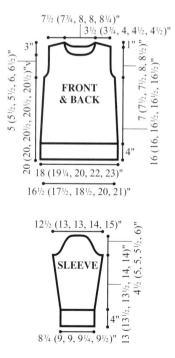

Fashion takes its cue from the Far East. Asymmetric styling and a brilliant shade of lacquer red shape up an exotic cardigan. Designed by Ann Denton. The Asymmetrical Cardigan first appeared in the Spring/Summer '98 issue of *Vogue Knitting*.

Asymmetrical Cardigan

SIZES
One size fits all.

KNITTED MEASUREMENTS
- Bust 48"/120cm.
- Length 19"/48cm.
- Upper arm 22"/56cm.

MATERIALS
- 26 1³/₄oz/50g balls (each approx 66yd/60m) of Trendsetter Yarns *Piatina* (viscose④) in #75 red
- One pair size 6 (4mm) needles OR SIZE TO OBTAIN GAUGE
- Stitch holders and markers
- Four 1"/25mm buttons
- 1yd/1m of ³/₄"/2cm bias tape
- Matching sewing thread

GAUGE
19 sts and 26 rows to 4"/10cm over pat st using size 6 (4mm) needles.
FOR PERFECT FIT, TAKE TIME TO CHECK GAUGE.

Note
Leave long ends of yarn when attaching new balls and attach at seam edges only.

STITCH GLOSSARY
Pattern Stitch
Row 1 (RS) K1 (selvage st), *k next st wrapping yarn around needle twice; rep from * to last st, k1 (selvage st).
Row 2 K1, *knit, dropping 2nd yarn wrap; rep from *, end k1.
Rows 3 and 4 Knit. Rep rows 1-4 for pat st.

BACK
Cast on 114 sts. K 8 rows. Work in pat st for 26 rows. Piece measures approx 5"/12.5cm from beg. Place markers each end of row.

Armhole shaping
Dec row (RS) K1, k2tog, work pat to last 3 sts, k2tog, k1. [Work 5 rows even. Work dec row. Work 7 rows even. Work dec row.] 4 times. Work 5 rows even. Work dec row—94 sts. Work even until piece measures 16"/40cm from beg, end with pat row 2.

Neck and shoulder shaping
Next row (RS) Bind off 5 sts, work until there are 29 sts on needle, sl center 26 sts to a holder for neck, join 2nd ball of yarn and work to end. Working both sides at once, bind off 5 sts from left shoulder once, then bind off from each shoulder edge 5 sts once more, 4 sts 4 times and AT SAME TIME, k2tog at neck edge every row 4 times.

LEFT FRONT
Cast on 66 sts. K 8 rows. Work in pat st for 26 rows. Place marker at beg of RS row (armhole edge).

Armhole shaping
(Note: Sts are inc'd at armhole edge only for asymmetrical fit of garment.)
Inc row 1 (RS) K1, M1, work pat to end of row.
Inc row 2 (WS) K1, work pat to last st, M1, k1.
Inc row 3 (RS) Rep inc row 1.
Row 4 Work even. Rep last 4 rows 11 times more—102 sts.

Shoulder shaping
Next row (RS) K1, k2tog, work pat to end. Work 1 row even. Rep last 2 rows 15 times more—86 sts. K 14 rows for front band. Bind off loosely.

RIGHT FRONT
Work as for left front, reversing shaping by inc at end of RS rows (for armhole) and dec at end of RS rows (for shoulder). K 4 rows for front band.
Buttonhole row (RS) K7, bind off 2 sts, *k15, bind off 2 sts; rep from * twice more, k26. On next row, cast on 2 sts over each set of bound-off sts. K 9 more rows. Bind off loosely.

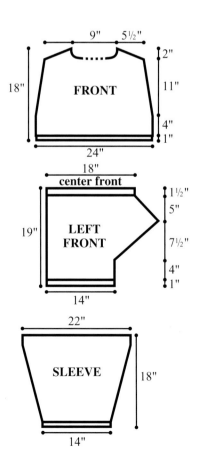

SLEEVES

Cast on 67 sts. K 8 rows. Then, work in pat st inc 1 st each side every 6th row 9 times, every 4th row 10 times—105 sts. Work even until piece measures 18"/45.5cm from beg. Bind off loosely on a RS row.

FINISHING
Back neckband

Pick up and k6 sts from right back neck, k26 sts from holder, pick up and k6 sts from left back neck—38 sts. K 3 rows.

Rows 5, 7, 11 and 13 (RS) K5, k2tog, k to last 7 sts, ssk, k5.

Rows 6, 8, 9, 10 and 12 Knit. Bind off firmly on 14th row. Block pieces lightly. Sew shoulder seams firmly. Reinforce with bias tape using sewing thread. Sew sleeves to armholes between markers. Sew side and sleeve seams. Sew on buttons. Sew length of yarn to inside of right seam edge and corresponding top of front garter band to tie garment closed on inside. •

Textured stitches and bright stripes add high impact to this pullover tee. It's loose-fitting with a rollneck and set-in short sleeves. A Vogue Original. Shown in size Small. The T-Shirt Pullover first appeared in the Spring/Summer '97 issue of *Vogue Knitting*.

T-Shirt Pullover

SIZES

To fit Small (Medium, Large). Directions are for smallest size with larger sizes in parentheses. If there is only one figure it applies to all sizes.

KNITTED MEASUREMENTS

● Bust 36 (38, 40)"/92 (97, 102)cm.
● Length 17 (18, 19)"/43 (46, 48)cm.
● Upper arm 12 (13, 14)"/30.5 (33, 35.5)cm.

MATERIALS

● 3 (3, 4) 1¾oz/50g balls (each approx 92yd/84m) of Filatura Di Crosa/Stacy Charles *Amico* (cotton③) in #34 red (R) and #210 fuchsia (F)
● 2 (2, 3) skeins #31 green (G)
● 1 skein #214 brown (B)
● One pair size 7 (4.5mm) needles OR SIZE TO OBTAIN GAUGE
● Size 6 (4mm) circular needle, 16"/41cm long

Note
The original colors used for this sweater are no longer available. Comparable color substitutes have been made, which are available at the time of printing.

GAUGE

24 sts and 36 rows to 4"/10cm over broken rib st using size 7 (4.5mm) needles. FOR PERFECT FIT, TAKE TIME TO CHECK GAUGE.

STITCH GLOSSARY

Broken Rib Stitch (on odd number of sts)

Row 1 (WS) K1, *p1, k1; rep from *.
Row 2 (RS) Purl.
Rep rows 1-2 for broken rib st.

BACK

With R, cast on 107 (113, 119) sts. Work in garter st for ½"/1.2cm. Work in broken rib st until 6½ (7, 7½)"/17 (18, 19)cm, ending with a WS row. * Change to B and k 2 rows for garter ridge. Change to G and work 10 rows in St st.* Rep from * to * once. Change to B and k 2 rows for garter ridge, ending with a WS row. Change to F.

Armhole shaping

Work in broken rib st and bind off 4 (5, 6) sts beg of 2 rows, dec 1 st each side every other row 5 (5, 6) times—89 (93, 95) sts, cont until armhole measures 7½ (8, 8½)"/19 (20, 22)cm.

Shoulder shaping

Bind off 8 sts beg of next 4 rows, 7 (8, 8) sts at beg of next 2 rows. Bind off rem 43 (45, 47) sts.

FRONT

Work as for back until armhole measures 5½ (6, 6½)"/14 (15, 17)cm, ending with WS row.

Neck shaping

Next row (RS) Work across 33 (34, 34) sts, join 2nd ball of yarn, bind off center 23 (25, 27) sts, work to end. Working both sides at once, bind off at each neck edge 2 sts twice. Dec 1 st at each neck edge every other row 6 times. Work on 23 (24, 24) sts each side until same length as back to shoulder.

Shoulder shaping

At shoulder edge, bind off 8 sts twice, then rem 7 (8, 8) sts each side.

SLEEVE

With B, cast on 71 (77, 83) sts. K 2 rows. Change to F and work in broken rib st for 2 (2¼, 2½)"/5 (6, 6.5)cm, ending with a WS row.

Cap shaping

Bind off 4 (5, 6) sts beg of next 2 rows, dec 1 st each side every other row 17 (19, 21) times. Work on 29 sts until 4 (4½, 5)"/10 (12, 13)cm from beg of cap shaping. Bind off 9 sts beg of next 2 rows. Bind off rem 11 sts.

FINISHING

Block pieces to measurements. Sew shoulder seams.

Collar

With RS facing, circular needle and B, beg at center back and pick up and k103 (105, 109) sts around entire neck opening, join to work in rnds. P 1 rnd, k 1 rnd for ridge. Change to F and k 12 rnds more. Bind off. Sew in sleeves. Sew side and sleeve seams matching pats. ●

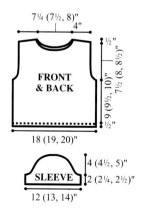

SIMPLE STRIPES

An easy
color switch
is all
it takes
to create
dramatic
impact

Seaworthy stripes in an easy pattern even a beginner can navigate. Drop shoulders and rolled edges make this jaunty classic perfect by land or sea. Designed by Anne Mieke Louwerens. Shown in size Large. The Easy Striped Pullover first appeared in the Spring/Summer '94 issue of *Vogue Knitting*.

Easy Striped Pullover

SIZES
To fit Small (Medium, Large, X-Large). Directions are for smallest size with larger sizes in parentheses. If there is only one figure it applies to all sizes.

KNITTED MEASUREMENTS
● Bust 42 (46, 50, 54)"/106.5 (117, 127, 137)cm.
● Length 18¹/₂ (19, 19¹/₂, 20)"/47 (48.5, 49.5, 51)cm.
● Upper arm 17 (18, 19, 20)"/43.5 (46, 48.5, 51)cm.

MATERIALS
● 4 (5, 5, 5) 3¹/₂oz/100g balls (each approx 185yd/168m) of Reynolds *Saucy* (cotton④) in #361 red (MC) and #817 ecru (CC)
● One pair size 8 (5mm) needles, OR SIZE TO OBTAIN GAUGE
● Size H/8 (5mm) crochet hook
● Stitch markers

GAUGE
18 sts and 24 rows to 4"/10cm over St st with size 8 (5mm) needles.
FOR PERFECT FIT, TAKE TIME TO CHECK GAUGE.

Note
Edges will curl; measure pieces with edges flat.

BACK
With MC, cast on 94 (104, 112, 122) sts.
Row 1 (RS) Knit.
Row 2 Purl. Rep last 2 rows twice (6 rows total). *Change to CC. Work 12 rows in St st (k on RS, p on WS). Change to MC. Work 12 rows in St st.* Rep between *'s until piece measures 18¹/₂ (19, 19¹/₂, 20)"/47 (48.5, 49.5, 51)cm from beg. Bind off all sts.

FRONT
Work as for back until piece measures 17¹/₂ (18, 18¹/₂, 19)"/44.5 (46, 47, 48.5)cm from beg, end with a WS row.

Neck shaping
Next row (RS) Work 31 (36, 40, 45) sts, join 2nd ball of yarn and bind off center 32 sts, work to end. Working both sides at once, purl 1 row.
Next row Work 28 (33, 37, 42) sts, k3tog (2 sts dec)—29 (34, 38, 43) sts. On left side, k3tog, work to end. Cont to shape neck by k3tog from each neck edge every other row twice. Bind off rem 25 (30, 34, 39) sts each side.

SLEEVES
With CC, cast on 48 (50, 52, 54) sts.
Row 1 (RS) Knit.
Row 2 Purl. Rep last 2 rows twice (6 rows total), inc 1 (1, 0, 0) sts on last row—49 (51, 52, 54) sts. Work stripe pat and incs (working inc sts into St st) simultaneously as foll: *Change to MC. Work 12 rows in St st. Change to CC. Work 12 rows in St st.* AT SAME TIME, inc 1 st each side every 4th row 0 (5, 11, 16) times, every 6th row 14 (10, 6, 2) times—77 (81, 86, 90) sts. Rep between *'s until piece measures 15¹/₂ (15, 14¹/₂, 14)"/39.5 (38, 37, 35.5)cm from beg. Bind off all sts.

FINISHING
Sew shoulder seams. With RS facing, crochet hook and MC, work 1 row sc around neck. Place markers 8¹/₂ (9, 9¹/₂, 10)"/21.5 (23, 24.5, 25.5)cm down from shoulders on front and back for armhole. Sew top of sleeves between markers. Sew side and sleeve seams. ●

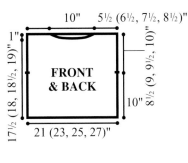

10" 5½ (6½, 7½, 8½)"
1"
17½ (18, 18½, 19)"
FRONT & BACK
8½ (9, 9½, 10)"
10"
21 (23, 25, 27)"

17 (18, 19, 20)"
SLEEVE
15½ (15, 14½, 14)"
10½ (11, 11½, 12)"

Worked in a cool cotton for a spring-to-summer look, Calvin Klein's playfully striped pullover is oversized with drop shoulders and features a boatneck with ribbed neckband. Shown in size 34-36. The Striped Boatneck Pullover first appeared in the Spring/Summer '87 issue of *Vogue Knitting*.

Striped Boatneck Pullover

SIZES
To fit 30-32 (34-36, 38-40, 42-44, 46-48)"/76-81 (86-91, 96-101, 106-112, 116-122)cm bust. Directions are for smallest size with larger sizes in parentheses. If there is only one set of figures it applies to all sizes.

KNITTED MEASUREMENTS
● Bust 37 (40, 44, 48, 52)"/93 (100, 110, 120, 129)cm.
● Length 25½ (26, 26, 26½, 27)"/64 (65, 65, 66.5, 67.5)cm.
● Upper arm 17 (18, 18, 19, 20)"/43 (45, 45, 48, 50)cm.

MATERIALS
Original Yarn
● 12 (13, 13, 14, 15) 1¾oz/50g balls (each approx 92yd/84m) of Wm. Unger *Pima* (cotton③) in #7254 grey (MC)
● 3 (3, 3, 4, 4) balls in #9999 white (CC)
Substitute Yarn
● 5 (5, 5, 5, 6) 4oz/125g balls (each approx 256yd/236m) of Classic Elite *Provence* (cotton④) in #2637 mushroom (MC)
● 1 (1, 2, 2, 2) balls in #2601 white (CC)
● One pair size 4 and 6 (3.5 and 4mm) needles OR SIZE TO OBTAIN GAUGE
Note
The original yarns used for this sweater are no longer available. Comparable substitutes have been made, which are available at the time of printing. Check gauge of substitute yarns very carefully before beginning.

GAUGE
22 sts and 30 rows to 4"/10cm over St st using size 6 (4mm) needles.
FOR PERFECT FIT, TAKE TIME TO CHECK GAUGE.

STITCH GLOSSARY
Stripe Pat (10 rows)
Rows 1-8 Work in St st (k on RS, p on WS) with MC.
Rows 9-10 Work in St st with CC.

BACK
With smaller needles and MC, cast on 86 (94, 105, 116, 126) sts. Work in k1, p1 rib for 2"/5cm. Change to larger needles. Cont in stripe pat and inc as foll: With CC, work 2 rows in St st, then work 10 rows of stripe pat 11 times, AT SAME TIME, inc 1 st each side every 12th row 8 times—102 (110, 121, 132, 142) sts—piece measures approx 17"/42.5cm from beg.

Armhole shaping
Cont in stripe pat, as foll:
Next row (RS) K2, k2tog, work to last 4 sts, ssk, k2.
Next row Purl. Rep last 2 rows 5 times more—90 (98, 109, 120, 130) sts. Cont in stripe pat until armhole measures 7¾ (8¼, 8¼, 8¾, 9¼)"/19.5 (20.5, 20.5, 22, 23)cm, end with a WS row.

Neckband
(Note: If last row is worked with CC, k 1 row with MC before working rib.)
With MC, work in k1, p1 rib for 1½"/4cm. Bind off knitwise.

FRONT
Work as for back.

SLEEVES
With smaller needles and MC, cast on 33 (39, 39, 45, 49) sts. Work in k1, p1, rib for 1"/2.5cm. Change to larger needles. Cont in stripe pat and inc as foll: With CC, work 2 rows in St st, then work 10 rows of stripe pat 9 (9, 9, 10, 10) times, AT SAME TIME, inc 1 st each side alternately every 2nd and 4th row (therefore 4 sts inc every 6 rows), until there are 93 (99, 99,

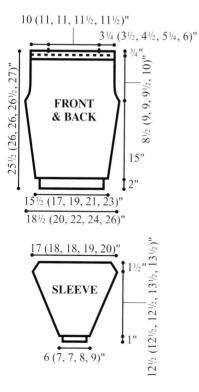

10 (11, 11, 11½, 11½)"
3¼ (3½, 4½, 5¼, 6)"
¾"
FRONT & BACK
8½ (9, 9, 9½, 10)"
25½ (26, 26, 26½, 27)"
15"
2"
15½ (17, 19, 21, 23)"
18½ (20, 22, 24, 26)"

17 (18, 18, 19, 20)"
1½"
SLEEVE
13½ (13½, 13½, 13½, 13½)"... 12½ (12½, 12½, 13½, 13½)"
1"
6 (7, 7, 8, 9)"

105, 109) sts—piece measures approx 13$\frac{1}{2}$ (13$\frac{1}{2}$, 13$\frac{1}{2}$, 14$\frac{1}{2}$, 14$\frac{1}{2}$)"/33 (33, 33, 36.5, 36.5)cm from beg.

Cap shaping

Dec 1 st each side every other row 6 times as for back. Bind off rem 81 (87, 87, 93, 97) sts.

FINISHING

Block pieces. Fold rib bands at top of front and back to WS and sew in place. Sew first and last 3$\frac{1}{4}$ (3$\frac{1}{2}$, 4$\frac{1}{2}$, 5$\frac{1}{4}$, 6)"/8 (9, 11.5, 13, 15)cm of front and back rib band tog for shoulder seams, leaving center 10 (11, 11, 11$\frac{1}{2}$, 11$\frac{1}{2}$)"/25 (26.5, 26.5, 29, 29)cm open for neck. Sew top of sleeve to straight edge of armhole. Sew dec armhole sts to dec sts of sleeve. Sew side and sleeve seams. •

Drop-Shoulder Striped Pullover

This clean-cut sport sweater is a breeze to knit—and wear. Bedecked with ship-shape navy and white stripes, it's oversized with drop shoulders, a crew neck, and set-in pocket. The navy stripes are stockinette; the white, garter stitch. Designed by Judy Ross. Shown in size 36. The Drop-Shoulder Striped Pullover first appeared in the Spring/Summer '87 issue of *Vogue Knitting*.

SIZES

To fit 30 (32, 34, 36, 38, 40, 42, 44)"/76 (81, 86, 91, 96, 101, 106, 112)cm bust. Directions are for smallest size with larger sizes in parentheses. If there is only one set of figures it applies to all sizes.

KNITTED MEASUREMENTS

- Bust 36 (38, 40$\frac{1}{2}$, 42, 44, 46$\frac{1}{2}$, 48, 50)"/91 (94, 102, 106, 111, 116, 120, 126)cm.
- Length 19 (19$\frac{3}{4}$, 20$\frac{1}{4}$, 20$\frac{3}{4}$, 21$\frac{1}{2}$, 22, 22$\frac{1}{2}$, 23$\frac{1}{4}$)"/48 (50, 51, 52.5, 54.5, 55.5, 56.5, 58.5)cm.
- Upper arm 19 (19$\frac{1}{2}$, 20, 20, 21, 22, 22, 23)"/47 (48, 50, 50, 52, 55, 55, 57)cm.

MATERIALS

Original Yarn

- 8 (9, 9, 9, 9, 10, 10, 10) 1$\frac{3}{4}$oz/50g balls (each approx 100yd/90m) of Nomotta/Leisure Arts *Alpha* (cotton③) in #75323 navy (MC)
- 4 (5, 5, 5, 5, 6, 6, 6) balls in #75316 white (CC)

Substitute Yarn

- 8 (9, 9, 9, 9, 10, 10, 10) 1$\frac{3}{4}$oz/50g hanks (each approx 108yd/100m) of Tahki Yarns *Cotton Classic* (cotton④) in #3861 navy (MC)
- 4 (5, 5, 5, 5, 6, 6, 6) hanks in #3001 white (CC)
- One pair each sizes 3 and 5 (3.25 and 3.75mm) needles OR SIZE TO OBTAIN GAUGE
- Stitch markers and holders

Note

The original yarns used for this sweater are no longer available. Comparable substitutes have been made, which are available at the time of printing. Check gauge of substitute yarns very carefully before beginning.

GAUGE

22 sts and 32 rows to 4"/10cm over stripe pat using size 5 (3.75mm) needles. FOR PERFECT FIT, TAKE TIME TO CHECK GAUGE.

STITCH GLOSSARY

Stripe Pat

With CC, K 4 rows, with MC work 10 rows in St st (k on RS, p on WS). Rep these 14 rows for stripe pat.

Note

For easier working, circle all numbers that pertain to your size and keep careful count of rows.

BACK

With smaller needles and MC, cast on 98 (104, 110, 116, 122, 128, 131, 137) sts.
Rib row 1 (RS) P2, *k1, p2; rep from * to end.
Rib row 2 K2, *p1, k2; rep from * to end. Rep last 2 rows once more, inc 2 (0, 2, 0, 0, 0, 1, 1) sts on last row—100 (104, 112, 116, 122, 128, 132, 138) sts. Change to larger needles. With MC, work in St st for 8 (4, 6, 8, 4, 6, 8, 4) rows. Work 14 rows of stripe pat 9 (10, 10, 10, 11, 11, 11, 12) times, then work first 8 (4, 6, 8, 4, 6, 8, 4) rows of pat once more—piece measures

approx 18$\frac{1}{4}$ (19, 19$\frac{1}{2}$, 20, 20$\frac{3}{4}$, 21$\frac{1}{4}$, 21$\frac{3}{4}$, 22$\frac{1}{2}$)"/46 (48, 49, 50.5, 52.5, 53.5, 54.5, 56.5)cm from beg.

Neck shaping

Next row (RS) Work 30 (31, 33, 35, 37, 39, 41, 42) sts, join 2nd ball of yarn and bind off center 40 (42, 46, 46, 48, 50, 50, 54) sts, work to end. Working both sides at once, dec 1 st at each neck edge every other row twice. Bind off rem 28 (29, 31, 33, 35, 37, 39, 40) sts each side.

POCKET LINING

(Note: Pocket lining is worked in St st *only* to lie flat.) With larger needles and MC, cast on 43 sts. Work in St st in foll stripes: [10 rows MC, 4 rows CC] 3 times, then work 10 rows MC in St st and knit next 4 rows in CC. Place sts on holder.

FRONT

Cast on and work rib and inc as for back. Change to larger needles. Work 8 (4, 6, 8, 4, 6, 8, 4) rows in MC, then 14 rows of stripe pat 5 times—piece measures approx 10$\frac{1}{4}$ (9$\frac{3}{4}$, 10, 10$\frac{1}{4}$, 9$\frac{3}{4}$, 10, 10$\frac{1}{4}$, 9$\frac{3}{4}$)"/26 (24.5, 25.5, 26, 24.5, 25.5, 26, 24.5)cm from beg.
Next row (RS) With CC, knit. Cont in pat as foll:

Pocket rib and joining lining

Row 1 (WS) With CC, k47 (51, 59, 63, 69, 75, 79, 85) sts, place marker, k2, [p1, k2] 13 times, place marker, k to end.
Row 2 With CC, k12, sl marker, [p2, k1] 13 times, p2, sl marker, k to end. Rep row 1 once more.

Next row (RS) With MC, k to marker, bind off next 41 sts knitwise, k to end.
Next row With MC, p to 1 st before sts on holder, with RS of pocket lining facing WS of front, p first st of pocket lining tog with next st on LH needle, p across lining sts on holder to last st, then p last st of lining tog with next st of front, p to end. Cont in pat until 14 rows of stripe pat have been worked 8 (8, 8, 9, 9, 9, 10, 10) times, then work first 0 (10, 12, 0, 10, 12, 0, 10) rows once more—piece measures approx 15½ (16¼, 16¾, 17¼, 18, 18½, 19, 19¾)"/39 (41, 42, 43.5, 45.5, 46.5, 47.5, 49.5)cm from beg.

Neck shaping
Next row (RS) Work 39 (40, 42, 44, 46, 48, 50, 51) sts, join 2nd ball of yarn and bind off center 22 (24, 28, 28, 30, 32, 32, 36) sts, work to end. Working both sides at once, dec 1 st at each neck edge every other row 11 times. Work even until same number of rows as back. Bind off rem 28 (29, 31, 33, 35, 37, 39, 40) sts each side for shoulders.

SLEEVES
With smaller needles and MC, cast on 62 (65, 68, 68, 71, 71, 71, 74) sts. Work in p2, k1 rib as for back. Change to larger needles. Inc 1 st each end every 4th row 21 (21, 21, 21, 22, 23, 23, 22) times, every other row 0 (0, 0, 0, 0, 2, 2, 4) times—104 (107, 110, 110, 115, 121, 121, 126), AT SAME TIME, work pat as foll: With MC, work in St st for 6 (6, 8, 8, 8, 6, 6, 6) rows. Work 14 rows of stripe pat 5 (5, 6, 6, 6, 6, 6, 6) times, then work first 12 (12, 0, 0, 0, 10, 10, 10) rows once more—piece measures approx 11½

(11½, 12, 12, 12, 13, 13, 13)"/29 (29, 30, 30, 30, 33, 33, 33)cm from beg. Bind off.

FINISHING
Block pieces. Sew left shoulder seam.

Neckband
With RS facing, smaller needles and MC, beg at right shoulder, pick up and k93 (96, 102, 102, 105, 108, 108, 114) sts evenly around entire neck edge. Work in p2, k1 rib as for back. Bind off knitwise. Sew right shoulder seam including neckband. Place markers 9½ (9¾, 10, 10, 10½, 11, 11, 11½)"/23.5 (24, 25, 25, 26, 27.5, 27.5, 28.5)cm down from shoulders on front and back for armholes. Sew top of sleeves between markers. Sew side and sleeve seams. Sew pocket lining to WS of front. •

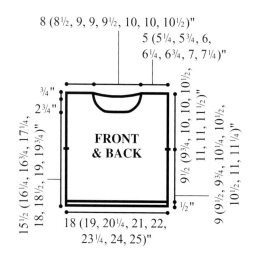

8 (8½, 9, 9, 9½, 10, 10, 10½)"

5 (5¼, 5¾, 6, 6¼, 6¾, 7, 7¼)"

¾"

2¾"

15½ (16¼, 16¾, 17¼, 18, 18½, 19, 19¾)"

FRONT & BACK

9½ (9¾, 10, 10, 10½, 11, 11, 11½)"

9 (9½, 9¾, 10¼, 10½, 10½, 11, 11¼)"

½"

18 (19, 20¼, 21, 22, 23¼, 24, 25)"

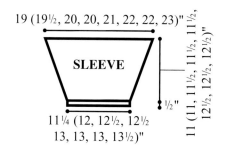

19 (19½, 20, 20, 21, 22, 22, 23)"

SLEEVE

11 (11, 11½, 11½, 11½, 12½, 12½, 12½)"

½"

11¼ (12, 12½, 12½ 13, 13, 13, 13½)"

Striped Twin Set

This stylish twin set in radiant stripes combines two perfect yarns—a lush angora blend for the sleeveless top; a comfy wool for the cardigan. The top hugs the body, while the crochet-edged V-neck open cardigan swings free. Both are easy to knit in stockinette stitch. Designed by Diane Delorean. The Striped Twin Set first appeared in the Fall/Winter '83 issue of *Vogue Knitting*.

Striped Twin Set

SIZES

To fit 32 (34, 36, 38)"/81 (86, 91, 96)cm bust. Directions are for smallest size with larger sizes in parentheses. If there is only one set of figures it applies to all sizes.

KNITTED MEASUREMENTS
CARDIGAN:
● Bust 35 (37, 39, 41)"/88 (92, 98, 102)cm.
● Length 25 (25$^1/_2$, 26, 26$^1/_2$)"/62 (64, 64.5, 66.5)cm.
● Upper arm 13 (14, 14$^1/_2$, 15$^1/_2$)"/32.5 (35, 36, 38.5)cm.
TOP:
● Bust 32 (33$^1/_2$, 36, 37$^1/_2$)"/80 (84, 90, 94)cm.
● Length 20$^3/_4$ (21, 21$^1/_4$, 21$^1/_2$)"/53 (53.5, 54, 55)cm.

MATERIALS
CARDIGAN:
Original Yarn
● 7 (7, 8, 8) 2oz/60g balls (each approx 100yd/90m) of Melrose *Cablenella* (wool/rayon⑤) in scarlet (A) and cardinal (B)
Substitute Yarn
● 9 (9, 10, 10) 1$^3/_4$oz/50g balls (each approx 82yd/75m) of Reynolds/JCA *Dover* (wool③) in #22 red (A) and #28 wine (B)
● One pair size 8 (5mm) needles OR SIZE TO OBTAIN GAUGE

● Size J (6mm) crochet hook
TOP:
Original Yarn
● 8 (8, 9, 9) $^1/_3$oz/10g balls (each approx 35yd/30m) of Melrose *French Rabbit Hair Angora* (angora⑤) in red (MC) and wine (CC)
Substitute Yarn
● 4 (4, 4, 5) .88oz/25g balls (each approx 80yd/73m) of Adrienne Vittadini/JCA *Angelina* (angora/lambswool/alpaca④) in #8010 red (MC) and #8020 wine (CC)
● One pair size 7 (4.5mm) needles OR SIZE TO OBTAIN GAUGE
● Size J (6mm) crochet hook
Note
The original yarns used for this twin set are no longer available. Comparable substitutes have been made, which are available at the time of printing. Check gauge of substitute yarns very carefully before beginning.

GAUGE
CARDIGAN:
16 sts and 23 rows to 4"/10cm over St st using size 8 (5mm) needles.
TOP:
20 sts and 28 rows to 4"/10cm over St st using size 7 (4.5mm) needles.
FOR PERFECT FIT, TAKE TIME TO CHECK GAUGES.

CARDIGAN

BACK
With size 8 (5mm) needles and A, cast on 70 (74, 78, 82) sts.
Row 1 *K1, p1; rep from * to end. Rep row 1 for k1, p1 rib for 1"/2.5cm, end with a WS row. *Change to B and work in St st (k on RS, p on WS) for 6 rows.

Change to A and work in St st for 6 rows. * Rep between * and * for stripe pat 6 times more. Change to B and work in St st for 6 rows—back measures 16$^1/_2$"/41cm from beg.

Raglan armhole shaping
Cont stripe pat, with A bind off 2 sts at beg of next 2 rows. Cont pat, dec 1 st each side of every other row 23 (25, 26, 28) times—20 (20, 22, 22) sts rem. Bind off.

LEFT FRONT
With size 8 (5mm) needles and A, cast on 37 (39, 41, 43) sts. Work in k1, p1 rib for 1"/2.5cm. Change to B and work in stripe pat as for back until same length as back to armhole.

Raglan armhole and neck shaping
Next row (RS) Bind off 2 sts at beg of row (armhole edge), k to last 2 sts, k2tog (for neck dec). Dec 1 st at neck edge every 6th row 0 (1, 2, 2) times then every 4th row 9 (8, 8, 8) times more, AT SAME TIME, dec 1 st at armhole edge every other row 23 (25, 26, 28) times—2 sts rem. Bind off.

RIGHT FRONT
Work as for left front reversing all shaping.

SLEEVES
With size 8 (5mm) needles and A, cast on 32 (34, 34, 36) sts. Work in k1, p1 rib for $^1/_2$ ($^1/_2$, 1, 1)"/1 (1, 2.5, 2.5)cm. Change to B and work in stripe pat inc 1 st each side of every 6th row 10 (11, 12, 13) times—52 (56, 58, 62) sts. Work even in pat until there are same number of rows as back to armhole—sleeve measures 16 (16, 16$^1/_2$, 16$^1/_2$)"/40.5 (40.5, 41.5, 41.5)cm from beg.

Raglan cap shaping

Bind off 2 sts at beg of next 2 rows. Dec 1 st each side of every other row 23 (25, 26, 28) times—2 sts rem. Bind off.

FINISHING

Sew side and sleeve seams. Set in sleeves matching stripes. To make front edge lie flat, fold in 2 sts along center front edges and baste in place (for facing). With crochet hook and A, working into 3rd st from the edge, sc evenly along front edges, top of sleeves and neck edge. Ch1, turn and work 1 sc in each sc. Fasten off. Press seams lightly on WS with damp cloth and warm iron.

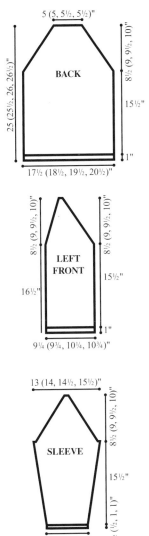

5 (5, 5½, 5½)"

8½ (9, 9½, 10)"

BACK

25 (25½, 26, 26½)"

15½"

1"

17½ (18½, 19½, 20½)"

8½ (9, 9½, 10)" 8½ (9, 9½, 10)"

LEFT FRONT

15½"

16½"

1"

9¼ (9¾, 10¼, 10¾)"

13 (14, 14½, 15½)"

8½ (9, 9½, 10)"

SLEEVE

15½"

½ (½, 1, 1)"

8 (8½, 8½, 9)"

TOP

BACK

With size 7 (4.5mm) needles and MC, cast on 80 (84, 90, 94) sts. Work in k1, p1 rib for 1"/2.5cm, end with a WS row. *Change to CC and work in St st (k 1 row, p 1 row) for 8 rows. Change to MC and work in St st for 8 rows.* Rep between * and * for stripe pat 4 times more. Change to CC and work in St st for 6 rows—back measures 13"/33cm from beg.

Armhole shaping

Cont in stripe pat, with CC bind off 5 sts at beg of next 2 rows. Dec 1 st each side of every other row 3 (3, 4, 4) times—64 (68, 72, 76) sts. Work even in stripe pat until armhole measures 7"/18cm, ending with last row of 9th CC stripe. Change to MC and work in k1, p1 rib for ¾ (1, 1¼, 1½)"/2 (2.5, 3, 4)cm. Bind off in rib.

FRONT

Work as for back.

FINISHING

Sew 12 (13, 13, 14) sts tog on each side of front and back for shoulders. Sew side seams. With crochet hook and MC, work 1 row of sc evenly around each armhole. •

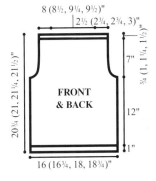

8 (8½, 9¼, 9½)"

2½ (2¾, 2¾, 3)"

20¾ (21, 21¼, 21½)"

¾ (1, 1¼, 1½)"

7"

FRONT & BACK

12"

1"

16 (16¾, 18, 18¾)"

This relaxed color-tipped polo offers polished comfort. It's loose-fitting, with shaped drop shoulders, buttoned front placket, polo collar, and ribbed edges. Designed by Christian de Falbe. Shown in size 38. The Color-Tipped Polo first appeared in the Winter Special '89/90 issue of *Vogue Knitting*.

Color-Tipped Polo

SIZES
To fit 32 (34, 36, 38, 40)"/81 (86, 91, 96, 101)cm bust. Directions are for smallest size with larger sizes in parentheses. If there is only one figure it applies to all sizes.

KNITTED MEASUREMENTS
● Bust 36 (38, 40, 42, 44)"/90 (95, 100, 105, 110)cm.
● Length 25 (25, 26, 26, 26)"/63.5 (63.5, 66, 66, 66)cm.
● Upper arm 19 (19, 20, 20, 20)"/48 (48, 50, 50, 50)cm.

MATERIALS
Original Yarn
● 11 (11, 11, 12, 12) 1³⁄₄oz/50g balls (each approx 131yd/120m) of Christian de Falbe/Cascade Yarns *Chandos* (merino/lambswool ③) in #10 white (MC)
● 1 ball in #02 black (CC)
Substitute Yarn
● 11 (11, 11, 12, 12) 1³⁄₄oz/50g balls (each approx 136yd/125m) of Filatura Di Crosa/Stacy Charles *501* (wool ③) in #106 off-white (MC)
● 1 ball in #115 black (CC)
● One pair each sizes 3 and 5 (3.25 and 3.75mm) needles OR SIZE TO OBTAIN GAUGE
● Three ¹⁄₂"/15mm buttons
Note
The yarns used for this sweater are no longer available. Comparable substitutes have been made, which are available at the time of printing. Check gauge of substitute yarns very carefully before beginning.

GAUGE
23 sts and 30 rows to 4"/10cm over St st using size 5 (3.75mm) needles. FOR PERFECT FIT, TAKE TIME TO CHECK GAUGE.

BACK
With smaller needles and CC, cast on 92 (98, 104, 110, 116) sts. Work in k1, p1 rib as foll: 1 row CC, 2 rows MC, 2 rows CC, 1 row MC, inc 11 sts evenly spaced across—103 (109, 115, 121, 127) sts. Change to larger needles. Work in St st with MC only until piece measures 15 (15, 16, 16, 16)"/38 (38, 40.5, 40.5, 40.5)cm from beg, end with a WS row. Inc 1 st each side on next row and rep inc every 6th row twice, every 8th row 5 times—119 (125, 131, 137, 143) sts. Work even until piece measures 23 (23, 24, 24, 24)"/58.5 (58.5, 61, 61, 61)cm from beg.

Shoulder shaping
Bind off 6 sts at beg of next 14 (8, 4, 0, 0) rows, 7 sts at beg of next 0 (6, 10, 12, 8) rows, 8 sts at beg of next 0 (0, 0, 2, 6) rows. Bind off rem 35 (35, 37, 37, 39) sts.

FRONT
Work as for back until piece measures 17¹⁄₂ (17¹⁄₂, 18¹⁄₂, 18¹⁄₂, 18¹⁄₂)"/44.5 (44.5, 47, 47, 47)cm from beg.

Placket and neck shaping
Cont inc at side edges, bind off center 5 sts on next row and work both sides at once with separate balls of yarn until placket measures 4¹⁄₂"/11.5cm. Bind off from each neck edge 5 sts once, 2 sts 3 (3, 4, 4, 4) times, dec 1 st every other row

4 (4, 3, 3, 4) times, AT SAME TIME, when same length as back to shoulder, shape shoulder as for back.

SLEEVES
With smaller needles and CC, cast on 40 (40, 44, 46, 46) sts. Work rib as for back, inc 8 sts evenly across last row—48 (48, 52, 54, 54) sts. Change to larger needles. Work in St st with MC only, inc 1 st each side every other row 15 (10, 10, 6, 6) times, every 4th row 16 (21, 21, 24, 24) times—110 (110, 114, 114, 114) sts. Work even until piece measures 14¹⁄₂ (15¹⁄₂, 15¹⁄₂, 16, 16)"/37 (39.5, 39.5, 40.5, 40.5)cm from beg. Bind off.

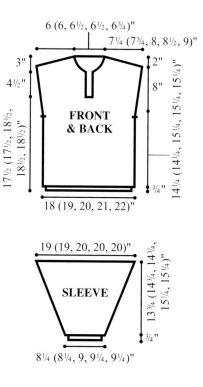

FINISHING
Block pieces. Sew shoulder seams.

Placket band
With RS facing, smaller needles and MC, pick up and k34 sts evenly along left front placket edge. Work in k1, p1 rib for 5 rows. Bind off in rib. Place markers on band for 3 buttons, the first $1^1/2$"/4cm from lower edge, the last $^1/2$"/1.5cm from top edge, the other evenly between. Work right front placket as for left, working buttonholes opposite markers on 3rd row by yo, k2tog.

Collar
With larger needles and CC, cast on 116 (116, 122, 122, 126) sts. Work stripes of rib as for back, then cont in rib with MC only for 8 rows. Change to smaller needles. Rib 6 rows more. Bind off in rib. Sew bound-off edge of collar around neck edge, leaving sides of placket bands free. Sew lower edges of placket bands, right over left. Place markers $9^1/2$ ($9^1/2$, 10, 10, 10)"/24 (24, 25, 25, 25)cm down from shoulders on front and back (measuring along shaped edge, not straight down from shoulders). Sew top of sleeves between markers. Sew side and sleeve seams. Sew on buttons. •

A striped basketweave pattern in a combination of warm earth tones gives this pullover glowing color and texture. Standard-fitting, the turtleneck pullover features angled armholes and poor-boy ribbed sleeves, and is paired with a matching skirt. A Vogue Original. Shown in size 32. The Basketweave Pullover & Skirt first appeared in the Winter Special '90/91 issue of *Vogue Knitting*.

Basketweave Pullover & Skirt

PULLOVER

SIZES
To fit 32 (34, 36, 38, 40)"/81 (86, 91, 96, 101)cm bust. Directions are for smallest size with larger sizes in parentheses. If there is only one figure it applies to all sizes.

KNITTED MEASUREMENTS
● Bust 38 (40½, 42½, 45, 48)"/95 (102, 105, 113, 120)cm.
● Length 22 (22½, 23, 23½, 24)"/55.5 (57, 58, 59.5, 61)cm.
● Upper arm 13 (13, 13¾, 13¾, 14½)"/33 (33, 34, 34, 36.5)cm.

MATERIALS
● 4 (5, 5, 6, 7) 1¾oz/50g balls (each approx 121yd/110m) of Baruffa/Lane Borgosesia *Maratona*® (wool③) in #8503 brown (A)
● 7 (8, 8, 9, 10) balls in #8525 rust (B)
● 3 (4, 4, 5, 6) balls in #20266 grey (C)
● One pair each sizes 6 and 7 (4 and 4.5mm) needles OR SIZE TO OBTAIN GAUGE
● Size 6 (4mm) circular needle, 16"/40cm long

Note
The original colors used for this sweater are no longer available. Comparable color substitutions have been made, which are available at the time of printing.

GAUGE
● 22 sts and 36 rows to 4"/10cm over basketweave pat using size 7 (4.5mm) needles.

● 28 sts and 32 rows to 4"/10cm over k2, p2 rib (slightly stretched) using size 7 (4.5mm) needles.
FOR PERFECT FIT, TAKE TIME TO CHECK GAUGES.

STITCH GLOSSARY
Stripe Pat
Work basketweave pat chart in stripes as foll: *8 rows C, 8 rows B, 8 rows A; rep from * (24 rows) for stripe pat.

BACK
With smaller needles and A, cast on 104 (112, 116, 124, 132) sts. Work in k1, p1 rib for 2½"/6.5cm, end with a WS row. Change to larger needles and C. Work in stripe and basketweave pat as foll:
Beg chart: Row 1 (RS) Beg with st 3 (3, 1, 1, 1), work 8-st rep 13 (14, 14, 15, 16) times, end with st 10 (10, 12, 12, 12). Cont in pats as established until piece measures 13 (13½, 13½, 14, 14)"/32.5 (34, 34, 35.5, 35.5)cm from beg.

Armhole shaping
Bind off 4 sts at beg of next 2 rows. Dec 1 st each side every other row 4 times—88 (96, 100, 108, 116) sts. Work even until armhole measures 8 (8, 8½, 8½, 9)"/20 (20, 21.5, 21.5, 23)cm.

Shoulder shaping
Bind off 6 (6, 7, 7, 6) sts at beg of next 2 rows, 5 (6, 6, 7, 8) sts at beg of next 8 rows. Bind off rem 36 (36, 38, 38, 40) sts.

FRONT
Work as for back until armhole measures 7½ (7½, 8, 8, 8½)"/19 (19, 20, 20, 21.5)cm, end with a WS row.

Neck and shoulder shaping
Next row (RS) Work 34 (38, 39, 43, 46) sts, join 2nd ball of yarn and bind off 20 (20, 22, 22, 24) sts, work to end. Working both sides at once, bind off from each neck edge 3 sts once, 2 sts once, 1 st every other row 3 times, AT SAME TIME, after 2 rows of neck shaping have been worked, shape shoulder as for back.

SLEEVES
With smaller needles and B, cast on 58 (58, 62, 62, 72) sts. Work in k2, p2 rib for 2"/5cm. Change to larger needles. Cont in rib, inc 1 st each side (working inc sts into rib) every 8th row 15 (15, 17, 17, 0) times, every 10th row 0 (0, 0, 0, 13), every 6th row 2 (2, 0, 0, 2) times—92 (92, 96, 96, 102) sts. Work even until piece measures 17½ (17½, 18, 18, 18½)"/44.5 (44.5, 46, 46, 47)cm from beg. Bind off in rib.

FINISHING
Block pieces. Sew shoulder seams.

Neckband
With RS facing, circular needle and B, pick up and k100 (100, 104, 104, 108) sts evenly around neck edge. Join. Work in k2, p2 rib for 6"/15cm. Bind off in rib. Pin sleeve into armhole, centering sleeve at shoulder and stretching to fit. Sew in place. Sew side and sleeve seams.

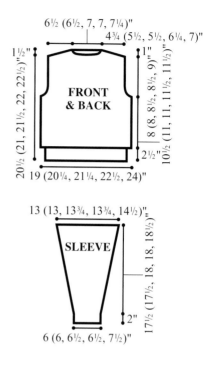

6½ (6½, 7, 7, 7¼)"

4¾ (5½, 5½, 6¼, 7)"

1½"

1"

FRONT & BACK

8 (8, 8½, 8½, 9)"

20½ (21, 21½, 22, 22½)"

10½ (11, 11, 11½, 11½)"

2½"

19 (20¼, 21¼, 22½, 24)"

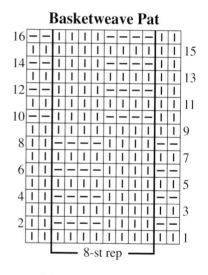

13 (13, 13¾, 13¾, 14½)"

SLEEVE

17½ (17½, 18, 18, 18½)"

2"

6 (6, 6½, 6½, 7½)"

Basketweave Pat

```
16 — — | | | | | — — — — | |
   | | | | | | | | | | | | |  15
14 — — | | | | | — — — — | |
   | | | | | | | | | | | | |  13
12 — — | | | | | — — — — | |
   | | | | | | | | | | | | |  11
10 — — | | | | | — — — — | |
   | | | | | | | | | | | | |  9
 8 | | | — — — — | | | | | |
   | | | | — — — — | | | | |  7
 6 | | | — — — — | | | | | |
   | | | | — — — — | | | | |  5
 4 | | | — — — — | | | | | |
   | | | | | | | | | | | — —  3
 2 | | | — — — — | | | — — —
   | | | | | | | | | | | | |  1
```

└── 8-st rep ──┘

Stitch Key

| I | K on RS, p on WS

| — | P on RS, k on WS

SKIRT

SIZES

To fit 34 (36, 38, 40, 42)"/86 (91, 96, 101, 106)cm hip. Directions are for smallest size with larger sizes in parentheses. If there is only one figure it applies to all sizes.

KNITTED MEASUREMENTS

● Hip 36 (37½, 39½, 41½, 43½)"/90 (94, 99,103, 108)cm.
● Length 22 (22, 22½, 22½, 23)"/56 (56, 57, 57, 58.5)cm.

MATERIALS

● 7 (8, 8, 9, 10) balls of Baruffa/Lane Borgosesia *Maratona®* in #41252 brown
● One pair each sizes 6 and 7 (4 and 4.5mm) needles OR SIZE TO OBTAIN GAUGE
● 1yd/1m of 1"/2.5cm waistband elastic

GAUGE

23 sts and 31 rows to 4"/10cm over St st using size 7 (4.5mm) needles. FOR PERFECT FIT, TAKE TIME TO CHECK GAUGE.

BACK

With smaller needles, cast on 130 (135, 143, 149, 156) sts. Work in k1, p1 rib for 2½"/ 6.5cm, dec 26 (27, 29, 30, 31) sts evenly spaced across last row—104 (108, 114, 119, 125) sts. Change to larger needles. Work in St st until piece measures 23¼ (23¼, 23¾, 23¾, 24¼)"/59 (59, 60, 60, 61.5)cm from beg. Bind off.

FRONT

Work as for back.

FINISHING

Block pieces. Sew side seams.

Waistband casing

Place markers 2½"/6.5cm down from top for waistband. Fold one half of waistband to WS. Sew in place, leaving opening. Draw elastic through casing, adjusting to fit. Sew casing closed. ●

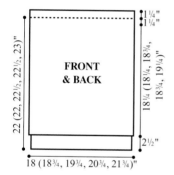

1¼"
1¼"

22 (22, 22½, 22½, 23)"

FRONT & BACK

18¼ (18¼, 18¾, 18¾, 19¼)"

2½"

18 (18¾, 19¾, 20¾, 21¾)"

Striped Snowflake Pullover

Warm up for winter with a striped pullover with front tasseled zipper and optional duplicate-stitch snowflakes on the back. Quick to make and fun to wear, it's oversized with raglan armholes and round neck. Designed by Anne Mieke Louwerens. Shown in size Medium. The Striped Snowflake Pullover first appeared in the Winter '94/95 issue of *Vogue Knitting*.

Striped Snowflake Pullover

Note
The original yarns used for this sweater are no longer available. Comparable substitutes have been made, which are available at the time of printing. Check gauge of substitute yarns very carefully before beginning.

SIZES
To fit Small (Medium, Large). Directions are for smallest size with larger sizes in parentheses. If there is only one figure it applies to all sizes.

FINISHED MEASUREMENTS
- Bust 44 (48, 52)"/112 (122, 132)cm.
- Length 23 (23¼, 23¾)"/58.5 (59, 60.5)cm.
- Upper arm 18 (18, 19)"/46 (46, 48.5)cm.

MATERIALS
Original Yarn
- 5 (5, 6) 1¾oz/50g balls (each approx 120yd/110m) of Filatura Di Crosa/Stacy Charles *Alpaca/Lana* (wool/alpaca/acrylic ④) in #929 red (A)
- 4 (4, 5) balls in #922 brown (B)
- 2 balls in #903 beige (C)

Substitute Yarn
- 6 (7, 8) 1¾oz/50g balls (each approx 99yd/91m) of Classic Elite *Maya* (llama/wool⑤) in #3058 red (A)
- 5 (5, 6) balls in #3076 brown (B)
- 3 balls in #3039 camel (C)
- One pair size 8 (5mm) needles OR SIZE TO OBTAIN GAUGE
- Stitch markers
- 7"/18cm zipper
- Matching sewing thread

GAUGE
17 sts and 24 rows to 4"/10cm over St st using size 8 (5mm) needles.
FOR PERFECT FIT, TAKE TIME TO CHECK GAUGE.

STITCH GLOSSARY
Stripe Pat
In St st, *6 rows B, 6 rows A; rep from * for stripe pat.

Full Fashioned Decs
K2, ssk at beg of rows, work to last 4 sts, k2tog, k2.
Note
On matching stripes: If adjusting length, work back, front and sleeves in stripe pat and end all pieces with 6 rows of the same color stripe. When working next stripe, beg raglan shaping on row 5 for back and front, on row 1 for sleeves.

BACK
With A, cast on 94 (102, 110) sts.
Row 1 *K1, p1; rep from *. Rep last row 5 times more. Change to B. Beg with a k row, work 70 rows in St st (k on RS, p on WS) and stripe pat—4 rows of 6th red stripe have been completed and piece measures approx 12½"/32cm from beg.

Raglan shaping
Bind off 5 (6, 6) sts at beg of next 2 rows—84 (90, 98) sts. Cont in pat, AT SAME TIME, beg with next RS row and dec 1 st each side (working full fashioned decs) [every other row, then every 4th row] 9 times—48 (54, 62) sts. Dec 1 st *every* row 8 (10, 12) times more. Bind off rem 32 (34, 38) sts.

FRONT
Work as for back until 2 (2, 3) sets of raglan decs have been completed—76 (82, 86) sts rem. Place marker after first 38 (41, 43) sts to divide work in half.
Beg neck slit: Next row (RS) Cont raglan shaping, work to marker, join 2nd ball of yarn and work to end. Cont stripe pat and raglan shaping until first (first, 2nd) dec of 8th set of raglan decs have been worked—54 (60, 64) sts rem.

Neck shaping
Cont raglan shaping, AT SAME TIME, beg with next RS row and bind off from each neck edge 6 (9, 9) sts once, 3 sts twice, 2 sts once, 1 st once. After completing 9 raglan decs and all neck decs, dec 1 st each side *every* row until 2 sts rem. Bind off.

LEFT SLEEVE
With A, cast on 38 (38, 40) sts. Work 6 rows in k1, p1 rib as for back. Change to B. Beg with a k row, work 90 rows in St st and stripe pat, AT SAME TIME, inc 1 st each side on first row, then every 4th row 19 times more—7th B stripe completed and ready to begin 7th A stripe and 78 (78, 80) sts.

Raglan shaping
Dec 1 st each side (working full fashioned decs) every other row 27 times, then *every* row 4 (4, 9) times more—16 (16, 8) sts. With RS facing, mark right side at top of sleeve.

For small (medium) At marked side, cont to dec *every* row 4 (6) times more. At rem side, bind off 3 (2) sts at beg of next WS row, then bind off 2 sts at beg of next WS row. Bind off rem 8 (6) sts.
For large At marked side, cont to dec every row 3 times. Bind off rem 5 sts.

RIGHT SLEEVE

Work as for left sleeve. Reverse shaping at top of sleeve.

FINISHING

Block pieces. Using photo as guide, duplicate st snowflake chart to back with C, then use chain st to outline snowflake. In same way, use C to chain st a free form scroll motif around front neck slit. Sew raglan seams, easing bound off sts on front and back to beg of raglan shaping on sleeves. Sew side and sleeve seams.

Neckband

With RS facing and A, pick up and k17 (19, 21) sts along right neck, 7 (6, 4) sts on right sleeve, 31 (33, 37) sts along back neck, 7 (6, 4) sts on left sleeve, 17 (19, 21) sts along left neck— 79 (83, 87) sts.
Next row (WS) *P1, k1; rep from *, end p1.
Next row (RS) *K1, p1; rep from *, end k1. Rep last 2 rows until neckband measures 1½"/4cm. Bind off in rib. With zipper pull at top of neckband, sew zipper along front neck slit and neckband, leaving zipper teeth visible. With C, make a 3"/8cm tassel and attach to zipper pull. •

Chart for Back

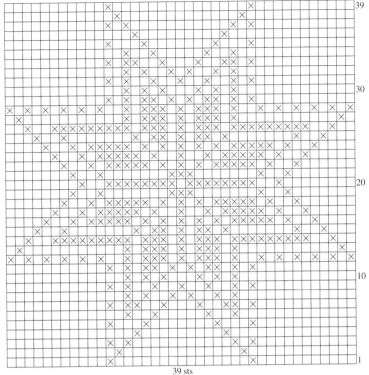

39

30

20

10

1

39 sts

Color Key
☐ Striped background

☒ Beige (CC)

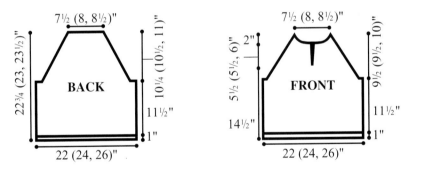

7½ (8, 8½)"
22¾ (23, 23½)"
BACK
10¼ (10½, 11)"
11½"
1"
22 (24, 26)"

7½ (8, 8½)"
2"
5½ (5½, 6)"
FRONT
9½ (9½, 10)"
11½"
14½"
1"
22 (24, 26)"

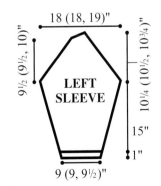

18 (18, 19)"
9½ (9½, 10)"
LEFT SLEEVE
10¼ (10½, 10¾)"
15"
1"
9 (9, 9½)"

Something for everyone— classic knits for all ages

Knit in cool white cotton, this man's or woman's alternating purl-and-block pattern pullover is the perfect casual summer cover-up. The sweater is oversized with drop shoulders and crew neck. Designed by Brigit Juhl. Shown in size 42. The Block-Pattern Pullover first appeared in the Spring/Summer '87 issue of *Vogue Knitting*.

Block-Pattern Pullover

SIZES
To fit 36 (38, 40, 42, 44)"/91 (96, 101, 106, 112)cm chest/bust. Directions are for smallest size with larger sizes in parentheses. If there is only one set of figures it applies to all sizes.

KNITTED MEASUREMENTS
● Chest/bust 42 (44, 46, 48, 50)"/105 (110, 115, 120, 125)cm.
● Length 23 (24, 25, 26, 27)"/58 (61, 63.5, 66, 68.5)cm.
● Upper arm 17 (18, 19, 20, 21)"/43 (46, 48, 51, 53)cm.

MATERIALS
Original Yarn
● 13 (14, 14, 15, 15) 1¾oz/50g balls (each approx 85yd/78m) of Wendy/White Buffalo Mills *Fiori* (cotton⑤) in #567 white
Substitute Yarn
● 14 (15, 15, 16, 16) 1¾oz/50g skeins (each approx 84yd/77m) of Berroco *Cotton 100* (cotton④) in #9100 white
● One pair each sizes 3 and 6 (3.25 and 4mm) needles OR SIZE TO OBTAIN GAUGE
Note
The original yarn used for this sweater is no longer available. A comparable substitute has been made, which is available at the time of printing. Check gauge of substitute yarns very carefully before beginning.

GAUGE
16 sts and 26 rows to 4"/10cm over block pat using size 6 (4mm) needles. FOR PERFECT FIT, TAKE TIME TO CHECK GAUGE.
Note
To work a gauge swatch, cast on 24 sts. Beg with 4th st of chart, work 6 sts, then 18-st rep. Work through row 32 of chart. Bind off. Block carefully as cotton will stretch. Blocked piece should measure 6" x 5" (15 x 12.5cm).

BACK
With smaller needles, cast on 74 (76, 78, 80, 82) sts.
Rib row 1 *K1, p1; rep from * to end. Rep last row for rib for 3"/7.5cm, inc 10 (12, 14, 16, 18) sts evenly across last row—84 (88, 92, 96, 100) sts.
Beg block pat: Row 1 (RS) Beg with 4th (2nd, 9th, 7th, 5th) st of chart, work to rep line, work 18-st rep of chart 4 (4, 5, 5, 5) times, then work first 6 (8, 1, 3, 5) sts of rep once more. Cont foll chart until piece measures 14½ (15, 15½, 16, 16½)"/36.5 (38, 39.5, 40.5, 42)cm from beg. Place markers each side of last row for arm-holes. Work even until armhole measures 8½ (9, 9½, 10, 10½)"/21.5 (23, 24, 25.5, 26.5)cm. Bind off all sts.

FRONT
Work as for back until armhole measures 5½ (6, 6½, 7, 7½)"/13.5 (15, 16, 17.5, 18.5)cm, end with a WS row.

Neck shaping
Next row (RS) Work 37 (39, 40, 41, 43) sts, join 2nd ball of yarn and bind off center 10 (10, 12, 14, 14) sts, work to end. Working both sides at once, bind off 2 sts from each neck edge twice, dec 1 st every other row 7 times. When same length as back, bind off rem 26 (28, 29, 30, 32) sts each side.

SLEEVES
With smaller needles, cast on 38 (40, 42, 44, 46) sts. Work in k1, p1 rib for 2½"/6.5cm, inc 6 (6, 6, 6, 4) sts evenly across last row—44 (46, 48, 50, 50) sts.
Beg block pat: Row 1 (RS) Beg with 6th (5th, 4th, 3rd, 3rd) st of chart, work to rep line, work 18-st rep of chart twice, then work first 4 (5, 6, 7, 7) sts of rep once more. Cont in block pat, AT SAME TIME, inc 1 st each side (working inc sts into pat) every 6th row 1 (2, 7, 9, 16) times, then every 8th row 11 (11, 7, 6, 1) times—68 (72, 76, 80, 84) sts. Work even until piece measures 18 (18½, 18½, 19, 19½)"/45.5 (46.5, 46.5, 47.5, 49)cm from beg. Bind off.

FINISHING
Block pieces. Sew left shoulder seam.

Neckband
With RS facing and smaller needles, beg at right shoulder, pick up and k32 (32, 34, 36, 36) sts along back neck, 38 (38, 40, 42, 42) sts along front neck—70 (70, 74, 78, 78) sts. Work in k1, p1 rib for 1"/2.5cm. Bind off. Sew right shoulder seam, including neckband. Sew top of sleeves to front and back between markers. Sew side and sleeve seams. ●

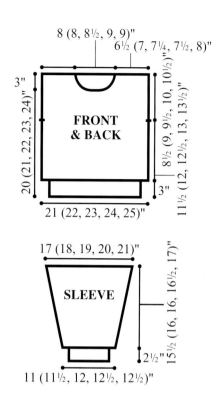

8 (8, 8½, 9, 9)"

6½ (7, 7¼, 7½, 8)"

3"

FRONT & BACK

20 (21, 22, 23, 24)"

8½ (9, 9½, 10, 10½)"

11½ (12, 12½, 13, 13½)"

3"

21 (22, 23, 24, 25)"

17 (18, 19, 20, 21)"

SLEEVE

15½ (16, 16, 16½, 17)"

2½"

11 (11½, 12, 12½, 12½)"

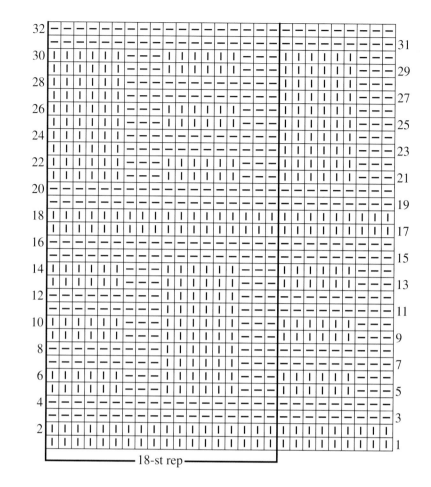

18-st rep

Stitch Key

$\boxed{I}$ K on RS, p on WS

$\boxed{-}$ P on RS, k on WS

Textured-Stitch Pullovers

His-and-her weekend warmth. The roomy comfort and easy-going good looks of textural stitches and sandy hues are captured in these oversized pullovers with drop shoulders and rolled highneck. Designed by Anne Mieke Louwerens. Both shown in size 38-40. The Textured-Stitch Pullovers first appeared in the Fall '89 issue of *Vogue Knitting*.

Textured-Stitch Pullovers

SIZES

To fit 36 (38-40, 42-44)"/91 (96-101, 106-112)cm bust/chest. Directions are for smallest size with larger sizes in parentheses. If there is only one figure it applies to all sizes.

KNITTED MEASUREMENTS

- Bust/chest 54 (56, 58)"/135 (140, 145)cm.
- Length 24 (25, 26)"/60 (63, 65)cm.
- Upper arm 21 (22, 23)"/53 (56, 57)cm.

MATERIALS

Original Yarn

- 9 (10, 11) 3½oz/100g balls (each approx 129yd/119m) of Tahki *Lana* (wool⑤) in #7023 mushroom

Substitute Yarn

- 18 (20, 22) 1¾oz/50g skeins (each approx 65yd/58m) of Berella®/Spinrite *Whistler* (wool⑤) in #9794 malt
- One pair each sizes 8 and 10 (5 and 6mm) needles OR SIZE TO OBTAIN GAUGE
- Size 8 (5mm) circular needle, 16"/40cm long
- Stitch markers and holders
- Cable needle (cn)

Note

The original yarn used for this sweater is no longer available. A comparable substitute has been made, which is available at the time of printing. Check gauge of substitute yarns very carefully before beginning.

GAUGE

16 sts and 20 rows to 4"/10cm over St st using size 10 (6mm) needles. FOR PERFECT FIT, TAKE TIME TO CHECK GAUGE.

STITCH GLOSSARY

Garter Ridge Pat

Row 1 (RS) Purl.

Rows 2-8 Work in St st (k on RS, p on WS). Rep rows 1-8 for garter ridge pat.

Chart Panel (over 42 sts)

Work 25 rows of chart I, 3 rows in St st, 23 rows of chart II, 3 rows of St st, 27 rows of chart III, 3 rows in St st. Work garter ridge and St st to end of piece as foll: 11 sts in St st, 20 sts in garter ridge pat, 11 sts in St st.

Right Twist (over 2 sts)

Skip next st on LH needle and k 2nd st in front of skipped st, then k skipped st, sl both from LH needle.

Left Twist (over 2 sts)

With RH needle behind LH needle, skip next st on LH needle, k 2nd st tbl, then k skipped st in front lp, sl both from LH needle.

Right Purl Twist (over 2 sts)

Skip next st on LH needle and k 2nd st in front of skipped st, then p skipped st, sl both from LH needle.

Left Purl Twist (over 2 sts)

Sl 1 st to cn and hold to *front*, p1, k1 from cn.

4-st Right Cross

Sl 1 st to cn and hold to *back*, k3, k1 from cn.

4-st Left Cross

Sl 3 sts to cn and hold to *front*, k1, k3 from cn.

8-st Left Cable

Sl 4 sts to cn and hold to *front*, k4, k4 from cn.

BACK

With smaller needles, cast on 92 (97, 102) sts.

Rib row 1 (RS) K2, *p3, k2; rep from * to end.

Rib row 2 P2, *k3, p2; rep from * to end. Rep last 2 rows for 4"/10cm, end with a RS row. Change to larger needles. Purl next row, inc 16 (15, 14) sts evenly across—108 (112, 116) sts.

Beg pats: Row 1 (RS) K12 (12, 14), place marker (pm), work garter ridge pat over 18 (20, 20) sts, pm, k3, pm, work chart panel over 42 sts, pm, k3, pm, work garter ridge pat over 18 (20, 20) sts, pm, k12 (12, 14). Cont in garter ridge and chart panel, working all other sts in St st, until piece measures 13½ (14, 14½)"/33.5 (35, 36.5)cm from beg. Place markers each side of last row for beg of armhole. Work even in pats until armhole measures 10½ (11, 11½)"/26.5 (28, 28.5)cm above markers. Bind off.

FRONT

Cast on and work rib as for back. Change to larger needles and work inc row—108 (112, 116) sts.

Beg pats: Row 1 (RS) K0 (1, 3), pm, chart panel over 42 sts, pm, k3, pm, work garter ridge st over 18 (20, 20) sts, pm, k3, pm, work chart panel over 42 sts, pm, k0 (1, 3). Cont in pats until armhole measures 8 (8½, 9)"/20.5 (22, 22.5)cm above markers, end with a WS row.

Neck shaping

Next row (RS) Work 40 (42, 44) sts, place center 28 sts on holder, join 2nd ball of yarn and work to end. Working both sides at once, dec 1 st at each neck edge *every* row 10 times. Work 1 row even. Bind off rem 30 (32, 34) sts each side for shoulders.

RIGHT SLEEVE

With smaller needles, cast on 42 (47, 47) sts. Work in k2, p3 rib as for back for 4"/10cm. Change to larger needles. Purl

next row, inc 10 (9, 11) sts evenly
across—52 (56, 58) sts.
Beg pats: Row 1 (RS) K17 (18, 19), pm,
work garter ridge pat over 18 (20, 20) sts,
pm, k17 (18, 19). Cont with garter ridge
pat inside markers and rem sts in St st,
inc 1 st each side every other row 6
times, every 4th row 10 (10, 11) times—
84 (88, 92) sts. Work even until piece
measures 15 (15½, 16)"/37.5 (39, 40)cm
from beg. Bind off.

LEFT SLEEVE
Cast on and rib as for right sleeve.
Change to larger needles and work inc
row—52 (56, 58) sts.
Beg pats: Row 1 (RS) K5 (7, 8), pm,
work chart panel over 42 sts, pm, k5 (7,
8). Keeping sts inside markers in chart
panel and rem sts in St st, work inc as for
right sleeve.

FINISHING
Block pieces. Sew shoulder seams.

Neckband
With RS facing and circular needle, beg at
right shoulder, pick up and k48 sts evenly
around back neck edge, 12 sts along left
neck edge, 28 sts from front neck holder
and 12 sts along right neck edge—100
sts. Join and k 4 rnds. *Purl 1 rnd. K 8
rnds. Rep from * once. K 4 rnds more.
Bind off. Band rolls naturally to RS. Sew
top of sleeves to front and back between
markers. Sew side and sleeve seams. •

Chart I

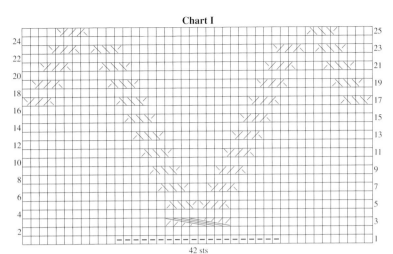

42 sts

Chart II

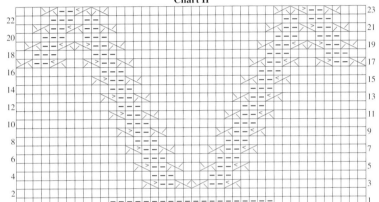

42 sts

Chart III

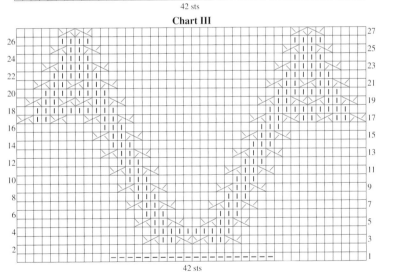

42 sts

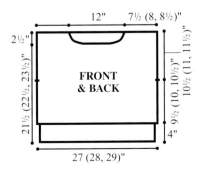

FRONT & BACK

12" 7½ (8, 8½)"
2½"
21½ (22½, 23½)"
10½ (11, 11½)"
9½ (10, 10½)"
4"
27 (28, 29)"

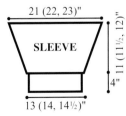

SLEEVE

21 (22, 23)"
11 (11½, 12)"
4"
13 (14, 14½)"

Stitch Key

☐ or ⊥ K on RS, p on WS

⊟ P on RS, k on WS

⊠ Right Twist

⊠ Left Twist

▨ Right Purl Twist

▨ Left Purl Twist

▧ 4-st Right Cross

▨ 4-st Left Cross

▧ 8-st Left Cable

Share a little quiet time with an oversized pullover styled for both men and women. Colorblocked in classic tones of blue, black, ecru and grey, this cozy cover-up features raglan armholes and an inset V-neck with ribbed foldback collar. Designed by Anne Mieke Louwerens. Shown in size 40. The Colorblocked Pullover first appeared in the Holiday '88 issue of *Vogue Knitting*.

Colorblocked Pullover

SIZES

To fit 36 (38, 40, 42, 44)"/91 (96, 101, 106, 112)cm chest/bust. Directions are for smallest size with larger sizes in parentheses. If there is only one figure it applies to all sizes.

KNITTED MEASUREMENTS

- Chest/bust 42 (44, 46, 48, 50)"/105 (110, 115, 120, 125)cm.
- Length 26¼ (26½, 27½, 27¾, 28¼)"/65.5 (66.5, 68.5, 69.5, 70.5)cm.
- Upper arm 18 (19, 19, 20, 21)"/45 (47.5, 47.5, 50, 52.5)cm.

MATERIALS

Original Yarn

- 2 (2, 2, 3, 3) 3½oz/100g balls (each approx 129yd/119m) of Tahki *Laña* (wool⑤) in #7021 black (A), #7015 ecru (B) and #7028 blue heather (C)
- 3 (3, 3, 4, 4) balls in #7024 grey (D)

Substitute Yarn

- 4 (4, 4, 6, 6) 1¾oz/50g balls (each approx 65yd/58m) of Berella®/Spinrite *Whistler* (wool⑤) in #9788 black (A), #9748 ecru (B), and #9799 blue (C)
- 6 (6, 6, 8, 8) balls in #9785 grey (D)
- One pair each sizes 8 and 10 (5 and 6mm) needles OR SIZE TO OBTAIN GAUGE
- Size 8 (5mm) circular needle, 16"/40cm long

Note

The original yarns used for this sweater are no longer available. Comparable substitutes have been made, which are available at the time of printing. Check gauge of substitute yarns very carefully before beginning.

GAUGE

16 sts and 20 rows to 4"/10cm over St st using size 10 (6mm) needles. FOR PERFECT FIT, TAKE TIME TO CHECK GAUGE.

BACK

With smaller needles and A, cast on 84 (88, 92, 96, 100) sts. Work in k1, p1 rib for 1¾"/4.5cm. Change to larger needles and B. P next row on WS. Cont in St st (k on RS, p on WS) until piece measures 15"/37.5cm from beg, end with a WS row.

Raglan shaping

Bind off 3 sts at beg of next 2 rows.
Next row (RS) K2, ssk, work to last 4 sts, k2tog, k2.
Next row Purl. Rep last 2 rows until 32 (34, 34, 36, 38) sts rem and armhole measures 9¾ (10, 11, 11¼, 11¾)"/24 (25, 27, 28, 29)cm. Bind off.

FRONT

Work rib as for back. Change to larger needles and C. Work as for back until 26 (28, 32, 34, 36) rows of armhole have been worked, and armhole measures 5¼ (5½, 6½, 6¾, 7¼)"/13 (14, 16, 17, 18)cm.

Neck shaping

Next row (RS) Mark center of row. Cont raglan armhole shaping, and shape neck as foll: work to 4 sts before center, k3tog, k1; join 2nd ball of yarn, k1, sl 1-k2tog-psso, work to end. Working both sides at once, work 1 row even. Rep last 2 rows 2 (3, 3, 4, 5) times more, then cont neck decs as foll:
Next row (RS) Work to 3 sts before center, k2tog, k1; on other side, k1, ssk, work to end. Work 1 row even. Rep last 2 rows 5 (4, 4, 3, 2) times more.
Next row (RS) K2, k2tog, k1.
Next row Purl.
Next row K2tog twice. Bind off 2 sts.

SLEEVES

With smaller needles and A, cast on 36 (38, 40, 40, 42) sts. Rib as for back for 1¾"/4.5cm. Change to larger needles and D. Work in St st, inc 1 st each side every 4th row 14 (16, 13, 18, 19) times, then every 6th row 4 (3, 5, 2, 2) times—72 (76, 76, 80, 84) sts. Work even until piece measures 18½ (19, 19, 19½, 20)"/46.5 (47.5, 47.5, 49, 50)cm from beg.

Raglan cap shaping

Bind off 3 sts at beg of next 2 rows.
Next row K2, sl 1-k2tog-psso, work to last 5 sts, k3tog, k2.
Next row Purl. Rep last 2 rows 2 (3, 1, 2, 3) times more.
Next row K2, ssk, work to last 4 sts, k2tog, k2.
Next row Purl. Rep last 2 rows until 14 sts rem. Bind off.

FINISHING

Block pieces. Sew raglan sleeve caps to raglan armholes.

Foldover neck

With RS facing, circular needle and A, pick up and k116 (124, 124, 130, 138) sts as foll: beg at center front neck, pick up sts along right front neck, right sleeve, back neck, left sleeve, and left front neck, end at center. Work back and forth as with straight needles in k1, p1 rib for 6"/15cm. Bind off in rib. Sew side edges to opposite front neck. Sew side and sleeve seams. •

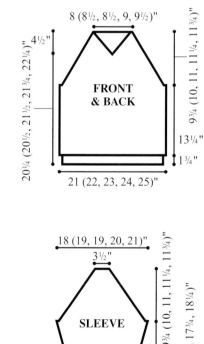

8 (8½, 8½, 9, 9½)"

4½"

FRONT & BACK

20¼ (20½, 21½, 21¾, 22¼)"

9¾ (10, 11, 11¼, 11¾)"

13¼"

1¾"

21 (22, 23, 24, 25)"

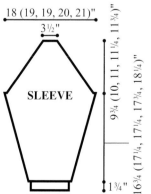

18 (19, 19, 20, 21)"

3½"

SLEEVE

9¾ (10, 11, 11¼, 11¾)"

16¾ (17¼, 17¼, 17¾, 18¼)"

1¾"

9 (9½, 10, 10, 10½)"

Perfect partners! These quick-knit his-and-her diamond-stitch pullovers are oversized with drop shoulders and a crew neck. A Vogue Original. Shown in woman's size 36 and man's size 42. The Diamond-Stitch Pullovers first appeared in the Holiday '87 issue of *Vogue Knitting*.

Diamond-Stitch Pullovers

SIZES
To fit 32 (34, 36, 38, 40, 42, 44)"/81 (86, 91, 96, 101, 106, 112)cm bust/chest. Directions are for smallest size with larger sizes in parentheses. If there is only one set of figures it applies to all sizes.

KNITTED MEASUREMENTS
● Bust/chest 39^1/2 (42, 44, 46, 47^1/2, 48^1/2, 50)"/98 (104, 110, 116, 118, 122, 124)cm.
● Length 24 (24^1/2, 25, 25^1/2, 25^1/2, 26, 26^1/2)"/60.5 (62, 63.5, 65, 65, 66, 67)cm.
● Upper arm 19 (19, 20, 20, 20, 21, 21)"/48 (48, 51, 51, 51, 53, 53)cm.

MATERIALS
Original Yarn
● 16 (17, 17, 18, 18, 19, 20) 1^3/4oz/50g balls (each approx 57yd/52m) of Wendy/White Buffalo Mills *Shetland Chunky* (wool⑤) in #86 ecru (man's) or #84 taupe (woman's)
Substitute Yarn
● 14 (15, 15, 16, 16, 17, 18) 1^3/4oz/50g skeins (each approx 65yd/58m) of Berella®/Spinrite *Whistler* (wool⑤) in #9748 ecru (man's) or #9793 taupe (woman's)
● One pair each sizes 9 and 10^1/2 (5.5 and 6.5mm) needles OR SIZE TO OBTAIN GAUGE
Note
The original yarn used for this sweater is no longer available. A comparable substitute has been made, which is available at the time of printing. Check gauge of substitute yarns very carefully before beginning.

GAUGE
14 sts and 20 rows to 4"/10cm over chart pat using size 10^1/2 (6.5mm) needles. FOR PERFECT FIT, TAKE TIME TO CHECK GAUGE.
Note
For easier working, circle all numbers that pertain to your size.

BACK
With smaller needles, cast on 68 (72, 76, 80, 80, 84, 84) sts.
Rib row 1 *K2, p2; rep from * to end. Rep row 1 for k2, p2 rib for 3"/7.5cm, inc 1 (1, 1, 1, 3, 1, 3) sts across last row—69 (73, 77, 81, 83, 85, 87) sts. Change to larger needles. Work chart pat, beg and end as indicated, until piece measures 23 (23^1/2, 24, 24^1/2, 24^1/2, 25, 25^1/2)"/58 (59.5, 61, 62.5, 62.5, 63.5, 64.5)cm from beg.

Shoulder shaping
Bind off 7 (8, 8, 9, 9, 9, 9) sts at beg of next 4 rows, 7 (7, 9, 8, 9, 10, 10) sts at beg of next 2 rows. Bind off rem 27 (27, 27, 29, 29, 29, 31) sts for back neck.

FRONT
Work as for back until piece measures 21 (21^1/2, 22, 22^1/2, 22^1/2, 23, 23^1/2)"/53 (54.5, 56, 57.5, 57.5, 58.5, 59.5)cm from beg, end with a WS row.

Neck shaping
Next row (RS) Work 27 (29, 31, 32, 33, 34, 34) sts, join 2nd ball of yarn and bind off center 15 (15, 15, 17, 17, 17, 19) sts, work to end. Working both sides at once, dec 1 st at each neck edge every other row 6 times, AT SAME TIME, when same length as back to shoulder, shape shoulder as for back.

SLEEVES
With smaller needles, cast on 28 (28, 28, 28, 32, 32, 32) sts. Work in k2, p2 rib for 3"/7.5cm, inc 5 (5, 7, 7, 3, 5, 5) sts evenly across last row—33 (33, 35, 35, 35, 37, 37) sts. Change to larger needles. Beg with 10th (10th, 9th, 9th, 9th, 8th, 8th) st of chart, work in chart pat, inc 1 st each end (working inc sts into pat) every 4th row 13 (12, 14, 12, 11, 11, 10) times, every 6th row 4 (5, 4, 6, 7, 7, 8) times— 67 (67, 71, 71, 71, 73, 73) sts. Work even in pat until piece measures 19 (19^1/2, 20, 20^1/2, 21, 21, 21^1/2)"/47.5 (49, 50, 51.5, 52.5, 52.5, 53.5) from beg. Bind off.

FINISHING
Block pieces. Sew left shoulder seam.

Neckband
With RS facing and smaller needles, beg at right shoulder, pick up and k72 (72, 72, 76, 76, 76, 80) sts evenly around neck edge. Work in k2, p2 rib for 1"/2.5cm. Bind off in rib. Sew right shoulder seam including neckband. Place markers 9^1/2 (9^1/2, 10, 10, 10, 10^1/2, 10^1/2)"/24 (24, 25.5, 25.5, 25.5, 26.5, 26.5)cm down from shoulders on front and back for armholes. Sew top of sleeves between markers. Sew side and sleeve seams.

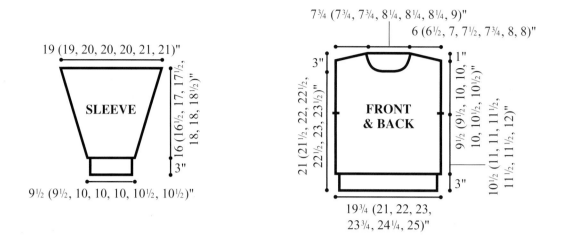

19 (19, 20, 20, 20, 21, 21)"

SLEEVE

16 (16½, 17, 17½, 18, 18, 18½)"

3"

9½ (9½, 10, 10, 10, 10½, 10½)"

7¾ (7¾, 7¾, 8¼, 8¼, 8¼, 9)"

6 (6½, 7, 7½, 7¾, 8, 8)"

3"

1"

FRONT & BACK

21 (21½, 22, 22½, 22½, 23, 23½)"

9½ (9½, 10, 10, 10, 10½)"

10½ (11, 11, 11½, 11½, 12)"

3"

19¾ (21, 22, 23, 23¾, 24¼, 25)"

Stitch Key

|I| K on RS, p on WS

|−| P on RS, k on WS

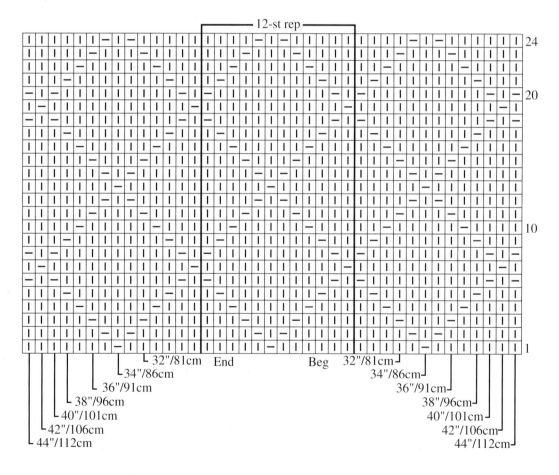

12-st rep

24

20

10

1

32"/81cm

End

Beg

32"/81cm

34"/86cm

36"/91cm

38"/96cm

40"/101cm

42"/106cm

44"/112cm

34"/86cm

36"/91cm

38"/96cm

40"/101cm

42"/106cm

44"/112cm

His-and-Hers Guernseys

These classic drop-shoulder guernsey pullovers pair a double moss-stitch yoke with a cable and diamond moss-stitch bodice. Her version is cropped and sports a high turtleneck; his is standard-fitting with a foldover standing crew neck. Designed by Michele Rose. Shown in woman's size Medium and man's size Small. The His-and-Hers Guernseys first appeared in the Winter Special '90/91 issue of *Vogue Knitting*.

His-and-Hers Guernseys

SIZES

To fit woman's (Small, Medium, Large); man's [Small, Medium, Large]. Directions for woman's sizes are in parentheses ( )'s; man's sizes are in brackets [ ]'s. If there is only one figure it applies to all sizes.

KNITTED MEASUREMENTS

● Bust/chest (40¹/₂, 43, 46)"/(101, 107, 115)cm; [43, 46, 49]"/[107, 115, 123]cm.
● Length (20¹/₂, 21, 21¹/₂)"/(52, 53.5, 54.5)cm; [25¹/₂, 26, 26¹/₂]"/[65.5, 66.5, 68]cm.
● Upper arm (18, 19, 20)"/(45, 48, 50)cm; [19, 20, 21]"/[48, 50, 53]cm.

MATERIALS

● (6, 6, 7); [8, 9, 9] 3¹/₂oz/100g balls (each approx 230yd/209m) of Plymouth *Galway* (wool④) in #93 beige (woman's) or #1 ecru [man's]
● One pair each sizes 6 and 8 (4 and 5mm) needles OR SIZE TO OBTAIN GAUGE
● Size 6 (4mm) circular needle, 16"/40cm long
● Stitch markers and cable needle (cn)

Note

One of the original colors used for this sweater is no longer available. A comparable color substitute has been made, which is available at the time of printing.

GAUGE

20 sts and 28 rows to 4"/10cm over ouble moss st using size 8 (5mm) needles. FOR PERFECT FIT, TAKE TIME TO CHECK GAUGE.

Note

For ease in working, circle the numbers that pertain to the size you are making.

STITCH GLOSSARY

5-St Cable

Sl 3 sts to cn and hold to *front*, k2; sl p st from cn to LH needle and p1, k2 from cn.

Moss St

Row 1 (RS) *K1, p1; rep from * to end.
Row 2 K the purl sts and p the knit sts. Rep row 2 for moss st.

Double Moss St

Row 1 (RS) *K1, p1; rep from * to end.
Row 2 K the knit sts and p the purl sts.
Row 3 *P1, k1; rep from * to end.
Row 4 Rep row 2. Rep rows 1-4 for double moss st.

BACK

With smaller needles, cast on (98, 106, 114); [106, 114, 122] sts. Work in k2, p2 rib for (1¹/₂"/4cm); [2¹/₂"/6.5cm], inc (3, 1, 1); [1, 1, 1] sts across last row—(101, 107, 115); [107, 115, 123] sts. Change to larger needles.
Beg chart pat: Row 1 (RS) Work (2, 5, 9); [5, 9, 13] sts in moss st, place marker (pm), beg with first st of chart, work to st (49); [49] (center st of piece), then working chart backwards from left to right, skip st (49); [49] and work sts (48-1); [48-1], pm, work (2, 5, 9); [5, 9, 13] sts in moss st. Cont in pats as established, sl markers every row, until (90); [120] rows have been worked in chart pat—piece measures approx (14¹/₂"/36cm);

[19¹/₂"/49.5cm] from beg. Cont in double moss st on all sts until piece measures (19¹/₂, 20, 20¹/₂)"/(49.5, 51, 52)cm; [24¹/₂, 25, 25¹/₂]"/[63, 64, 65.5]cm from beg.

Shoulder and neck shaping

Bind off (11, 12, 13); [11, 13, 13] sts at beg of next 4 rows, (12, 12, 14); [12, 12, 14] sts at beg of next 2 rows, AT SAME TIME, bind off center (21, 23, 23); [25, 25, 29] sts and working both sides at once, bind off from each neck edge (4); [4] sts once, (2); [3] sts once.

FRONT

Work as for back until piece measures (18, 18¹/₂, 19)"/(45.5, 47, 48)cm; [23, 23¹/₂, 24]"/[59, 60, 61.5]cm from beg, end with a WS row.

Neck and shoulder shaping

Next row (RS) Work (43, 45, 49); [44, 48, 50] sts, join 2nd ball of yarn and bind off (15, 17, 17); [19, 19, 23] sts, work to end. Working both sides at once, bind off from each neck edge (4); [4] sts once, (2); [3] sts once, dec 1 st every other row (3); [3] times, AT SAME TIME, when same length as back to shoulder, shape shoulder as for back.

SLEEVES

With smaller needles, cast on (42); [42] sts. Work in k2, p2 rib for (1¹/₂, 2, 2)"/(4, 5, 5)cm; [1¹/₂, 2, 2¹/₂]"/[4, 5, 6.5]cm, inc (3); [3] sts evenly across last row—(45); [45] sts. Change to larger needles.
Beg chart pat: Row 1 (RS) Beg with st (27); [27] of chart, work to st (49); [49], then working chart backwards, from left to right, skip st (49); [49] and work sts (48-27); [48-27]. Cont in pat as established, inc 1 st each side (working inc sts into

double moss st) every 4th row (9, 18, 24); [10, 16, 25] times, every 6th row (13, 7, 3); [15, 11, 5] times—(89, 95, 99); [95, 99, 105] sts. Work even in pat until (120); [136] rows have been worked in chart pat—piece measures approx (18½, 19, 19)"/(47, 48, 48)cm; [21, 21½, 22]"/[52.5, 53.5, 55]cm from beg. Bind off.

FINISHING
Block pieces. Sew shoulder seams.

Neckband
With RS facing and circular needle, pick up and k(88, 92, 92); [96, 96, 100] sts evenly around neck edge. Join. Work in k2, p2 rib for (8"/20.5cm); [5"/13cm]. Bind off in rib. *Man's version only:* Fold band in half to WS and sew in place. Place markers (9, 9½, 10)"/(22.5, 24, 25)cm; [9½, 10, 10½]"/[24, 25, 26.5]cm down from shoulders on front and back for armholes. Sew top of sleeves between markers. Sew side and sleeve seams. •

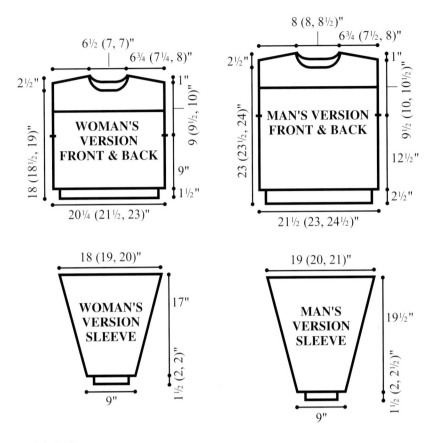

Stitch Key
☐ K on RS, p on WS

⊟ P on RS, k on WS

5-st Cable

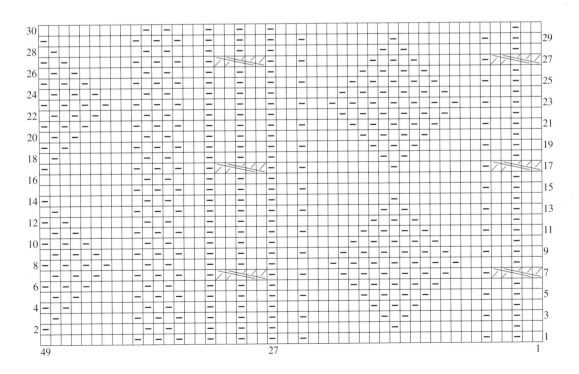

Tweedy wool yarns in soft earth tones lend autumn richness to this man's ribbed pullover. A weekend classic, the easy-fitting crew neck is striped at the chest and upper arm. A Vogue Original. Shown in size Large. The Man's Ribbed Pullover first appeared in the Fall '98 issue of *Vogue Knitting*.

Man's Ribbed Pullover

SIZES
To fit Small (Medium, Large, X-Large). Directions are for smallest size with larger sizes in parentheses. If there is only one figure it applies to all sizes.

KNITTED MEASUREMENTS
- Chest 38½ (43, 48, 53)"/96 (108, 120, 132)cm.
- Length 26 (26½, 27, 28)"/66 (67, 68.5, 71)cm.
- Upper arm 17¼ (19, 20, 22½)"/43 (47, 50, 56)cm.

MATERIALS
- 7 (8, 8, 9) 3½oz/100g hanks (each approx 137yd/127m) of Manos del Uruguay/Simpson Southwick Co. *700 Tex* (wool④) in #108 grey multi (MC)
- 2 (2, 2, 3) hanks in #1 tan (CC)
- One pair size 8 (5mm) needles OR SIZE TO OBTAIN GAUGE
- Size 6 (4mm) circular needle, 16"/40cm long
- Stitch holders

GAUGE
20 sts and 24 rows to 4"/10cm over k4, p2 rib pat (slightly stretched), using size 8 (5mm) needles. FOR PERFECT FIT, TAKE TIME TO CHECK GAUGE.

STITCH GLOSSARY
K4, P2 Rib Pat (multiple of 6 sts)
Row 1 (RS) K2, *p2, k4; rep from *, end last rep k2 instead of k4.
Row 2 K the knit sts and p the purl sts.
Rep row 2 for k4, p2 rib pat.

BACK
With size 8 (5mm) needles and MC, cast on 96 (108, 120, 132) sts. Work in k4, p2 rib pat for 11"/28cm. *With CC, work 12 rows in rib. With MC, work 4 rows in rib. With CC, work 12 rows in rib*. Cont with MC only in rib until piece measures 17"/43cm from beg, end with a WS row.

Armhole shaping
Dec row 1 (RS) K2, k3tog, work to last 5 sts, SK2P, k2.
Next row (WS) P3, rib to last 3 sts, p3. Rep last 2 rows 1 (2, 3, 4) times more.
Dec row 2 (RS) K2, k2tog, work to last 4 sts, SKP, k2.
Next row (WS) P3, rib to last 3 sts, p3. Rep last 2 rows 3 (2, 1, 0) times more—80 (90, 100, 110) sts. Work even until armhole measures 9 (9½, 10, 11)"/23 (24, 25.5, 28)cm. Bind off all sts in rib.

FRONT
Work as for back until armhole measures 6 (6½, 7, 8)"/15.5 (16.5, 18, 20.5)cm, end with a WS row.

Neck shaping
Next row (RS) Work 31 (35, 40, 44) sts, join a 2nd ball of yarn and bind off center 18 (20, 20, 22) sts, work to end. Working both sides at once, bind off from each neck edge 3 sts once, 2 sts twice, dec 1 st every other row 3 times. When same length as back, bind off rem 21 (25, 30, 34) sts each side for shoulders.

SLEEVES
With size 8 (5mm) needles and MC, cast on 44 (44, 44, 50) sts. Beg and end with k3, work in k4, p2 rib pat for 2"/5cm. Inc

1 st each side on next row (working inc sts into rib), then every 4th row 6 (18, 27, 24) times more, every 6th (6th, 0, 2nd) rows, 14 (6, 0, 6) times—86 (94, 100, 112) sts. AT SAME TIME, when piece measures 16"/40.5cm from beg, rep between *'s as on back for stripe, then cont in MC only until piece measures 22"/56cm from beg, end with a WS row.

Cap shaping
Work as for back armhole shaping. Bind off rem 70 (76, 80, 90) sts.

FINISHING
Block pieces to measurements. Sew shoulder seams. Set in sleeves. Sew side and sleeve seams.

Neckband
With RS facing, circular needle and MC, pick up and k66 (70, 70, 74) sts evenly around neck edge. Join and work in k1, p1 rib for 2"/5cm. Bind off in rib. ●

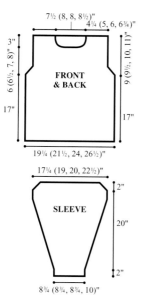

A mosaic of stitch patterns forms a plaid grid on this comfy man's or woman's oversized pullover with doubled crew neck and drop shoulders. Designed by Norah Gaughan. Shown in size 40-42. The Textured Pullover first appeared in the Winter Special '89/90 issue of *Vogue Knitting*.

Textured Pullover

SIZES
To fit 36-38 (40-42, 44-46)"/91-96 (101-106, 112-116)cm bust/chest. Directions are for smallest size with larger sizes in parentheses. If there is only one figure it applies to all sizes.

KNITTED MEASUREMENTS
● Bust/chest 43 (47, 51)"/108 (118, 127)cm.
● Length 27 (28, 29)"/68.5 (71, 73.5)cm.
● Upper arm 21 (23, 23)"/53 (58, 58)cm.

MATERIALS
● 9 (10, 10) 3¹/₂oz/100g balls (each approx 164yd/150m) of Rowan/Westminster Fibers *Magpie* (wool④) in #312 beige
● One pair each sizes 5 and 7 (3.75 and 4.5mm) needles OR SIZE TO OBTAIN GAUGE
● Size 5 (3.75mm) circular needle, 16"/40cm long

Note
The original color used for this sweater is no longer available. A comparable color substitute has been made, which is available at the time of printing.

GAUGE
17 sts and 24 rows to 4"/10cm over St st using size 7 (4.5mm) needles. FOR PERFECT FIT, TAKE TIME TO CHECK GAUGE.

STITCH GLOSSARY
Broken Rib Pat (over an even # of sts)
Row 1 (RS) Knit.

Row 2 *P1, k1; rep from * to end.
Row 3 Rep row 2.
Row 4 Purl.
Row 5 *K1, p1; rep from * to end.
Row 6 Rep row 5.
Rows 7-24 Rep rows 1-6 for 3 times.
Rows 25 and 26 Rep rows 1 and 2.

Rib and Welt Pat (multiple of 8 sts)
Row 1 (RS) *K1, p1, k1, p5; rep from * to end.
Row 2 and all WS rows K the knit sts and p the purl sts.
Row 3 K1, p1, *k5, p1, k1, p1; rep from *, end k5, p1.
Row 5 K1, *p5, k1, p1, k1; rep from *, end p5, k1, p1.
Row 7 *K5, p1, k1, p1; rep from * to end.
Row 9 P4, *k1, p1, k1, p5; rep from *, end [k1, p1] twice.
Row 11 K3, *p1, k1, p1, k5; rep from *, end p1, k1, p1, k2.
Row 13 P2, *k1, p1, k1, p5; rep from *, end k1, p1, k1, p3.
Row 15 K1, *p1, k1, p1, k5; rep from *, end p1, k1, p1, k4.
Row 17 Rep row 1.
Row 19 Rep row 3.
Row 21 Rep row 5.
Row 23 Rep row 7.
Row 25 Rep row 9.
Row 26 Rep row 2.

BACK
With smaller needles, cast on 82 (90, 98) sts. Work in k1, p1 rib for 2¹/₂"/6.5cm, end with a RS row. P next row on WS, inc 10 sts evenly across—92 (100, 108) sts. Change to larger needles.
Beg pat: Row 1 (RS) Work St st over 6 (10, 14) sts, [row 1 of broken rib over 16 sts, St st over 16 sts] twice, row 1 of bro-

ken rib over 16 sts, St st over 6 (10, 14) sts. Cont in pat for a total of 6 (10, 12) rows. *K 1 row, p 1 row.
Next row (RS) Work row 1 of broken rib over 6 (10, 14) sts, [row 1 of rib and welt over 16 sts, row 1 of broken rib over 16 sts] twice, row 1 of rib and welt over 16 sts, row 1 of broken rib over 6 (10, 14) sts. Cont in pat for 25 rows more. K 1 row, p 1 row.
Next row (RS) Work St st over 6 (10, 14) sts, [row 1 of broken rib over 16 sts, St st over 16 sts] twice, row 1 of broken rib over 16 sts, St st over 6 (10, 14) sts. Cont in pat for 25 rows more. Rep from* (56 rows) until piece measures 27 (28, 29)"/68.5 (71, 73.5)cm from beg. Bind off.

FRONT
Work as for back until piece measures 24 (25, 26)"/61 (63.5, 66)cm from beg, end with a WS row.

Neck shaping
Next row (RS) Work 39 (42, 46) sts, join 2nd ball of yarn, bind off 14 (16, 16) sts, work to end. Working both sides at once, bind off from each neck edge 3 sts once, 2 sts twice, dec 1 st every other row 3 times. When same length as back, bind off rem 29 (32, 36) sts each side.

SLEEVES
With smaller needles, cast on 40 (42, 42) sts. Work in k1, p1 rib for 2"/5cm, end with a RS row. P next row on WS, inc 6 sts evenly across—46 (48, 48) sts. Change to larger needles. Work pat and incs simultaneously as foll:
Beg pat: Row 1 (RS) Work St st over 15 (16, 16) sts, row 1 of broken rib over 16 sts, St st over 15 (16, 16) sts. Cont in pat

as for back, AT SAME TIME, inc 1 st each side (working inc sts into pat) every 4th row 10 (15, 15) times, every 6th row 12 (10, 10) times—90 (98, 98) sts. Work even in pat until piece measures 21 (22, 22)"/53 (56, 56)cm from beg. Bind off.

FINISHING
Block pieces. Sew shoulder seams.

Neckband
With RS facing and circular needle, pick up and k88 (92, 92) sts around neck edge. Join, and work in k1, p1 rib for 3½"/9cm. Bind off in rib. Fold band in half to WS and sew in place. Place markers 10½ (11½, 11½)"/26.5 (29, 29)cm down from shoulders on front and back for armholes. Sew top of sleeves between markers. Sew side and sleeve seams. •

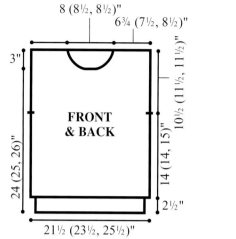

8 (8½, 8½)"

6¾ (7½, 8½)"

3"

FRONT & BACK

24 (25, 26)"

10½ (11½, 11½)"

14 (14, 15)"

2½"

21½ (23½, 25½)"

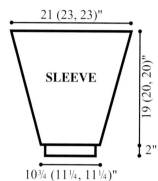

21 (23, 23)"

SLEEVE

19 (20, 20)"

2"

10¾ (11¼, 11¼)"

Child's Embroidered Cardigan

Play time! A child's drawing is interpreted into simple embroidery on this easy-to-knit cardigan with rolled edges and crew neck. Follow the diagram provided or use one of your own favorite drawings. Designed by Agi Revesz. Shown in size 4. The Child's Embroidered Cardigan first appeared in the Spring/Summer '96 issue of *Vogue Knitting*.

Child's Embroidered Cardigan

SIZES

To fit child's size 2 (4, 6). Directions are for smallest size with larger sizes in parentheses. If there is only one figure it applies to all sizes.

KNITTED MEASUREMENTS

- Chest (buttoned) 25 (28, 31)"/63.5 (71, 78.5)cm.
- Length 14¼ (15, 16)"/36 (38, 40.5)cm.
- Upper arm 11½ (12, 13)"/29 (30.5, 33)cm.

MATERIALS

- 6 (6, 7) 1¾oz/50g balls (each approx 95yd/86m) of Dale of Norway *Kolibri* (cotton③) in #9025 lime (MC)
- 1 ball in #0090 black
- One pair each sizes 4 and 5 (3.5 and 3.75mm) needles OR SIZE TO OBTAIN GAUGE
- Stitch holders
- Six decorative buttons

Note
The original colors used for this sweater are no longer available. Comparable color substitutes have been made, which are available at the time of printing.

GAUGE

24 sts and 32 rows to 4"/10cm over St st using size 5 (3.75mm) needles. FOR PERFECT FIT, TAKE TIME TO CHECK GAUGE.

STITCH GLOSSARY

K2, P1 Rib (multiple of 3 sts)
Row 1 (RS) K1, *p1, k2; rep from *, end k1.
Row 2 K the knit sts and p the purl sts. Rep row 2 for k2, p1 rib.

BACK

With smaller needles and MC, cast on 75 (84, 93) sts. Work in St st for 2 rows, then work in k2, p1 rib for 1"/2.5cm, inc 0 (0, 1) st on last row—75 (84, 94) sts. Change to larger needles and work in St st until piece measures 13¼ (14, 15)"/33.5 (35.5, 38)cm from beg, end with a WS row.

Neck shaping

Next row (RS) Work 24 (27, 32) sts, join 2nd ball of yarn, bind off center 27 (30, 30) sts, work to end. Working both sides at once, bind off 3 sts from each neck edge once. Work even until piece measures 14¼ (15, 16)"/36 (38, 40.5)cm from beg. Bind off rem 21 (24, 29) sts each side for shoulders.

POCKET LINING (make one)

With larger needles and MC, cast on 23 (23, 24) sts and work in St st for 1¾"/4.5cm. Place sts on holder.

LEFT FRONT

With smaller needles and MC, cast on 36 (39, 45) sts and work in St st and rib as for back, dec 1 (0, 1) st on last row—35 (39, 44) sts. Change to larger needles and work in St st until piece measures 2½ (3, 3½)"/6.5 (7.5, 9)cm from beg, end with a WS row.

Pocket joining

Next row (RS) Work 6 (8, 10) sts, place next 23 (23, 24) sts on holder, with RS facing, k sts of pocket lining, work to end. Work even until piece measures 12¼ (13, 14)"/31 (33, 35.5)cm from beg, end with a RS row.

Neck shaping

Next row (WS) Bind off 5 (6, 6) sts (neck edge), work to end. Cont to bind off from neck edge 3 sts twice, 2 sts once, 1 st once. When same length as back, bind off rem 21 (24, 29) sts for shoulder.

RIGHT FRONT

Work as for left front, reversing neck shaping and omitting pocket.

SLEEVES

With smaller needles and MC, cast on 40 (42, 44) sts. Work St st and rib as for back. Change to larger needles. Work in St st, inc 1 st each side every 4th row 5 (1, 5) times every 6th row 10 (14, 12) times—70 (72, 78) sts. Work even until piece measures 12 (13, 13½)"/30.5 (33, 34.5)cm from beg. Bind off all sts.

FINISHING

Block pieces to measurements. Embroider motif with A on fronts foll diagram and photo, or use your own drawing. Sew shoulder seams.

Neckband

With RS facing, smaller needles and MC, beg at right front neck, pick up and k64 (70, 70) sts evenly around neck edge.
Next row (WS) K1, *p2, k1; rep from * to end. Cont in k2, p1 rib as established for 6 rows more. Work in St st for 2 rows. Bind off all sts.

Button band

With RS facing, smaller needles and MC, pick up and k 77 (80, 86) sts evenly along right front (for boy's) or left front (for girl's) including side of neckband. Work in k2, p1 rib for 1"/2.5cm. Bind off in rib. Place markers for 6 buttons, the first one 1/2"/.5cm from neck edge, last one 1"/2.5cm from lower edge and 4 others spaced evenly between.

Buttonhole band

Work as for button band on opposite side, working buttonholes on row 4 opposite markers as foll: bind off 3 sts for each buttonhole. On foll row, cast on 3 sts over bound off sts. Complete as for button band.

Pocket band

With RS facing, smaller needles and MC, work in k2, p1 rib across sts from pocket holder for 4 rows then work in St st for 2 rows. Bind off. Place markers 5¾ (6, 6½)"/14.5 (15, 16.5)cm down from shoulder seams on front and back for armholes. Sew top of sleeves between markers. Sew side and sleeve seams. Sew on buttons. •

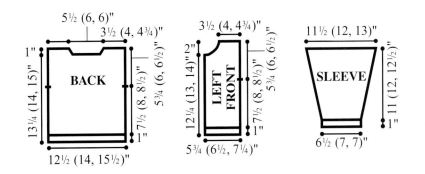

Tennis anyone? This kid's cardigan with drop shoulders and contrast crocheted trim is a snap to knit in stockinette. For extra fun the matching cap is topped with fanciful cat ears. Designed by Abigail Liles. Shown in size 4. The Child's Cardigan & Matching Cap first appeared in the Spring/Summer '96 issue of *Vogue Knitting*.

Child's Cardigan & Matching Cap

SIZES
To fit child's size 2 (4, 6). Directions are for smallest size with larger sizes in parentheses. If there is only one figure it applies to all sizes.

KNITTED MEASUREMENTS
● Chest 25 (28, 31)"/63.5 (71, 78.5)cm.
● Length (after crochet edge) 14½ (15, 16)"/37 (38, 40.5)cm.
● Upper arm 11½ (12, 13)"/29 (30.5, 33)cm.
● Head circumference 16 (18, 20½)"/40.5 (46, 52)cm.

MATERIALS
CARDIGAN:
● 6 (6, 7) 1¾oz/50g balls (each approx 50yd/45m) of Reynolds/JCA *Colors* (cotton⑤) in #106 cream (MC)
● 1 ball each in #113 fuchsia (A), #114 purple (B) and #111 red (C)
● One pair size 10 (6mm) needles OR SIZE TO OBTAIN GAUGE
● Size G (4.5mm) crochet hook
● Six decorative buttons
HAT:
● 1 ball in MC: small amounts of A, B and C
● One pair each sizes 8 and 10 (5 and 6mm) needles OR SIZE TO OBTAIN GAUGE

GAUGE
14 sts and 20 rows to 4"/10cm over St st using size 10 (6mm) needles. FOR PERFECT FIT, TAKE TIME TO CHECK GAUGE.

CARDIGAN

BACK
With larger needles and MC, cast on 44 (49, 55) sts. Work in St st until piece measures 13½ (14, 15)"/34.5 (35.5, 38)cm from beg, end with a WS row.

Neck shaping
Next row (RS) Work 12 (14, 17) sts, join 2nd ball of yarn and bind off center 20 (21, 21) sts for neck, work to end. Work both sides at once until piece measures 14 (14½, 15½)"/35.5 (37, 39.5)cm from beg. Bind off all sts each side for shoulders.

LEFT FRONT
With larger needles and MC, cast on 20 (23, 26) sts. Work in St st until piece measures 12 (12½, 13½)"/30.5 (31.5, 34.5)cm from beg, end with a RS row.

Neck shaping
Next row (WS) Bind off 3 sts (neck edge), work to end. Cont to bind off from neck edge 2 sts twice, 1 st 1 (2, 2) times. When same length as back, bind off rem 12 (14, 17) sts for shoulder.

RIGHT FRONT
Work as for left front, reversing neck shaping.

SLEEVES
With larger needles and MC, cast on 24 (24, 26) sts. Work in St st, inc 1 st each side every 6th row 8 (9, 10) times—40 (42, 46) sts. Work even until piece measures 11½ (12½, 13)"/29 (31.5, 33)cm from beg. Bind off.

FINISHING
Block pieces to measurements. Sew shoulder seams.

Neckband
With RS facing, crochet hook and A, work 2 rows sc evenly around neck edge. Fasten off.

Lower edge band
With RS facing, crochet hook and B, work 2 rows sc evenly along lower edge of fronts and back. Fasten off.

Button band
With A, work 2 rows sc along left front (for girl's) or right front (for boy's).

Buttonhole band
Sew six buttons on button band, the first and last ½"/.5cm from top and bottom edge, and the others spaced evenly between. With A, work 2 rows sc along opposite front edge, working buttonholes on 2nd row opposite buttons as foll: ch 2, skip 2 sc for each buttonhole.

Cuffs
With C, work 2 rows sc evenly around lower edge of each sleeve. Place markers 5¾ (6, 6½)"/14.5 (15, 16.5)cm down from shoulders on front and back for armholes. Sew top of sleeves between markers. Sew side and sleeve seams.

HAT

With larger needles and A, cast on 56 (64, 72) sts. Work in St st for 4 rows. Change to MC and cont in St st until piece measures 3½ (4, 5)"/9 (10, 12.5)cm from beg, end with a WS row.

Shape top

Next row (RS) [K6, k2tog] 7 (8, 9) times—49 (56, 63) sts. P 1 row.

Next row (RS) [K5, k2tog] 7 (8, 9) times—42 (48, 54) sts. P 1 row. Cont in this way to dec 7 (8, 9) sts every other row until there are 14 (16, 18) sts. K2tog across last (RS) row. Fasten off, leaving an end for sewing. Pull end through rem sts, draw tog tightly and sew back seam.

CAT EARS (make 2)

Outer Ear With smaller needles and B, cast on 12 sts. P 1 row. K 1 row. P 1 row.

Next row (RS) K5, k2tog, k5. P 1 row.

Next row K4, k3tog tbl, k4. P 1 row.

Next row K3, k3tog tbl, k3. P 1 row.

Next row K2, k3tog tbl, k2.

Next row P1, p3tog, p1.

Next row K3tog tbl. Fasten off.

Inner Ear With smaller needles and C, cast on 8 sts. P 1 row. K 1 row. P 1 row.

Next row (RS) K3, k2tog, k3. P 1 row.

Next row K2, k3tog tbl, k2. P 1 row.

Next row K1, k3tog tbl, k1. P 1 row. K 3tog, tbl. Fasten off. Sew inner and outer ear tog and attach on top of hat. •

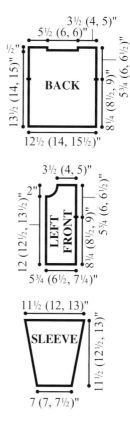

EASY EVENING

Stunning
sweaters
for a
night
wrapped
in luxury

Irresistibly soignée, the shrug makes a striking silhouette. This incredibly easy-to-knit one-piece cover-up is luxurious in a rich angora blend. A Vogue Original. The Evening Shrug first appeared in the Winter '98/99 issue of *Vogue Knitting*.

Evening Shrug

SIZES
One size.

KNITTED MEASUREMENTS
● Bust 42"/106cm.
● Length (cuff to cuff) 60"/152cm.
● Upper arm 22"/56cm.

MATERIALS
● 9 .88oz/25g balls (each approx 80yd/73m) of Adrienne Vittadini/JCA *Angelina* (angora/lambswool/alpaca④) in #7878 black
● One pair each sizes 5 and 7 (3.75 and 4.5mm) needles OR SIZE TO OBTAIN GAUGE
● Stitch markers

GAUGE
22 sts and 32 rows to 4"/10cm over k1, p2 rib (slightly stretched) using size 7 (4.5mm) needles.
FOR PERFECT FIT, TAKE TIME TO CHECK GAUGE.

STITCH GLOSSARY
K1, P2 Rib (multiple of 3 sts plus 1)
Row 1 (RS) K1, *p2, k1; rep from * to end.
Row 2 K the knit sts and p the purl sts. Rep row 2 for k1, p2 rib.

Note
Shrug is worked in one piece from cuff to cuff.

BODY
With smaller needles, cast on 49 sts. Work in k1, p1 rib for 4"/10cm, inc 4 sts evenly across last row—53 sts. Change to larger needles and cont as foll:
Next row (RS) Work 5 sts in garter st, work k1, p2 rib over next 43 sts, work 5 sts in garter st. Cont as established, inc 1 st each side (inside of 5 sts garter st and into rib pat) alternately every 2nd and 4th row until there are 119 sts. Work even until piece measures 19½"/49.5cm from beg. Place a marker each side of row for end of sleeve. Work even until piece measures 21"/53cm above marker. Place another marker each side of row for beg of next sleeve. Work 3½"/9cm more, then dec 1 st each side on next row, then alternately every 2nd and 4th row until there are 53 sts. Work even until piece measures 15½"/39.5cm from last marker. Change to smaller needles and work in k1, p1 rib, dec 4 sts evenly across first row—49 sts. When rib measures 4"/10cm, bind off in rib.

FINISHING
Block piece to measurements. Sew sleeve seams from rib to marker. ●

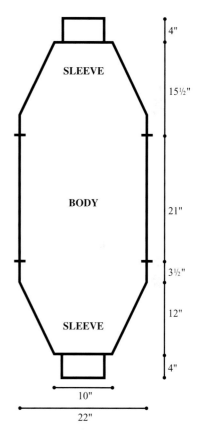

Knit the night fantastic! This glittering metallic mesh pullover is standard-fitting, with drop shoulders, ribbed sleeves and a bateau neck. Designed by Jacqueline Van Dillen. Shown in size 36. The Mesh-Stitch Pullover first appeared in the Winter '91/92 issue of *Vogue Knitting*.

Mesh-Stitch Pullover

SIZES
To fit 32 (34, 36, 38, 40)"/81 (86, 91, 96, 101)cm bust. Directions are for smallest size with larger sizes in parentheses. If there is only one figure it applies to all sizes.

KNITTED MEASUREMENTS
● Bust 35½ (38, 41, 44, 47)"/90 (96.5, 104, 111.5, 119.5)cm.
● Length 25½ (25½, 26½, 26½, 27½)"/64.5 (64.5, 67.5, 67.5, 70)cm.
● Upper arm 14 (15, 16, 17, 18)"/35.5 (38, 40.5, 43, 45.5)cm.

MATERIALS
● 31 (32, 33, 34, 35) ⅞oz/25g balls (each approx 50yd/46m) of Anny Blatt *Antique* (viscose/polyester③) in #2427 silver
● One pair size 7 (4.5mm) needles OR SIZE TO OBTAIN GAUGE
● Size G (4.5mm) crochet hook

GAUGE
● 23 sts and 32 rows to 4"/10cm over mesh st pat using size 7 (4.5mm) needles.
● 24 sts and 32 rows to 4"/10cm over rib pat (slightly stretched) using size 7 (4.5mm) needles.
FOR PERFECT FIT, TAKE TIME TO CHECK GAUGES.

STITCH GLOSSARY
Mesh St (multiple of 4 sts + 2 extra)
Row 1 (RS) Knit.
Row 2 (WS) Purl.
Row 3 K1, *k2tog, yo, SKP; rep from *, end k1.
Row 4 P1, *p1, k in front and back of yo lp, p1; rep from *, end p1.
Row 5 Knit.
Row 6 Purl.
Row 7 K1, *yo, SKP, k2tog; rep from *, end last rep yo, k1.
Row 8 P1, k1 in yo, *p2, k in front and back of yo lp; rep from *, end last rep p2, k1 in yo, p1.
Rep rows 1-8 for mesh st.

Rib Pat (multiple of 5 sts + 2 extra)
Row 1 (RS) P2, *k3, p2; rep from * to end.
Row 2 (WS) K2, *p3, k2; rep from * to end. Rep rows 1 and 2 for rib pat.

BACK
Cast on 102 (110, 118, 126, 134) sts. Work in mesh st pat until piece measures 25 (25, 26, 26, 27)"/63.5 (63.5, 66, 66, 68.5)cm. Bind off.

FRONT
Work as for back until piece measures 22½ (22½, 23½, 23½, 24½)"/57 (57, 59.5, 59.5, 62)cm, end with a WS row.

Neck shaping
Next row (RS) Work 46 (49, 52, 55, 59) sts, join 2nd ball of yarn and bind off 10 (12, 14, 16, 16) sts, work to end. Cont in pat, working both sides at once, bind off from each neck edge 3 sts twice, 2 sts 6 times, dec 1 st every other row once. When same length as back to shoulders, bind off rem 27 (30, 33, 36, 40) sts each side for shoulders.

SLEEVES
Cast on 37 (37, 42, 42, 47) sts. Work in rib pat, inc 1 st each side (working inc sts into rib) every 4th row 6 (15, 15, 22, 23) times, then every 6th row 18 (12, 12, 8, 8) times—85 (91, 96, 102, 109) sts.

Work even until piece measures 17 (17, 17, 18, 18)"/43 (43, 43, 45.5, 45.5)cm from beg. Bind off in rib.

FINISHING
Wet block only.

Neckband
With RS facing, pick up and k102 (110, 118, 126, 134) sts evenly across back neck edge. Work in St st for 8 rows. Bind off loosely. Work front neckband as for back. Mark center 8¼ (8½, 9, 9½, 9½)"/21 (21.5, 23, 24, 24)cm for neck on front and back neckband. Whipstitch shoulders tog, lapping front band over back. Place markers 7 (7½, 8, 8½, 9)"/17.5 (19, 20.5, 21.5, 23)cm down from shoulders on front and back for armholes. Sew top of sleeves between markers. Sew side and sleeve seams. With RS facing and crochet hook, sc evenly along lower edge of front and back. Join with sl st. Fasten off. ●

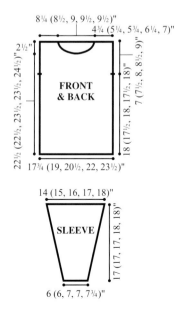

An alluring red angora blend gives this short-sleeved pullover star quality. Designed by fashion great Perry Ellis, it's standard-fitting with angled armholes and crew neck. Shown in size 34. The Angora Pullover first appeared in the Fall/Winter '87 issue of *Vogue Knitting*.

Angora Pullover

SIZES
To fit 30 (32, 34, 36, 38)"/76 (81, 86, 91, 96)cm bust. Directions are for smallest size with larger sizes in parentheses. If there is only one set of figures it applies to all sizes.

KNITTED MEASUREMENTS
● Bust 33 (34, 36, 38, 40)"/83 (85, 90, 96, 99)cm.
● Length 20 (20, 21, 21, 22)"/51 (51, 53, 53, 56)cm.
● Upper arm 16 (16, 17, 17, 18)"/41 (41, 43, 43, 46)cm.

MATERIALS
Original Yarn
● 27 (28, 28, 29, 29) ¹/₃oz/10g balls (each approx 35yd/30m) of Melrose *French Rabbit Hair Angora* (angora③) in red
Substitute Yarn
● 8 (8, 8, 9, 9) .88oz/25g balls (each approx 80yd/73m) of Adrienne Vittadini/JCA *Angelina* (angora/lambswool/alpaca④) in #8010 red
● One pair each sizes 5 and 7 (3.75 and 4.5mm) needles OR SIZE TO OBTAIN GAUGE
Note
The original yarn used for this sweater is no longer available. A comparable substitute has been made, which is available at the time of printing. Check gauge of substitute yarns very carefully before beginning.

GAUGE
22 sts and 26 rows to 4"/10cm over St st using size 7 (4.5mm) needles.

FOR PERFECT FIT, TAKE TIME TO CHECK GAUGE.

BACK
With smaller needles, cast on 81 (85, 85, 91, 95) sts. Work in k1, p1 rib for 2¹/₂"/6.5cm, inc 10 (8, 14, 14, 14) sts evenly across last row—91 (93, 99, 105, 109) sts. Change to larger needles. Work in St st (k on RS, p on WS) until piece measures 12 (12, 12¹/₂, 12¹/₂, 13)"/30.5 (30.5, 31.5, 31.5, 33)cm from beg.

Armhole shaping
Dec 1 st each side every other row 6 (6, 7, 9, 9) times—79 (81, 85, 87, 91) sts. Work even until armhole measures 8 (8, 8¹/₂, 8¹/₂, 9)"/20.5 (20.5, 21.5, 21.5, 23)cm. Bind off.

FRONT
Work as for back until armhole measures 5 (5, 5¹/₂, 5¹/₂, 6)"/13 (13, 14, 14, 15.5)cm, end with a WS row.

Neck shaping
Next row (RS) Work 34 (34, 36, 37, 39) sts, join 2nd ball of yarn and bind off center 11 (13, 13, 13, 13) sts, work to end. Working both sides at once, bind off from each neck edge 3 sts once, 2 sts 3 (3, 3, 4, 4) times, then dec 1 st every other row 4 (4, 4, 3, 4) times. When same length as back, bind off rem 21 (21, 23, 23, 24) sts each side.

SLEEVES
With smaller needles, cast on 61 (63, 63, 67, 69) sts. Work in k1, p1 rib for ³/₄"/2cm, inc 4 (2, 4, 0, 4) sts evenly across last row—65 (65, 67, 67, 73) sts. Change to larger needles. Work in St st,

inc 1 st each side every other row 12 (12, 13, 13, 13) times—89 (89, 93, 93, 99) sts. Work even until piece measures 5 (5, 5¹/₂, 5¹/₂, 6)"/13 (13, 14, 14, 15.5)cm from beg, end with a WS row.

Cap shaping
Dec 1 st each side every other row 6 (6, 7, 9, 9) times—77 (77, 79, 75, 81) sts. Bind off.

FINISHING
Block pieces. Sew left shoulder seam.

Neckband
With RS facing and smaller needles, beg at right shoulder, pick up and k104 (108, 108, 112, 114) sts evenly around entire neck edge. Work in k1, p1 rib for ³/₄"/2cm. Bind off in rib. Sew right shoulder seam including neckband. Sew top of sleeves to straight edge of armholes, then sew dec sts of front and back armholes to dec sts of sleeve. Sew side and sleeve seams. ●

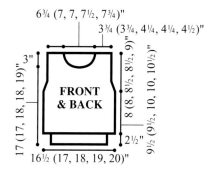

6³/₄ (7, 7, 7¹/₂, 7³/₄)"
3³/₄ (3³/₄, 4¹/₄, 4¹/₄, 4¹/₂)"
3"
17 (17, 18, 18, 19)"
8 (8, 8¹/₂, 8¹/₂, 9)"
9¹/₂ (9¹/₂, 10, 10, 10¹/₂)"
FRONT & BACK
2¹/₂"
16¹/₂ (17, 18, 19, 20)"

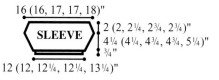

16 (16, 17, 17, 18)"
2 (2, 2¹/₄, 2³/₄, 2³/₄)"
4¹/₄ (4¹/₄, 4³/₄, 4³/₄, 5¹/₄)"
³/₄"
SLEEVE
12 (12, 12¹/₄, 12¹/₄, 13¹/₄)"

An ultra-chic jacket for a big night out. It's loose-fitting, with angled armholes and crocheted edging. Decorative braid adds a feminine finish. Designed by Lily Chin. Shown in size 36. The Chenille Jacket first appeared in the Winter '91/92 issue of *Vogue Knitting*.

Chenille Jacket

SIZES
To fit 32 (34, 36, 38, 40)"/81 (86, 91, 96, 101)cm bust. Directions are for smallest size with larger sizes in parentheses. If there is only one figure it applies to all sizes.

KNITTED MEASUREMENTS
● Bust (closed) 37½ (39½, 41½, 43½, 45½)"/95 (100.5, 105.5, 110.5, 115.5)cm.
● Length 18½ (18½, 19, 20, 21)"/47 (47, 48, 51, 53.5)cm.
● Upper arm 17 (17½, 18½, 19, 19½)"/43 (44.5, 47, 48, 49.5)cm.

MATERIALS
● 6 (6, 7, 7, 8) 3½oz/100g balls (each approx 72yd/67m) of Trendsetter *Cenci* (viscose/acrylic ⑥) in #99 black (MC)
● 2 1¾oz/50g balls (each approx 66yd /61m) of Trendsetter *Piatina* (viscose④) in #99 black (CC)
● One pair size 10½ (7mm) needles OR SIZE TO OBTAIN GAUGE
● Size G (4.5mm) crochet hook
● One large hook and eye (or fur hook)
● 3yd/2.75m of decorative black trim

GAUGE
8 sts and 14 rows to 4"/10cm over St st with MC using size 10½ (7mm) needles. FOR PERFFECT FIT, TAKE TIME TO CHECK GAUGE.

BACK
With MC, cast on 37 (39, 41, 43, 45) sts. Work in St st (k on RS, p on WS) until piece measures 10 (10, 10, 11, 11)"/25.5 (25.5, 25.5, 28, 28)cm from beg.

Armhole shaping
Dec 1 st each side every other row 4 (4, 4, 5, 5) times—29 (31, 33, 33, 35) sts. Work even until armhole measures 8½ (8½, 9, 9, 10)"/21.5 (21.5, 23, 23, 25.5)cm. Bind off.

LEFT FRONT
With MC, cast on 19 (20, 21, 22, 23) sts. Work in St st until same length as back to armhole. Work armhole shaping at side edge only (beg of RS rows) as for back—15 (16, 17, 17, 18) sts. Work even in pat until armhole measures 6 (6, 6½, 6½, 7½)"/15 (15, 16.5, 16.5, 19)cm, end with a RS row.

Neck shaping
Next row (WS) Bind off 3 (4, 4, 5, 5) sts (neck edge), work to end. Bind off 2 sts from neck edge once, then dec 1 st every other row twice. When same length as back to shoulders, bind off 8 (8, 9, 8, 9) sts.

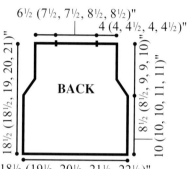

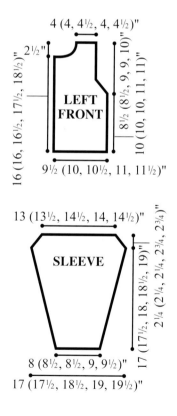

RIGHT FRONT

Work as for left front, beg neck shaping on a RS row to reverse shaping.

SLEEVES

With MC, cast on 16 (17, 17, 18, 19) sts. Work in St st, inc 1 st each side every 6th row 9 (9, 10, 10, 10) times—34 (35, 37, 38, 39) sts. Work even until piece measures 17 (17$\frac{1}{2}$, 18, 18$\frac{1}{2}$, 19)"/43 (44.5, 45.5, 47, 48)cm from beg.

Cap shaping

Dec 1 st each side every other row 4 (4, 4, 5, 5) times—26 (27, 29, 28, 29) sts. Bind off.

FINISHING

Wet block pieces. Do not press. Sew shoulder seams. Sew top of sleeves to straight edge of armholes, then sew dec sts of front and back armholes to dec sts of sleeve. Sew side and sleeve seams.

Edging

With RS facing, crochet hook and CC, beg at right front lower edge, sc along front edge, neck edge, left front edge and lower edge, working 3 sc in corners. Join. Work 1 rnd of backwards crochet (crab st). Fasten off. Work 1 row of sc around sleeve edges. Join. Work 1 rnd of backwards crochet. Fasten off. Sew trim on inside (WS) edge of crochet edging. Sew hook and eye at neck edge. •

That famous Missoni magic is captured in a close-fitting crewneck pullover with set-in sleeves and ridge-patterned details. Shown in size 32. The Short-Sleeve Pullover first appeared in the Spring/Summer '89 issue of *Vogue Knitting*.

Short-Sleeve Pullover

SIZES
To fit 32 (34, 36, 38, 40)"/81 (86, 91, 96, 101)cm bust. Directions are for smallest size with larger sizes in parentheses. If there is only one figure it applies to all sizes.

KNITTED MEASUREMENTS
● Bust 32½ (34½, 36, 38, 40½)"/81 (86, 91, 96, 102)cm.
● Waist 28 (29½, 31½, 32½, 36)"/69 (74, 78.5, 84, 90)cm.
● Length 23¾ (24¼, 24¼, 24¾, 24¾)"/60.5 (61.5, 61.5, 63, 63)cm.
● Upper arm 12 (12¾, 12¾, 13, 13)"/30 (31.5, 31.5, 32.5, 32.5)cm.

MATERIALS
Original Yarn
● 7 (8, 8, 9, 10) 1¾oz/50g balls (each approx 208yd/190m) of Filatura Di Crosa/Stacy Charles *Lipari* (cotton/polyester①) in #107 purple
Substitute Yarn
● 7 (8, 8, 9, 10) .88oz/25g balls (each approx 216yd/200m) of Mondial/Skacel Collection *Cablé 5* (cotton①) in #634 red
● One pair each sizes 1 and 2 (2.25 and 2.75mm) needles OR SIZE TO OBTAIN GAUGE
Note
The original yarn used for this sweater is no longer available. A comparable substitute has been made, which is available at the time of printing. Check gauge of substitute yarns very carefully before beginning.

GAUGE
● 33 sts and 42 rows to 4"/10cm over St st using size 2 (2.75mm) needles.
● 33 sts and 60 rows to 4"/10cm over ridge pat using size 2 (2.75mm) needles. FOR PERFECT FIT, TAKE TIME TO CHECK GAUGES.

STITCH GLOSSARY
Ridge Pat
*P 1 row (RS), k 1 row, p 2 rows, k 1 row, p 1 row, k 2 rows, p 1 row, k 2 rows, p 1 row, k 1 row, p 1 row; rep from * (14 rows) for ridge pat.

BACK
With smaller needles, cast on 132 (140, 148, 156, 168) sts. Work in k2, p2 rib for ¾"/2cm, inc 2 (2, 2, 2, 0) sts evenly across last row—134 (142, 150, 158, 168) sts. Change to larger needles. Work in St st (k on RS, p on WS) until piece measures 3¾"/9.5cm from beg. Dec 1 st each side on next row and rep dec every 4th row 9 times more—114 (122, 130, 138, 148) sts. Work even until piece measures 8"/20.5cm from beg. Inc 1 st each side on next row, then rep inc every 6th row 7 times more, end with a WS row—130 (138, 146, 154, 164) sts. Work in ridge pat, AT SAME TIME, cont inc every 6th row twice more—134 (142, 150, 158, 168) sts. Work even until piece measures 14¾"/37.5cm from beg.

Armhole shaping
Cont ridge pat, dec 1 st each side every 4th row 9 times—116 (124, 132, 140, 150) sts. Work even until armhole measures 7½ (8, 8, 8½, 8½)"/19 (20, 20, 21.5, 21.5)cm.

Neck and shoulder shaping
Next row (RS) Work 50 (53, 55, 58, 61) sts, join 2nd ball of yarn and bind off 16 (18, 22, 24, 30) sts, work to end. Working both sides at once, bind off from each neck edge 3 sts twice, 2 sts 5 times, then dec 1 st every other row 4 times, AT SAME TIME, when armhole measures 8 (8½, 8½, 9, 9)"/20.5 (21.5, 21.5, 23, 23)cm, bind off from each shoulder edge 5 (4, 5, 5, 5) sts twice, 4 (5, 5, 5, 5) sts twice, 4 (5, 5, 6, 7) sts 3 times.

FRONT
Work as for back until armhole measures 5½ (6, 6, 6½, 6½)"/14 (15, 15, 16.5, 16.5)cm, end with a WS row.

Neck shaping
Next row (RS) Work 53 (56, 58, 61, 64) sts, join 2nd ball of yarn and bind off 10 (12, 16, 18, 24) sts, work to end. Working both sides at once, bind off from each neck edge 2 sts 3 times, then dec 1 st every other row 13 times, then every 4th row 4 times, AT SAME TIME, when same length as back to shoulder, shape shoulder as for back.

SLEEVES
With smaller needles, cast on 84 (88, 88, 92, 92) sts. Work in k2, p2 rib for ¾"/2cm, inc 10 sts evenly spaced across last row—94 (98, 98, 102, 102) sts. Change to larger needles. Work in ridge pat, inc 1 st each side every 8th row 3 times—100 (104, 104, 108, 108) sts. Work even until piece measures 2¾"/7cm from beg.

Cap shaping

Cont ridge pat, *dec 1 st each side of next row. Work 3 rows even. Dec 1 st each side of next row. Work 1 row even.* Rep between *'s 16 (18, 18, 18, 18) times more. Dec 1 st each side every other row 2 (0, 0, 6, 6) times, every row 12 (12, 12, 8, 8) times. Bind off rem 4 sts.

FINISHING

Block pieces. Sew left shoulder seam.

Neckband

With RS facing and smaller needles, pick up and k128 (132, 136, 140, 144) sts around entire neck edge. Work in k2, p2 rib for ¾"/2cm. Bind off in rib. Sew right shoulder seam, including neckband. Set in sleeves. Sew side and sleeve seams. •

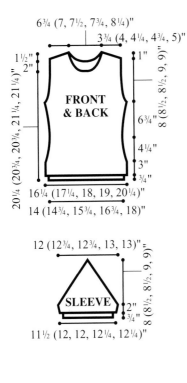

A simply elegant tunic knit in luminous metallic silver with side slits and a flattering ballet neckline. The tunic is oversized with crocheted edges and features fully-fashioned raglan sleeves. A Vogue Original. Shown in size Medium. The Ballet-Neck Tunic first appeared in the Winter '95/96 issue of *Vogue Knitting*.

Ballet-Neck Tunic

SIZES
To fit Small (Medium, Large, X-Large). Directions are for smallest size with larger sizes in parentheses. If there is only one figure it applies to all sizes.

KNITTED MEASUREMENTS
● Bust 44 (47, 51, 54)"/111.5 (119, 129.5, 137)cm.
● Length 24 (24^1/$_2$, 25, 25^1/$_2$)"/61 (62, 63.5, 65)cm.
● Upper arm 13 (13^1/$_2$, 14, 14^1/$_2$)"/33 (34, 35.5, 37)cm.

MATERIALS
Original Yarn
● 10 (11, 11, 12) 1^3/$_4$oz/50g balls (each approx 98yd/85m) of Classic Elite/Tiber *Rayon de Soleil* (viscose/polyamide③) in #2654 silver (A)
● 11 (12, 12, 13) 1oz/25g balls (each approx 92yd/84m) of Classic Elite/Tiber *Doreale* (viscose/rayon③) in #4601 silver (B)
Substitute Yarn
● 18 (20, 20, 21) .88oz/25g hanks (each approx 85yd/78m) of Berroco, Inc. *Metallica* (rayon/metallic③) in #1002 silver
● One pair size 10^1/$_2$ (6.5mm) needles OR SIZE TO OBTAIN GAUGE
● Size H (5mm) crochet hook
Note
The original yarn used for this sweater is no longer available. A comparable substitute has been made, which is available at the time of printing. Check gauge of substitute yarns very carefully before beginning.

GAUGE
15 sts and 20 rows to 4"/10cm over St st using 2 strands held tog and size 10^1/$_2$ (6.5mm) needles.
FOR PERFECT FIT, TAKE TIME TO CHECK GAUGE.
Note
Use 2 strands held tog throughout.

STITCH GLOSSARY
SKP Sl 1, k1, psso.
SK2P Sl 1, k2tog, psso the k2tog.

BACK
With 2 stands held tog, cast on 84 (90, 98, 103) sts.
Row 1 (RS) Knit.
Row 2 K1, (selvage st), p to last st, k1 (selvage st). Rep rows 1 and 2 for St st for 40 rows or approx 8"/20.5 cm. Place yarn markers at each end of row for side slits. Cont in St st until piece measures 14^1/$_2$"/37cm from beg, end with a WS row.

Raglan armhole shaping
Bind off 3 (4, 4, 4) sts at beg of next 2 rows. Work 2 rows even.
***Dec row 1 (RS)** k3, k3tog (for 2 sts dec), k to last 6 sts, SK2P (2 sts dec), k3. Work 3 rows even.
Dec row 2 (RS) k3, k2tog (for 1 st dec), k to last 5 sts, SKP (1 st dec), k3. Work 3 rows even *. Rep between *'s 3 (4, 3, 3) times more. On next row, dec 1 (0, 2, 2) sts each side and rep this dec every 4th row 1 (0, 2, 3) times. Work 1 (0, 1, 1) row even on 50 (52, 54, 55) sts.

Neck shaping
Next row (RS) Work 15 (15, 16, 16), join 2nd balls of yarn and bind off center 20 (22, 22, 23) sts, work to end. Working both sides at once, bind off 4 sts from each neck edge twice—7 (7, 8, 8) sts rem each side. P 1 row, then bind off rem sts for shoulders.

FRONT
Work as for back until armhole measures approx 6^1/$_2$ (7, 7^1/$_2$, 8)"/16.5 (18, 19, 20.5)cm and there are 54 (58, 62, 63) sts, end with a WS row.

Neck shaping
(Note: Cont to work raglan armhole shaping as on back.)
Next row (RS) Work 17 (18, 20, 20), join 2nd ball of yarn and bind off center 20 (22, 22, 23) sts, work to end. Working both sides at once, bind off 2 sts from each neck edge 4 times. After armhole decs, work even on shoulder sts until same length as back. Bind off rem sts for shoulders.

SLEEVES
With 2 strands held tog, cast on 32 (34, 34, 36) sts. Work in St st as for back (with selvage sts) inc 1 st each side every 8th (8th, 6th, 6th) row 9 (9, 10, 10) times—50 (52, 54, 56) sts. Work even until piece measures 15^1/$_2$"/39.5 cm from beg.

Raglan cap shaping
Bind off 3 (4, 4, 4) sts at beg of next 2 rows. Work 0 (0, 0, 2) rows even. Rep between *'s on back raglan armhole a total of 4 (5, 5, 5) times. ** Dec 1 st each side of next row. Work 1 row even **. Rep between **'s 3 (0, 1, 2) times more. Dec 2 sts each side of next row. Work 1 row even. Bind off rem 8 sts.

FINISHING

Block pieces to measurements. Sew raglan sleeves to armholes. Sew sleeve seams. Sew side seams to markers leaving 8"/20.5cm side slits. With crochet hook and 2 stands held tog, work sc evenly around neck edge. Ch1, do not turn, and working *backwards* (from left to right) work 1 backwards sc in each sc around. Work sc and backwards sc edge in same way around sleeve cuffs and around lower edge and side slits. •

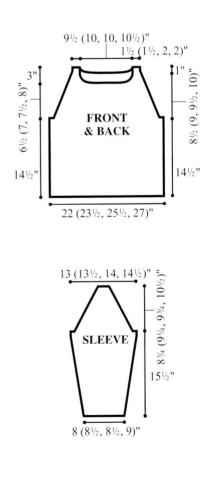

9½ (10, 10, 10½)"

1½ (1½, 2, 2)"

3"

1"

6½ (7, 7½, 8)"

8½ (9, 9½, 10)"

FRONT & BACK

14½"

14½"

22 (23½, 25½, 27)"

13 (13½, 14, 14½)"

8¾ (9¼, 9¾, 10½)"

SLEEVE

15½"

8 (8½, 8½, 9)"

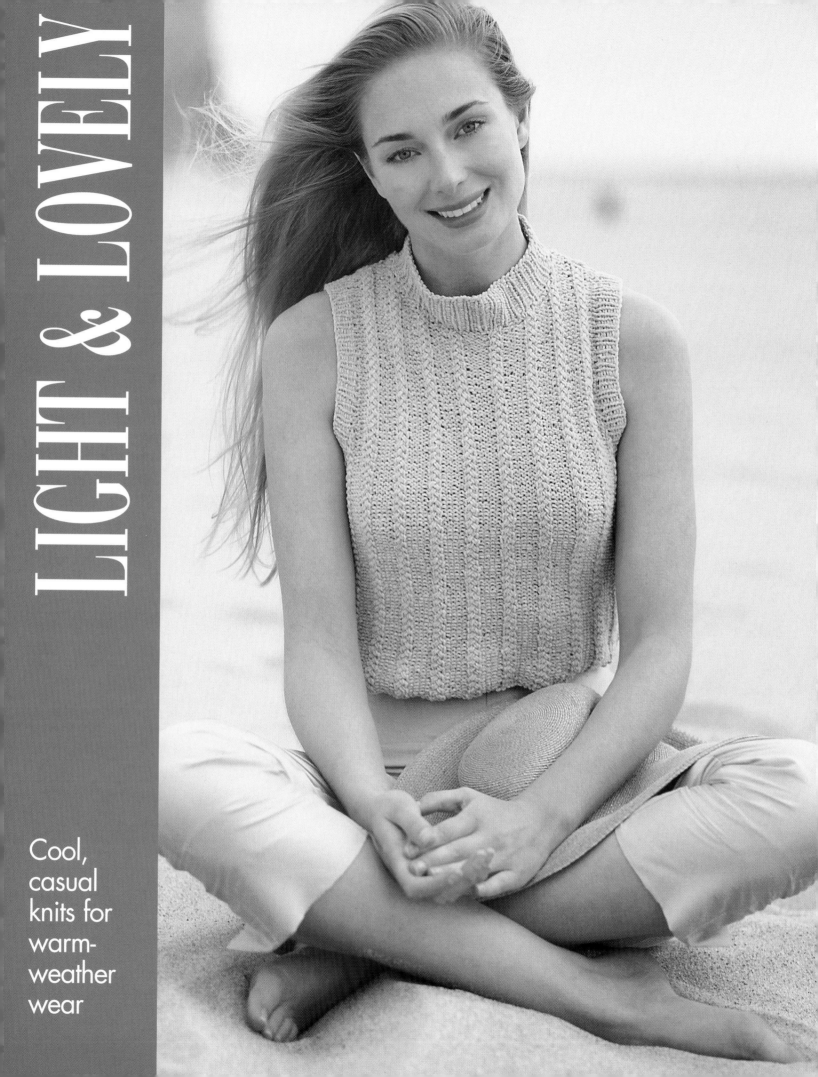

LIGHT & LOVELY

Cool, casual knits for warm-weather wear

Candy color and a braided rib pattern turn a fashion basic into a weekend winner. The sleeveless crop top is standard-fitting with a stylish mock-turtleneck. Keep the top short or lengthen to suit your figure. Designed by Melissa Leapman. Shown in size Medium. The Braided-Rib Crop Top first appeared in the Spring/Summer '97 issue of *Vogue Knitting*.

Braided-Rib Crop Top

SIZES
To fit Small (Medium, Large). Directions are for smallest size with larger sizes in parentheses. If there is only one figure it applies to all sizes.

KNITTED MEASUREMENTS
● Bust 35½ (38, 41)"/90 (96.5, 104)cm.
● Length 16 (16, 17½)"/40.5 (40.5, 44.5)cm.

MATERIALS
● 4 (5, 6) 1¾oz/50g balls (each approx 143yd/130m) of GGH/Muench *Cotton Velours* (cotton④) in #2 lilac
● One pair each sizes 5 and 6 (3.75mm and 4mm) needles OR SIZE TO OBTAIN GAUGE

GAUGE
21 sts and 28 rows to 4"/10cm over Braided Rib pat, using size 6 (4mm) needles.
FOR PERFECT FIT, TAKE TIME TO CHECK GAUGE.

STITCH GLOSSARY
2-st Left Twist (LT) (worked on RS rows)
With RH needle behind work, k 2nd st on LH needle through back lp (tbl), leave st on needle; then k first st through front lp; sl both sts from needle.

2-st Right Twist (RT) (worked on WS rows)
P 2nd st on LH needle, leave st on needle; p first st; sl both sts from needle.

Braided Rib Pat (over a multiple of 7 sts, plus 2)
Row 1 (RS) P1, *p2, 2LT, k1, p2; rep from *, end p1.
Row 2 K1, *k2, 2RT, p1, k2; rep from *, end k1. Rep rows 1 and 2 for Braided Rib Pat.

BACK
With larger needles, cast on 93 (100, 107) sts. Work in Braided Rib Pat until piece measures 8 (8, 9)"/20.5 (20.5, 23)cm from beg, end with a WS row.

Armhole shaping
Bind off 6 sts at beg of next 2 rows, 3 sts at beg of next 4 rows, 2 sts at beg of next 2 rows. Dec 1 st each side on next row, then every other row 2 (5, 5) times more—59 (60, 67) sts. Work even until armhole measures 7 (7, 7½)"/17.5 (17.5, 19)cm, end with a WS row.

Shoulder shaping
Next row (RS) Bind off 4 (4, 5) sts at beg of next 4 rows, 3 (4, 5) sts at beg of next 2 rows. Bind off rem 37 (36, 37) sts.

FRONT
Work as for back until armhole measures 6 (6, 6½)"/15 (15, 16.5)cm, end with a WS row.

Neck shaping
Next row (RS) Work in pat across 22 (23, 26) sts, join 2nd ball of yarn and bind off center 15 (14, 15) sts, work to end. Working both sides at once, bind off from each neck edge 4 sts once, 3 sts once, 2 sts once, then dec 1 st at each neck edge every other row twice, AT SAME TIME, when piece measures same length as back to shoulder, shape shoulders each side as for back.

FINISHING
Block pieces. Sew left shoulder seam.

Neckband
With RS facing and smaller needles, beg at right back shoulder, pick up and k70 sts evenly around neck edge. Work in k1, p1 rib for 1¼"/3cm. Bind off loosely in rib. Sew right shoulder seam, including neckband.

Armhole bands
With RS facing and smaller needles, beg at underarm and pick up and k90 (90, 94) sts evenly around armhole edge. Work in k1, p1 rib for ¾"/2cm. Bind loosely in rib. Sew side seams, including armhole bands. ●

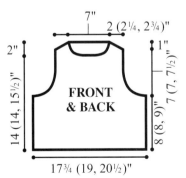

Fluid ribbon yarn and trapeze shaping transform a basic pullover into a summer standout. The sweater is sleeveless and loose-fitting with a scooped neck and ribbed armhole and neck bands. Designed by Laurie MacMillan. Shown in size 36. The Trapeze-Shaped Pullover first appeared in the Spring/Summer '92 issue of *Vogue Knitting*.

Trapeze-Shaped Pullover

SIZES
To fit 32 (34, 36, 38)"/81 (86, 91, 96)cm. Directions are for smallest size with larger sizes in parentheses. If there is only one figure it applies to all sizes.

KNITTED MEASUREMENTS
● Bust 36 (38, 40, 42$\frac{1}{2}$)"/91.5 (96.5, 101.5, 108)cm.
● Length 19$\frac{1}{2}$ (20$\frac{1}{2}$, 21, 22)"/49.5 (52, 53.5, 56)cm.

MATERIALS
● 8 (9, 9, 10) 1$\frac{3}{4}$oz/50g balls (each approx 109yd/100m) of Anny Blatt *Victoria* (polyamide③) in #160 tan
● One pair each sizes 6 and 7 (4 and 4.5mm) needles OR SIZE TO OBTAIN GAUGE
● Size 6 (4mm) circular needle, 24"/60cm long
● Stitch markers

Note
The original color used for this sweater is no longer available. A comparable color substitute has been made, which is available at the time of printing.

GAUGE
22 sts and 29 rows to 4"/10cm over St st using size 7 (4.5mm) needles. FOR PERFECT FIT, TAKE TIME TO CHECK GAUGE.

BACK
With smaller needles, cast on 179 (193, 207, 221) sts. Work in k1, p1 rib for $\frac{3}{4}$"/2cm, dec 44 (48, 52, 56) sts evenly across last WS row—135 (145, 155, 165) sts. Change to larger needles. Work in St st (k on RS, p on WS) for 8 rows.
Dec row (RS) K1, place marker (pm), ssk, k62 (67, 72, 77), k2tog, pm, k1, pm, ssk, k62 (67, 72, 77), k2tog, pm, k1. Cont in St st, dec 1 st before or after each marker as established every 8th row 8 (9, 7, 7) times, every 6th row 0 (0, 3, 4) times—99 (105, 111, 117) sts. Work even until piece measures 11$\frac{1}{2}$ (12, 12$\frac{1}{2}$, 13)"/29 (30.5, 32, 33)cm from beg, end with a WS row.

Armhole shaping
Bind off 5 (5, 6, 6) sts at beg of next 2 rows, 3 sts at beg of next 2 (2, 4, 4) rows, 2 sts at beg of next 4 rows. Dec 1 st each side every other row 7 (7, 6, 7) times—61 (67, 67, 71) sts. Work even until armhole measures 6 (6$\frac{1}{2}$, 6$\frac{1}{2}$, 7)"/15 (16.5, 16.5, 18)cm, end with a WS row.

Neck shaping
Next row (RS) K16 (17, 17, 18) sts, join 2nd ball of yarn and bind off 29 (33, 33, 35) sts, work to end. Working both sides at once, bind off from each neck edge 2 sts twice, dec 1 st every other row 4 times. When armhole measures 8 (8$\frac{1}{2}$, 8$\frac{1}{2}$, 9)"/20.5 (21.5, 21.5, 23)cm, bind off rem 8 (9, 9, 10) sts each side.

FRONT
Work as for back until piece measures 3 (3$\frac{1}{2}$, 3$\frac{1}{2}$, 4)"/7.5 (9, 9, 10)cm from beg of armhole shaping, end with a WS row.

Neck shaping
Next row (RS) K23 (26, 26, 28) sts. Join 2nd ball of yarn and bind off 15 sts, work to end. Working both sides at once, bind off from each neck edge 2 sts twice, dec 1 st every other row 9 (12, 12, 13) times, then 1 st every 4th row 2 (1, 1, 1) times. When piece measures same length as back to shoulder, bind off rem 8 (9, 9, 10) sts each side.

FINISHING
Block pieces. Do not press. Sew shoulder seams.

Neckband
With RS facing and circular needle, pick up and k144 (150, 150, 154) sts evenly around neck opening. Join, mark beg of rnd. Work in k1, p1 rib for $\frac{3}{4}$"/2cm. Bind off loosely.

Armhole bands
With RS facing and smaller needles, pick up and k101 (107, 107, 111) sts along armhole edge. Work in k1, p1 rib for $\frac{3}{4}$"/2cm. Bind off. Sew side seams, including armhole bands.●

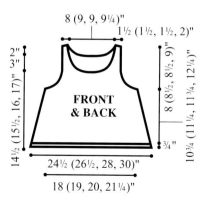

Relaxed lines and chic texture lend this scooped tank top casual appeal. The loose-fitting, elongated sleeveless pullover can be knit in either a solid or striped ribbed pattern. Designed by Adri. The Ribbed Tank first appeared in the Spring/Summer '83 issue of *Vogue Knitting*.

Ribbed Tank

SIZES
To fit 32 (34, 38)"/81 (86, 96)cm bust. Directions are for smallest size with larger sizes in parentheses. If there is only one set of figures it applies to all sizes.

KNITTED MEASUREMENTS
- Bust 36 (38, 40)"/90 (96, 99)cm.
- Length 26"/66cm.

MATERIALS
Original Yarn
PLAIN TANK:
- 8 (9, 10) 1¾oz/50g balls (each approx 110yd/100m) of Scheepjeswol *Granada* (cotton②) in #549 light turquoise (CC)

STRIPED TANK:
- 5 (6, 7) balls in #540 khaki (MC)
- 5 (6, 7) balls in #549 light turquoise (CC)

Substitute Yarn
PLAIN TANK:
- 8 (9, 10) 1¾oz/50g balls (each approx 113yd/113m) of Phildar *Phil Flamme* (cotton/acrylic/viscose④) in #003 jean's (CC)

STRIPED TANK:
- 5 (6, 7) balls in #056 marine (MC)
- 5 (6, 7) balls in #003 jean's (CC)
- Size 7 (4.5mm) circular needle, 24"/60cm long OR SIZE TO OBTAIN GAUGE
- Stitch markers and holders

Note
The original yarn used for this sweater is no longer available. A comparable substitute has been made, which is available at the time of printing. Check gauge of substitute yarns very carefully before beginning.

GAUGE
20 sts and 36 rows to 4"/10cm over garter st using size 7 (4.5mm) needle. FOR PERFECT FIT, TAKE TIME TO CHECK GAUGE.

PLAIN TANK

BACK
With CC (and using CC throughout), cast on 92 (98, 101) sts. Working back and forth on circular needles, beg big rib pat as foll:
Row 1 (RS) P2, *k1, p2; rep from * to end.
Row 2 *K2, p1; rep from *, end k2. Rep rows 1 and 2 until piece measures 2"/5cm, end with a WS row. Then beg working garter st (k every row), for 1¾"/4.5cm, end with a WS row. Cont working big rib pat for 2"/5cm and garter st for 1¾"/4.5cm alternately until piece measures 17"/43cm from beg, end with a WS row. Place marker at each end of row.

Armhole shaping
Cont in pat, dec 1 st each side of every other row 13 (14, 14) times—66 (70, 73) sts. Work even in pat until piece measures 3½"/9cm from armhole marker, end with a WS row.

Neck shaping
Work 22 (24, 24) sts in pat, place rem 44 (46, 49) sts on holder. Bind off 2 sts at neck edge on every other row 3 (4, 4) times—16 sts. Dec 1 st at neck edge on every other row 8 times—8 sts. Work even in pat until armhole measures 9"/23cm. Bind off. Leaving 22 (22, 25) sts on holder for center front, work rem 22 (24, 24) sts in pat. Work one row in pat. Bind off 2 sts at neck edge on every other row 3 (4, 4) times—16 sts. Dec 1 st at neck edge on every other row 8 times—8 sts. Work even in pat until armhole measures 9"/23cm. Bind off.

FRONT
Work as for back.

FINISHING
Do not press. Sew shoulder seams.

Neckband
With RS facing beg at right shoulder neck edge, pick up and k34 (36, 36) sts along right back neck edge, k22 (22, 25) sts from center back holder, pick up and k34 (36, 36) sts along left back neck edge to shoulder, pick up and k34 (36, 36) sts along left front neck edge, k22 (22, 25) sts from center front holder, pick up and k34 (36, 36) sts along right front neck edge to shoulder—180 (188, 194) sts. Join, mark beg of rnd. Work in k1, p1 rib for 5/8"/1.5cm. Bind off in rib.

Armhole bands
With RS facing beg at armhole marker, pick up and k46 sts to shoulder, pick up and k46 sts from shoulder to armhole marker—92 sts. Work in k1, p1 rib for 5/8"/1.5cm. Bind off in rib. Sew side seams including armhole bands

STRIPED TANK

Note
Work big rib pat stripe in MC and garter st stripe in CC.

BACK

With MC, cast on 92 (98, 101) sts. Beg big rib pat stripe as foll:

Row 1 (RS) P2, *k1, p2; rep from * to end.
Row 2 *K2, p1; rep from *, end k2. Rep rows 1 and 2 until piece measures 2"/5cm, end with a WS row. Change to CC and work in garter st (k every row), for 1¾"/4.5cm, end with a WS row. Change to MC and k one row (RS). Beg with row 2 (WS) of big rib pat, rep rows 1 and 2 as above for 2"/5cm, end with a WS row. Cont working big rib pat stripe with MC for 2"/5cm and garter st with CC for 1¾"/4.5cm alternately until piece measures 17"/43cm from beg, end with a WS row. Work armhole shaping, neck shaping, front and finishing as for plain tank top, but keeping to pat as set for striped tank top. •

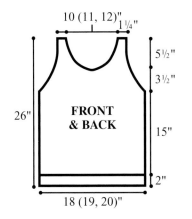

Calvin Klein incorporates simple lines, a spare shape and comfortable cotton fibers in this ultra-cool cropped tank. The close-fitting top features a buttoned scoop-back neck and crochet edging. The Scoop-Back Crop Top first appeared in the Spring/Summer '85 issue of *Vogue Knitting*.

Scoop-Back Crop Top

SIZES
To fit 32 (34, 36, 38)"/81 (86, 91, 96)cm bust. Directions are for smallest size with larger sizes in parentheses. If there is only one set of figures it applies to all sizes.

KNITTED MEASUREMENTS
● Bust 32 (34, 36, 38)"/80 (84, 89, 96)cm.
● Length 14½ (15, 15½, 16)"/36.5 (38, 39.5, 40.5)cm.

MATERIALS
Original Yarn
● 6 (6, 7, 7) 1¾oz/50g balls (each approx 140yd/127m) of Phildar *Detente* (cotton④) in #10 white
Substitute Yarn
● 8 (8, 9, 9) 1¾oz/50g balls (each approx 108yd/100m) of Garnstudio/Aurora Yarns *Muskat* (cotton③) in #18 white
● One pair size 9 (5.5mm) needles OR SIZE TO OBTAIN GAUGE
● Size F (4mm) crochet hook
● Three ⅝"/15mm buttons
Note
The original yarn used for this sweater is no longer available. A comparable substitute has been made, which is available at the time of printing. Check gauge of substitute yarns very carefully before beginning.

GAUGE
18 sts and 25 rows to 4"/10cm over St st with 2 strands of yarn using size 9 (5.5mm) needles.
FOR PERFECT FIT, TAKE TIME TO CHECK GAUGE.
Note
Use 2 strands of yarn held tog throughout.

FRONT
With 2 strands of yarn, cast on 64 (66, 68, 72) sts. Work in St st (k on RS, p on WS), inc 1 st each side every 6th row 4 (5, 6, 7) times—72 (76, 80, 86) sts. Work even until piece measures 6 (6, 6½, 6½)"/15 (15, 16.5, 16.5)cm from beg, end with a WS row.

Armhole shaping
Bind off 3 sts at beg of next 2 rows. Dec 1 st each side every other row twice—62 (66, 70, 76) sts. Work even until armhole measures 5½ (6, 6, 6½)"/14 (15.5, 15.5, 16.5)cm, end with a WS row.

Neck shaping
Next row (RS) Work across first 23 (24, 25, 27) sts, join 2nd ball of yarn and bind off center 16 (18, 20, 22) sts, work to end. Working both sides at once, bind off from each neck edge 3 sts twice, 2 sts once, 1 st 4 (3, 2,1) times—11 (13, 15, 18) sts each side. Work even until armhole measures 8½ (9, 9, 9½)"/21.5 (23, 23, 24)cm. Bind off all sts.

RIGHT BACK
With 2 strands of yarn, cast on 34 (35, 36, 38) sts. Work in St st, inc 1 st at beg of every 6th (RS) row 4 (5, 6, 7) times, AT SAME TIME, when piece measures 4½ (5, 5½, 6)"/11.5 (13, 14, 15.5)cm from beg, end with a RS row.

Neck shaping
Next row (WS) Cont inc at side edge, bind off from neck edge (beg of WS rows) 9 sts once, then 3 sts once, 2 sts once, 1 st 3 times, then dec 1 st every 4th row 5 times, AT SAME TIME, when piece measures same length as front to armhole, bind off 3 sts from armhole edge once, then dec 1 st at same edge twice—11 (13, 15, 18) sts. Work even

until piece measures same length as front. Bind off all sts. Mark back edge for 3 buttons, first in 2nd row from beg, last 2 rows below first neck dec, rem marker spaced evenly between.

LEFT BACK
Work as for right back reversing all shaping, and working buttonholes opposite markers as foll:
Buttonhole row 1 (RS) K1, bind off 2 sts, k to end.
Buttonhole row 2 Purl, casting on 2 sts over bound-off sts.

FINISHING
Block pieces to measurements. Sew shoulder and side seams.

Armhole edging
With RS facing, crochet hook and 2 strands of yarn, beg at side seam, work 1 row of sc evenly around armhole. Fasten off.

Outside edging
With RS facing, crochet hook and 2 strands of yarn, beg at right side seam, work 1 row of sc evenly along bottom edge, center back edges and neck edge, working 3 sc in each corner. Sew on buttons. ●

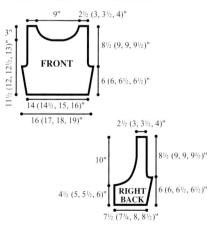

Perfect for hot summer days, this close-fitting ballerina top knit in bright white features ribbed panels, short dolman sleeves and a scooped boatneck. Designed by Katarina Ronnlund-Linden. Shown in size 34. The Short-Sleeve Ribbed Pullover first appeared in the Spring/Summer '87 issue of *Vogue Knitting*.

Short-Sleeve Ribbed Pullover

SIZES
To fit 30 (32, 34, 36)"/76 (81, 86, 91)cm bust. Directions are for smallest size with larger sizes in parentheses. If there is only one set of figures it applies to all sizes.

KNITTED MEASUREMENTS
- Bust 30 (32, 34, 36)"/76 (81, 86, 91)cm.
- Length 19 (20, 20½, 21½)"/47.5 (49.5, 51, 53.5)cm.
- Width from sleeve band to sleeve band 24 (25, 25½, 27½)"/59 (63, 65, 69)cm.

MATERIALS
Original Yarn
- 5 (6, 6, 7) 1¾oz/50g balls (each approx 110yd/100m) of Bernat *Gloucester Sport* (cotton③) in #36242 white
Substitute Yarn
- 3 (4, 4, 5) 3½oz/100g skeins (each approx 185yd/170m) of Reynolds/JCA *Saucy* (cotton③) in #800 white
- One pair each sizes 5 and 7 (3.75 and 4.5mm) needles OR SIZE TO OBTAIN GAUGE
- Stitch markers and holders
Note
The original yarn used for this sweater is no longer available. A comparable substitute has been made, which is available at the time of printing. Check gauge of substitute yarns very carefully before beginning.

GAUGE
21 sts and 28 rows to 4"/10cm over St st using size 7 (4.5mm) needles.

FOR PERFECT FIT, TAKE TIME TO CHECK GAUGE.
Notes
1 For easier working of pats, keep careful count of rows.
2 K first and last st of every row for selvage sts.

BACK
With smaller needles, cast on 72 (80, 84, 92) sts. Beg rib pat:
Row 1 (RS) K1 (selvage st), *k2, p2; rep from *, end k2, k1 (selvage st).
Row 2 K1, p2, *k2, p2; rep from *, end k1. Rep last 2 rows for 1"/2.5cm from beg. Change to larger needles and cont in rib until piece measures 5½ (6, 6½, 7)"/14 (15, 16.5, 17.5)cm from beg. Cont in rib and inc for dolman as foll:
Row 1 (RS) K1, work next 6 in St st (k on RS, p on WS), rib to last 7 sts, work 6 sts in St st, k1. Work 4 rows even, then inc 1 st each end (working inc sts in St st) every 4th row twice, every other row 19 times, AT SAME TIME, work pat as foll:
Next 5 rows K the k sts and p the p sts.
Next row (RS) K1, work next 10 sts in St st, rib to last 11 sts, work next 10 sts in St st, k1. Cont in pat working 4 less sts in rib every 6th row until 10 (10, 14, 14) sts rem in rib. Cont working these center sts in rib and work all other sts in St st. After all inc have been worked, there are 114 (122, 126, 134) sts and piece measures approx 12½ (13, 13½, 14)"/32 (33, 34.5, 35.5)cm from beg. Mark each side of last row for beg of sleeve. Work even until piece measures 17 (18, 18½, 19½)"/42.5 (44.5, 46, 48.5)cm from beg, end with a WS row.

Neck and shoulder shaping
Next row (RS) Work across 49 (51, 53, 55) sts, join 2nd ball of yarn and bind off next 3 (5, 3, 5) sts, rib center 10 (10, 14, 14) sts and place on a holder, bind off next 3 (5, 3, 5) sts, work to end. Working both sides at once, bind off 3 sts from each neck edge 6 times, AT SAME TIME, after 1"/2.5cm of neck shaping has been worked, bind off from each armhole edge 10 (11, 12, 13) sts twice, 11 sts once.

FRONT
Work as for back.

FINISHING
Block pieces. Sew left shoulder seam.

Neckband
With RS facing and smaller needles, beg at right shoulder, pick up and k29 (33, 29, 33) sts to center rib sts, rib across sts from holder, pick up and k58 (66, 58, 66) sts to center rib sts on front, rib across sts from holder, pick up and k29 (33, 29, 33) sts to end—136 (152, 144, 160) sts.
Next row (WS) K1, p2, *k2, p2, rep from *, end k1. Cont in k2, p2 rib (making sure to match center rib sts), for 1"/2.5cm. Bind off in rib. Sew right shoulder seam, including neckband.

Sleeve bands
With RS facing and smaller needles, beg at underarm edge, pick up and k78 (82, 82, 86) sts along sleeve edge. Work in k2, p2 rib for 1"/2.5cm. Bind off in rib. Sew side seams including sleeve band.●

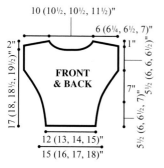

10 (10½, 10½, 11½)"

6 (6¼, 6½, 7)"

2"

17 (18, 18½, 19½)"

1"

FRONT & BACK

7"

5½ (6, 6, 6½)"

12 (13, 14, 15)"

15 (16, 17, 18)"

5½ (6, 6½, 7)"

Fashion meets fitness in a body-baring racerback crop top edged in delicate crochet. Designed by Carla Patrick Scott. Shown in size 34. The Racerback Top first appeared in the Spring/Summer '86 issue of *Vogue Knitting*.

Racerback Top

SIZES
To fit 32 (34, 36, 38)"/81 (86, 91, 96)cm bust. Directions are for smallest size with larger sizes in parentheses. If there is only one set of figures it applies to all sizes.

KNITTED MEASUREMENTS
● Bust 34 (36, 38, 40)"/86 (90, 94, 100)cm.
● Length 18 (19, 19½, 20½)"/45.5 (48.5, 49.5, 52)cm.

MATERIALS
Original Yarn
● 2 (2, 3, 3) 3½oz/100g balls (each approx 109yd/100m) of Tahki *Creole* (cotton⑤) in #715 red/orange
Substitute Yarn
● 5 (5, 7, 7) 1¾oz/50g balls (each approx 50yd/46m) of Reynolds/JCA *Colors* (cotton⑤) in #111 red
● One pair each sizes 7 and 9 (4.5 and 5.5mm) needles OR SIZE TO OBTAIN GAUGE
● Size G (4.5mm) crochet hook
Note
The original yarn used for this sweater is no longer available. A comparable substitute has been made, which is available at the time of printing. Check gauge of substitute yarns very carefully before beginning.

GAUGE
14 sts and 21 rows to 4"/10cm over St st (blocked) using size 9 (5.5mm) needles. FOR PERFECT FIT, TAKE TIME TO CHECK GAUGE.
Note
After making gauge swatch, wet swatch. Lay it flat and dry thoroughly. Then measure swatch for gauge.

BACK
With smaller needles, cast on 53 (55, 59, 61) sts.
Rib row 1 *K1, p1; rep from *, end k1.
Rib row 2 *P1, k1; rep from *, end p1.
Rep last 2 rows for 1"/2.5cm, inc 7 (8, 7, 9) sts evenly spaced across last row—60 (63, 66, 70) sts. Change to larger needles. Cont in St st (k on RS, p on WS) until piece measures 8½ (9, 9½, 10)"/21.5 (23, 24, 25.5)cm from beg, or desired length to underarm, end with a WS row.

Armhole shaping
Bind off 10 (10, 11, 11) sts at beg of next 2 rows, 3 sts at beg of next 2 rows, 2 sts at beg of next 2 rows, then dec 1 st each side every other row 9 (10, 10, 11) times—12 (13, 14, 16) sts. Then inc 1 st each side every other row 5 (6, 6, 6) times, then every 4th row 5 times, AT SAME TIME, when there are 24 (27, 28, 30) sts, end with a WS row and work as foll:

Neck shaping
Next row (RS) Cont inc at side edge, work until there are 11 (12, 13, 14) sts on RH needle, join 2nd ball of yarn and bind off center 2 (3, 2, 2) sts, work to end. Working both sides at once, bind off from each neck edge 3 sts 0 (1, 1, 1) times, 2 sts 2 (1, 2, 3) times, 1 st 5 (5, 4, 3) times. Bind off rem 6 sts each side.

FRONT
Work as for back to armhole.

Armhole shaping
Bind off 2 (2, 3, 3) sts at beg of next 2 rows. Dec 1 st each side every 4th row 3 (3, 3, 4) times—50 (53, 54, 56) sts. Work even until armhole measures 3 (3½, 3½, 4)"/8 (9.5, 9.5, 10.5)cm.

Neck shaping
Work across 17 sts, join 2nd ball of yarn and bind off center 16 (19, 20, 22) sts, work to end. Working both sides at once, bind off from each neck edge 3 sts once, 2 sts twice, 1 st 4 times—6 sts each side. Work even until armhole measures 9½ (10, 10, 10½)"/24 (25.5, 25.5, 26.5)cm. Bind off rem sts each side.

FINISHING
Block pieces to measurements. Sew shoulder seams. Sew side seams. With RS facing and crochet hook, work 1 rnd sc evenly around neck and armhole edges.

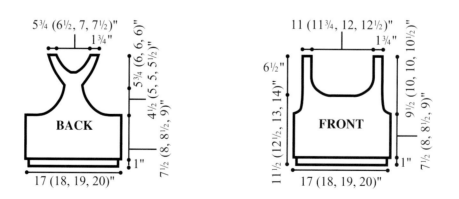

5¾ (6½, 7, 7½)"

1¾"

5¾ (6, 6, 6)"

5¾ (5, 5, 5½)"

4½ (8, 8½, 9)"

BACK

1"

7½ (8, 8½, 9)"

17 (18, 19, 20)"

11 (11¾, 12, 12½)"

1¾"

6½"

11½ (12½, 13, 14)"

9½ (10, 10, 10½)"

FRONT

1"

7½ (8, 8½, 9)"

17 (18, 19, 20)"

Front-Cable Racerback Top

A pretty cable draws the center line down a breezy summer racerback top. It's a snap to make in a cool cotton blend for warm-weather wear. Designed by Teri Leve. The Front-Cable Racerback Top first appeared in the Spring/Summer '84 issue of *Vogue Knitting*.

Front-Cable Racerback Top

SIZES
To fit 32 (34, 36, 38)"/81 (86, 91, 96)cm bust. Directions are for smallest size with larger sizes in parentheses. If there is only one set of figures it applies to all sizes.

KNITTED MEASUREMENTS
● Bust 31 (33, 35, 37)"/78 (82, 88, 92)cm.
● Length 21 (21, 21 1/4, 21 1/4)"/53 (53, 54, 54)cm.

MATERIALS
Original Yarn
● 4 (4, 5, 5) 3 1/2oz/100g balls (each approx 120yd/110m) of Anny Blatt Flirt'Anny (cotton/rayon/linen⑥) in #1223 grey
Substitute Yarn
● 10 (10, 12, 12) 1 3/4oz/50g skeins (each approx 100yd/92m) of Berroco, Inc. Linor (rayon/cotton/linen④) in #3730 stone
● One pair size 7 (4.5mm) needles OR SIZE TO OBTAIN GAUGE
● Cable needle (cn)
● Stitch markers
Note
The original yarn used for this sweater is no longer available. A comparable substitute has been made, which is available at the time of printing. Check gauge of substitute yarns very carefully before beginning.

GAUGE
16 sts and 24 rows to 4"/10cm over seed st with 2 strands of yarn using size 7 (4.5mm) needles.
FOR PERFECT FIT, TAKE TIME TO CHECK GAUGE.
Note
Use 2 strands of yarn held tog throughout.

FRONT
With 2 strands held tog, cast on 70 (74, 78, 82) sts.

Row 1 (RS) K1, *p1, k1; rep from * until 29 (31, 33, 35) sts have been worked, place marker, p2, k8, p2, place 2nd marker, k1, **p1, k1, rep from ** across rem 29 (31, 33, 35) sts.
Row 2 K1, *p1, k1, rep from * to first marker, sl marker, k2, p8, k2 to 2nd marker, sl marker, k1, **p1, k1, rep from ** to end.
Row 3 K1, *p1, k1, rep from * to first marker, sl marker, p2, sl 4 sts onto cn and hold to back, k next 4 sts, k4 sts from cn (cable twist made), p2, sl marker, k1, **p1, k1, rep from ** to end.
Rows 4, 6, 8, 10, and 12 Rep row 2.
Rows 5, 7, 9, and 11 Rep row 1.
Row 13 Rep row 3 (cable twist row). Rep rows 4-13 working seed st on two outer panels and cable over center panel between markers, until front measures 3"/7.5cm from beg, end with a WS row. Cont in pat, dec 1 st at each side of next row, then dec 1 st at each side every 3"/7.5cm 4 times in all—62 (66, 70, 74) sts. Work even in pat until front measures 13"/33cm, end with a pat row 4.

Armhole shaping
Cont in pat, bind off 2 (3, 4, 5) sts at beg of next 2 rows. Dec 1 st at each side every other row 7 times—44 (46, 48, 50) sts.

Neck shaping
Next row (RS) Cont in pat, work across 16 (16, 17, 17) sts, join a 2nd ball of yarn, bind off next 12 (14, 14, 16) sts, work to end. Working both sides at once cont in seed st, dec 1 st at each armhole edge on next and then on every 4th row AT SAME TIME, dec 1 st at each neck edge every other row until 4 (4, 5, 5) sts rem on each side.
FOR 2 SMALLER SIZES ONLY:
Next row (RS) Dec 1 st at each neck edge.
FOR 2 LARGER SIZES ONLY:
Next row (RS) Dec 1 st at each neck edge and armhole edge.

STRAPS
FOR ALL SIZES:
Work even in seed st on 3 rem sts for each side until straps measure 6 1/2 (6 1/2, 7, 7)"/16.5 (16.5, 18, 18)cm slightly stretched. Bind off in seed st.

BACK
With 2 stands held tog, cast on 69 (73, 77, 81) sts. Work in seed st as for front (omitting cable) shaping sides as for front until back measures 13"/33cm from beg, end with a WS row—61 (65, 69, 73) sts.

Armhole shaping
Cont in seed st pat, bind off 8 (10, 10, 12) sts at beg of next 2 rows—45 (45, 49, 49) sts. Bind off 4 sts at beg of next 4 rows—29 (29, 33, 33) sts. Dec 1 st at each side *every* row 8 (8, 10, 10) times—13 sts. Work even in pat on 13 sts until back measures 18 1/2"/47cm from beg. Bind off in seed st.

FINISHING
Sew side seams. Sew straps to back. Press lightly on WS side with warm iron. ●

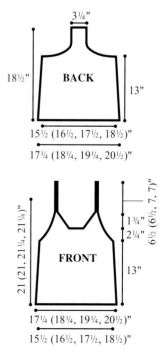

Resources

Write to the yarn companies listed below for yarn purchasing and mail-order information.

AD HOC
distributed by
Stacy Charles Collection
1059 Manhattan Ave.
Brooklyn, NY 11222

ADRIENNE VITTADINI
distributed by JCA
35 Scales Lane
Townsend, MA 01469

ANNY BLATT
7796 Boardwalk
Brighton, MI 48116

AURORA YARNS
PO Box 3068
Moss Beach, CA 94038

**BAABAJOES WOOL
COMPANY**
PO Box 260604
Lakewood, CO 80215

BARUFFA
distributed by Lane Borgosesia
PO Box 217
Colorado Springs, CO 80903

BERELLA®
distributed by Spinrite Yarns, Ltd.
PO Box 40
Listowel, ON
N4W 3H3 Canada

BERROCO, INC.
14 Elmdale Road
PO Box 367
Uxbridge, MA 01569

BROWN SHEEP CO., INC.
100662 County Road 16
Mitchell, NE 69357

CHERRY TREE HILL YARN
PO Box 254
East Montpelier, VT 05651

CLASSIC ELITE
300 Jackson Street, #5
Lowell, MA 01854

CLECKHEATON
distributed by Plymouth Yarn
PO Box 28
Bristol, PA 19007

COLINETTE YARNS, LTD
distributed by Unique Kolours
1428 Oak Lane
Downingtown, PA 19335
UK: Units 2-5
Banwy Workshops
Llanfair Caereinion
Powys SY21 0SG

FILATURA DI CROSA
distributed by
Stacy Charles Collection
1059 Manhattan Ave.
Brooklyn, NY 11222

GARNSTUDIO
distributed by Aurora Yarns
PO Box 3068
Moss Beach, CA 94038

GGH
distributed by Muench Yarns
285 Bel Marin Keys Blvd. Unit J
Novato, CA 94949

JCA
35 Scales Lane
Townsend, MA 01469

JUDI & CO.
18 Gallatin Drive
Dix Hills, NY 11746

LANE BORGOSESIA U.S.A.
PO Box 217
Colorado Springs, CO 80903

MANOS DEL URUGUAY
distributed by Simpson Southwick
55 Curtiss Place
Maplewood, NJ 07040

MONDIAL
distributed by Skacel Collection
PO Box 88110
Seattle, WA 98138-2110
UK: Spring Mill House
Baildon, Shipley
West Yorkshire BD17 6AD

MUENCH YARNS
285 Bel Marin Keys Blvd. Unit J
Novato, CA 94949

PHILDAR
distributed by Lane Borgosesia
PO Box 217
Colorado Springs, CO 80903

PLYMOUTH YARN
PO Box 28
Bristol, PA 19007

REYNOLDS
distributed by JCA
35 Scales Lane
Townsend, MA 01469

ROWAN
distributed by Westminster Fibers
5 Northern Blvd.
Amherst, NH 03031
UK: Green Lane Mill
Holmfirth
West Yorkshire HD7 1RW

SIMPSON SOUTHWICK
55 Curtiss Place
Maplewood, NJ 07040

SKACEL COLLECTION
PO Box 88110
Seattle, WA 98138-2110
UK: Spring Mill House
Baildon, Shipley
West Yorkshire BD17 6AD

SPINRITE YARNS, LTD.
PO Box 40
Listowel, ON
N4W 3H3 Canada

**STACY CHARLES
COLLECTION**
1059 Manhattan Ave.
Brooklyn, NY 11222

STAHL WOLLE
distributed by Tahki Imports, Ltd.
11 Graphic Place
Moonachie, NJ 07074

TAHKI IMPORTS, LTD.
11 Graphic Place
Moonachie, NJ 07074

TRENDSETTER YARNS
16742 Stagg St.
Suite 104
Van Nuys, CA 91406

UNIQUE KOLOURS
1428 Oak Lane
Downingtown, PA 19335

WESTMINSTER FIBERS
5 Northern Blvd.
Amherst, NH 03031

**WOLF—NOTHING BUT
CUTLERY**
35 Jane Street #2
Toronto, ON
M6S 3Y3 Canada

WOOL PAK YARNS NZ
distributed by
Baabajoes Wool Company
PO Box 260604
Lakewood, CO 80215

**Vogue Knitting
161 Avenue of the Americas
New York, NY 10013-1252
Fax 212-620-2731
www.vogueknitting.com**

**In UK and Europe:
Vogue Knitting
New Lane
Havant Hants PO9 2ND, England
Tel 01705 486221
Fax 01705 492769**

We have made every effort to ensure the accuracy of the contents of this publication. We are not responsible for any human or typographical errors.

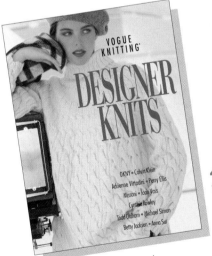

ACKNOWLEDGEMENTS

There are many people who contributed to the making of this book. In particular, and most importantly, we would like to thank the previous editors of *Vogue Knitting* magazine, including Polly Roberts, Marilyn F. Cooperman, Lola Ehrlich, Margaret C. Korn, Meredith Gray Harris, Sonja Bjorklund Dagress, Nancy J. Thomas, Margery Winter, Carla S. Scott, and Gay Bryant, for their vision and impeccable design selections. We would also like to extend our warmest appreciation and gratitude to all of the dedicated and knowledgeable *Vogue Knitting* staff members, past and present, for their skill and countless hours of hard work in bringing the best of knitting to their readers. Special thanks also goes to the tireless knitters and contributing technical experts, without whom the magazine would not be possible.

PHOTO CREDITS

Paul Amato (pages 21, 25, 47, 49, 57, 83, 85, 121), Richard Bailey (pages 71, 99), Eric Boman (page 149), Alessandro D' Andrea (page 10), Carlo Dalla Chiesa (page 51), Patrick Demarchelier (pages 81, 93, 106, 147, 151), Roger Eaton (pages 35, 133, 137), Arthur Elgort (page 155), Bob Frame (pages 91, 115), William Garrett (page 123), Tim Geaney (page 27), Michael Halsband (page 139), Bob Hiemstra (page 39), Barry Hollywood (pages 64, 145), Jim Jordan (pages 87, 142), Francois Lamy (page 77), Barry Lategan (page 95), Rudy Molacek (pages 69, 103, 153), Gordon Munro (page 31), Dewey Nicks (page 75), Elisabeth Novick (pages 19, 73), Dick Nystrom (page 32), Michael O' Brien (page 135), Peggy Sirota (pages 109, 113), Danny Sit (pages 23, 61), Otto Stupakoff (pages 101, 117), Paul Sunday (page 29), Alberto Tolot (pages 13, 15, 88), Robert Trachtenberg (pages 45, 125, 129, 140), Nick Vaccaro (pages 17, 41, 79, 130), Antoine Verglas (page 53)